GUNNER
ON THE
SOMME

The Memoir of
William Robert Price,
1st South Midland 1914–1917

W.R. Price
Introduced by Mark Pottle

The History Press

First published 2016

The History Press
The Mill, Brimscombe Port
Stroud, Gloucestershire, GL5 2QG
www.thehistorypress.co.uk

British Library Cataloguing in Publication Data.
A catalogue record for this book is available from the British Library.

ISBN 978 0 7509 6982 6

Typesetting and origination by The History Press
Printed and bound in Great Britain by TJ International Ltd

CONTENTS

FOREWORD BY
JEREMY DAVIDSON

My maternal grandfather, William Robert Price, known as Robin Price throughout his life, was born in 1886, a few months after the untimely death, at the young age of 46, of his father William Edwin Price, Liberal MP for Tewkesbury and ex-professional soldier. Robin and his elder brother, Morgan Philips Price, were brought up by their mother on the 2,000-acre Gloucestershire estate left by their father, and received a conventional landed gentry upbringing. Both went to Harrow and then Trinity College, Cambridge, from where my grandfather graduated in 1908 with a BA in natural sciences specialising in botany. The following year he joined the Royal Botanic Gardens, Kew, as an assistant in the Herbarium. In 1911, following the death of his mother, he set off with fellow Kew botanist Henry John Elwes on a year-long plant-collecting expedition to Formosa (today Taiwan), then a tropical paradise under Japanese administration. He discovered several species new to science, one of which, *Pleione Pricei*, was named after him. He continued on his own to Japan, Korea and China for a further six months and returned 'hardened by rough travel', no doubt expecting to dedicate his life, in the tradition of eighteenth-century plant collectors, to field botany. The Great War put paid to his ambitions.

Like so many of his contemporaries, Robin Price volunteered at the outbreak of war in August 1914, in his case electing to join the Royal Field Artillery. But why did this public school and Cambridge-educated young man enlist as a gunner (private soldier)? First of all, although only a fleeting allusion to it is made in this memoir, he suffered from a severe and debilitating stutter, which he recognised would preclude him from being an officer and giving orders. Secondly, he identified with ordinary working men, as did his brother (who in later life was Labour MP for the Forest of Dean, 1935–50), and perhaps hoped that he would find uncomplicated comradeship in joining the ranks.

It is worth recording, however, that his brother was opposed to the war, and that their maternal cousin, the Liberal MP Sir Charles Trevelyan, who was a member of Asquith's government between 1908 and 1914, helped to found the Union of Democratic Control (UDC), a cross-party organisation opposed to the war. Trevelyan resigned from the government over the declaration of war; he was one of only three ministers to do so. Morgan Price later joined the UDC, registered as a conscientious objector and served as a war correspondent for the *Manchester Guardian* in Russia, 1914–18. It is possible that my grandfather wished to leave the shadow of his ambitious and self-confident brother by joining up.

There is no doubt whatsoever that he found true comradeship in the ranks, fighting alongside ordinary men who came from the same part of England as he did. Although his different social background would have been obvious to his comrades, it is clear he was treated as 'one of us'. On several occasions he had high-quality clothing, footwear, food and even a record player sent over from England, for the benefit of his fellow gunners; these items were dispatched by his maternal aunt Miss Anna Philips – the 'faithful factotum' referred to in the text of his memoir, and effectively his next of kin. It also emerges that he made little attempt to befriend officers even though it must have been tempting to do so, and he was in general highly complimentary of the officers in his brigade.

My grandfather was also a keen photographer and managed to smuggle a German-made Goerz camera to the front, which was used to take all but one of the photographs in this book, the exception being the splendid if thoroughly conventional full-length portrait that opens the plates section, and which was clearly taken by a professional photographer with a mobile studio somewhere near the front. More than 150 of my grandfather's photographs from his early war experiences have survived, and we have only been able to reproduce a small selection here, but we feel that they illustrate his memoir tremendously well.

I saw my grandfather regularly in my childhood, as my parents lived abroad, and clearly remember him hunched over a venerable Smith Corona typewriter at an elegant Georgian desk (now a prized possession of my brother), painstakingly hammering out the manuscript for this memoir, and labouring over its detailed maps as if they were botanical illustrations.

He was always happy to talk about his experiences in the Great War – at times giving the impression that it had been a 'big adventure' – though he recognised that he had been very lucky to get through it in one piece. He was discharged as a result of injuries received from a direct hit on his gun emplacement during the Third Battle of Ypres in September 1917. Later in his life he was to suffer from severe arthritis, which he claimed to be a result of sleeping on the ground during his time at the front.

After demobilising, he married Comfort Watney, in 1920, and in the early years of their marriage particularly she did much to help him mitigate his speech impediment and improve his self-confidence. They had one daughter, Jacqueline, my mother. They lived in Gloucestershire at Cockleford Mill, Cowley, where my grandfather continued his botanical studies until the end of the Second World War. He served in the Home Guard during that conflict. Between the wars he wrote a number of learned papers on such esoteric subjects as 'Some Aboriginal Tribes of South-Eastern China' (1929), 'The Lilies of Formosa' (1936), 'The Flora of Taitan Island, Amoy' and 'The Flora of Gloucestershire' (co-authored 1948).

In 1946 my grandparents moved to London, and he resumed his work at Kew, classifying obscure plant collections until two years before his death in 1975. When his wife died in 1965 he seemed to acquire a new lease of life, and undertook a three-month tour of the Far East on his own, including a return to Taiwan. Much to his astonishment, he was received with reverence by the botanical community there, and awarded an Honorary Doctorate by National Taiwan Normal University.

He was a tall, strikingly handsome man. A true natural scientist, he was observant, a meticulous note-taker and intellectually curious, which makes this memoir all the more interesting. In common with many 'gentlemen' of his generation, he had sufficient private means to be able to indulge his interests. Emotionally reticent and self-sufficient, he appeared to have no old friends and rarely, if ever, sought out those he had fought alongside. His speech impediment must have made normal conversation and establish-ing friendships difficult. My mother said he was a doting father and was a constant presence in her childhood. An affectionate grandfather, he would take my brother and I, and sometimes our sister, out of school in Sussex for trips on the nearby Bluebell Railway and treat us to sumptuous cream teas. On dropping us back at school he would slip a pound note into our pockets – a fortune in those days. He was a lifelong member of the Liberal Party and a committed Humanist. As a young man he played the clarinet, and claimed that he had played under the baton of Edward Elgar at a village concert. When I was 18 he gave me his clarinet and I have played it ever since.

My brother, late sister Sally, to whom my grandfather was particularly close, and I have nothing but the fondest memories of this gentle, generous and thoughtful man – qualities we hope emerge from this unpretentious and personal account of a gunner in the Great War.

I am especially grateful to the military historians Evelyn and Chris Wilcock who, while researching 240th Brigade of the Royal Field Artillery, discovered my grandfather's manuscript in the Imperial War Museum, where it had been filed anonymously. They managed to identify the author, and then track me down as his oldest surviving heir, and subsequently put me in touch with Michael Leventhal of The History Press, who felt that this memoir merited publishing. Mark Pottle, of Wolfson College, Oxford, was appointed editor, and it has been a real pleasure working with him.

Jeremy Davidson
eldest grandson of W. R. Price

Editorial Note and Acknowledgements

The text presented here is based upon a typescript deposited in the Imperial War Museum, and citations to that work should take the form 'W.R. Price, *Gunner on the Somme*, Imperial War Museum, London (66/164/1)'. Every effort has been made to render an accurate transcription of that typescript, but where readers are in doubt they should refer to the original.

WRP (as Price will be referred to hereafter in editorial matter) did not expect a scholarly treatment of his memoir: he would not have imagined biographical notes in the text, or other footnotes, and we have respected this: the contemporary record is the thing, not the editorial apparatus that accompanies it, and reader here finds the memoir exactly as it was written, unencumbered by footnotes.

That said, there is at times an obvious need for some kind of editorial comment. The memoir was written long after the events that it describes, and although a contemporary diary – which has not survived – was the basis for much of its content, there are inevitable slips. In the Notes section at the back of the book we have tried to correct any errors, and give such additional information as might augment WRP's account, or simply entertain the reader. We have adopted the format of endnotes without cues in the text: each note is preceded by the page number, and a short extract of the text to which it refers, allowing the original context to be more readily remembered. Doubtless we have not always succeeded in supplying the necessary information, but we have made every effort within the limits of our resources, and readers who seek a definitive account of the operations, army deployments and movements described herein are advised to refer to the many authoritative and specialist works that are available. The chapter headings (i.e. 'Tranquil Days', etc.) are those given by WRP.

Small errors in WRP's typescript have been silently corrected, for example, the spelling of place names; we have also altered punctuation to make the text more readable and the meaning clearer. WRP sometimes put phrases in quotation marks that are obviously not quotations, but rather what he considered to be truisms, and these have been retained. Elsewhere, passages that are clearly quotations from published sources are not necessarily accurate: where the changes are minimal (i.e. a comma for a semi-colon, etc.) we have made silent corrections, but where WRP's quotation differs in substance from the original we have made a note of this (included at the relevant point in the Notes section).

To assist the reader we have also included a brief chronology of the First World War and a glossary. We have produced two maps ourselves, one of the Western Front, and one of the Somme offensive; but we also include within the text the five maps painstakingly drawn by WRP himself to illustrate the text. We have placed these as near as possible to their original placement in the narrative.

The text and photographs of *Gunner on the Somme* are copyright to the heirs of the author, William Price, and may not be further reproduced in whole or in part without their authority.

Acknowledgements

In addition to friends and family, with the mention especially of David Langstow and Steffen Gross, we would like to thank: the staff at the Bodleian Library, Oxford; the Imperial War Museum; and Wolfson College, Oxford. We would like to pay special tribute to Evelyn and Christopher Wilcock, for bringing the text to wider attention, and for their work both in making the initial transcription and identifying the artillerymen mentioned therein. In their own notes on the text, Evelyn and Christopher wrote that they owed a great deal to Derek Driscoll, for his generosity with information about 240th Brigade of the Royal Field Artillery, and for the Bristol Gunners website that he began but which, for reasons of ill health, he was unable to complete. We too would like to acknowledge Derek's contribution.

Lastly, we would like to thank our expert publishers at The History Press, namely Michael Leventhal, who commissioned the work and helped in its evolution, and Christine McMorris and Andrew Latimer, who turned the digitised memoir into a published book, complete with a wonderful jacket.

Interest in the First World War in Britain over the last 100 years has been phenomenal, and is perhaps the best memorial to those who served. Since the advent of the World Wide Web, a host of individuals – be they local historians, regimental historians, family members, or simply Great War enthusiasts – and established institutions have created websites providing information on different aspects of the war. We would like to acknowledge their work, and especially that of the Western Front Association, the Commonwealth War Graves Commission, and Chris Baker's *The Long, Long Trail*. We would also like to identify here three particular sources on which we have relied, namely Dale Clarke, *British Artillery 1914–19: Field Army Artillery* (Oxford, 2004); Paul Strong and Sanders Marble, *Artillery in the Great War* (Barnsley, 2011); and F. S. Gedye, *An Outline of the War History of the 240th* (1st South Midland: Gloucestershire) Brigade R.F.A. (T) (nd), 4 (hereafter referred to as 240th Brigade).

JD, MP, February 2016

INTRODUCTION BY
MARK POTTLE

Reading 'Gunner' Robin Price's account of his life as a volunteer soldier with a territorial battery of the Royal Field Artillery (RFA) on the Western Front between April 1915 and September 1917, one understands better how, for men such as he, the experience could have been both the best of times and the worst of times.

Price attests to the horrors of the war. Approaching some curious-looking 'heaps of old rags' outside the ruined village of Flaucourt in January 1917, he discovered the 'shrivelled white faces and skeleton hands' of fifty or so dead French infantrymen, mown down by a German machine gun months earlier and now lying frozen on the ground. Such visions of Hell sat alongside glimpses of Paradise: the luxury of falling asleep in the summer grass in a 'pretty country of small meadows and orchards, little villages and poplar-lined roads' during a fortnight at rest camp in 1917; or returning to his battery several months later, after a memorable dinner, and stopping his horse from galloping in order to savour the beauty of an autumn night:

> I thought, this won't do, we shall be back too soon, I must spin this heavenliness
> out a little; I shall never enjoy anything like this again in France, or perhaps ever.
> I slowed him down into his beautiful walk, which was better than any gallop.
> There was no sound and even the guns were silent. If I had listened, I am sure
> I should have heard the nightjar.

Weeks after this interlude he was invalided out of the war when a shrapnel bullet lodged in his back during Third Ypres. He had got the hoped-for 'Blighty one', but it was bittersweet: 'There would never be comradeship like this again. [...] I kept on saying to myself, "I'm leaving these fellows", and I couldn't bear it.' In terms of social standing and education Price would have been considered officer material. His family owned a large estate in Gloucestershire, and he was educated at Harrow and Trinity College, Cambridge. A paralysing stutter, however, compelled him to enlist in the ranks, and the friendship and acceptance that he found there was never forgotten.

The greatest accolade that his comrades bestowed was when they nick-named him 'Gunner'. This meant more than any official decoration possibly could. It was a recognition that he was 'one of them'; and yet, at the same time, it was an acknowledgement that he was different. He could afford, for example, during an especially wet period in the autumn of 1916, to order from a manufacturer in England oilskin slacks for all of the men in his sub-section. On another occasion, with a pocket full of francs, he stood his friends round after round of *vin rouge* in an *estaminet*: 'Then came "*Finis, Messieurs, partir*", and out we poured with *au revoirs* onto the common and sang our way back to the lines over the grass in the dim light of that perfect summer evening.' His last recollection of that night was of his friend Gunner Wiggin 'trying to run races with himself'.

Price had fretted over the oilskin slacks, fearing that he might be sus-pected of currying favour either with the officers or men, but ultimately he reproached himself for not having kitted out the whole battery. It was typical of him to make the gesture and then worry about its consequences. Inhabiting a halfway house as he did, somewhere between the officers and the rank and file, he understood the social realities that were at play: he had an unusual vantage point, and he observed from it well. He rated the officers in his battery very highly, not least because of their obvious concern for the well-being of their men. In one of the most touching passages in his memoir, Price writes of the stoicism of a young new subaltern who, when the battery had reached a gun position on a windswept slope, 'walked miserably up and down in the rain all night', the major having given orders 'that the men were to get themselves dug into the dry before any work was done on officers' quarters'. In what army but the British, Price wonders, could this happen? Realising that the young officer would probably never order the men to dig him a shelter, Price took the initiative: '"Can't we make a dugout for you, sir?" He smiled and said, "Oh, thank you, Gunner Price".' Price and two others set to work, and 'had a large enough hole dug by night to be able to put a bit of roof on it'. The socially unifying effect of the trenches, which influenced the attitudes of such diverse and important characters as Clement Attlee and

Harold Macmillan, can doubtless be exaggerated, but Price's account shows ways in which it was profoundly true.

Trained as a botanist, Price had a natural eye for detail, and his memoir conveys wonderfully well the rhythm of life at the front for an artillery gunner. Intervals of intense excitement, and even exhilaration, were separated by long spells of tedium, and overshadowing all was the fear of death, the 'ever increasing dull foreboding', the constant calculation and recalculation of the odds whenever the battery came within range of enemy guns. Reflections on the hated German 5.9 led into a matter-of-fact discussion of that most disabling of emotions, fear: 'After the first few times, it came upon us all, when we heard the shells on the way, and it was, of course, in the form of shaking knees [...] We seemed not to have proper control of our legs'. Eventually Price and his fellow gunners became hardened, so much so that they reacted with a complete lack of feeling towards 'a mere boy' of a reinforcement who lost his head under fire:

> I often thought afterwards how brutal we must have been to that poor lad. I remembered his bewildered, scared face, unable to understand anything yelled at him in the din of the bombardment and being pushed away and told to get out of the way. I wish I could remember ever having said a kind word to him afterwards.

This episode notwithstanding, there was abundant compassion in the ranks, and large doses of humour, which were meted out to defy even the most depressing of circumstances. Standing up to their knees in mud, the men of Price's battery would address any passers-by with the mordant observation: 'Here's the shit (pointing, and two second pause) and we're in it.' It was a 'gag' attributed to Price himself, and when done properly it was 'difficult for the Sergeant-Major not to laugh', while officers turned away. They were, of course, all in it together; but it was the ordinary soldier who had the most right to complain.

The most pitiful suffering, perhaps, was that of the least articulate members of every artillery unit in this war, namely the horses. Forget what Price dismissively calls 'Haig's pets, the Cavalry', and think instead of the beasts of burden, the 140 or so animals in every RFA battery that hauled the dead weight of guns and ammunition across uncrossable terrain, and were then made to stand up to their fetlocks in a sea of liquid mud, into which they trampled their hay because they grew so agitated at the sight of food. In training, Price and his comrades 'soon learnt that horses came before men, they cost more', but the reality was that they were expendable, and NCOs carried revolvers to shoot them when they became bogged down. The erection of the Animals in War Memorial in London's Park Lane in 2004, the 90th anniversary of the outbreak of the war, was a long time in coming.

Price makes no claim to a heroic role on the Western Front. He saw action on two of its great stages, the Somme and Passchendaele, but in his own words his battery played only 'an average part' in these battles and was 'on the whole lucky as regards casualties'. The understatement here, which is entirely characteristic of him, belies the contribution that the 240th Brigade made during the Somme, notably at Pozières in September 1916, and later at Third Ypres. In mid-August 1917 his sub-section received a direct hit from a German shell, mortally wounding three of his friends, and rendering a fourth – the aforementioned Gunner Wiggin – an invalid. By one of those inexplicable quirks of fate, Price and the sixth member of the gun team escaped injury: having been given permission to rest, they had left the gun not long before it was hit. It was his third 'near miss', and he did not expect to be so lucky as to be afforded another. He was not: the fourth close encounter ended his war, although luckily not his life.

Forty years elapsed before Price wrote his account of his experiences with the 240th, and by then the war memoir was an established literary genre. There was much competition to get into print. Price was a reflective and thoughtful man, with a remarkably modern outlook on life, but he nevertheless believed that he did not possess imagination: certainly he did not strive for literary effect in the writing of his memoir. Instead he meant 'merely to portray the day to day life of a Territorial Battery' at the front. He offered his typescript to a publisher, but it was rejected in March 1962, an unidentified reader's report suggesting that it lacked the literary and imaginative appeal to command a sale: 'I hate to say it, but it isn't "phoney" enough to attract the people who read "phoney" war books today.'

It is important to note, at this point, that *Gunner on the Somme* is neither a contemporary record, unaffected by later judgements, nor a memoir written in old age, without reference to original materials. Rather, it is a meeting of the two. Price based his account upon a contemporary diary, which sadly has not survived: the narrative suggests that he followed it very closely, but it is impossible to be sure, and there are occasions when one would like to know. Was the disillusionment that he reported at the end of the Somme his feeling at the time, or a retrospective judgement cast in the present tense? Perhaps it is best to treat his account as an internal dialogue: in 1958 the veteran revisited the Western Front, metaphorically and literally, and wandered around it in the company of his younger self. What ensued is *Gunner on the Somme.*

As a philosophical man with a strongly rationalist bent, Price saw clearly the futility of wars in general, and of this one in particular. There is no reason to doubt that this principle was a constant throughout his life. And yet his pride in his role in the Great War, and that of the 48th (South Midland) Division, 240th Brigade, 'C' Battery, and 'A' sub-section of the RFA, shine brightly throughout his memoir. He wanted to be the best gunner he could possibly be, and at the same time he came to doubt the war he was fighting in, and especially the way that it was conducted. There is no moral inconsistency here, no circle that cannot be squared: such, after all, is the complexity of human nature. Price and his contemporaries were able to give their all without surrendering their right to think freely and to criticise, which was one of the greatest blessings of the still evolving democracy they were defending.

In an understandably emotional postscript to the memoir, which recounts his 1958 return to the battlefields around Ypres, 'Gunner' pays fulsome tribute to the British army that had fought there, a body of men that 'suffered probably more than any other army from prehistoric leadership in the doctrine of frontal assaults upon entrenched positions, and in Haig's ridiculous cavalry complex'. Such outspoken critical sentiments run against the grain of current historical writing on British military leadership and tactics during the war, but lest they be dismissed as the views of an amateur or, worse, as misplaced emotionalism, it should be remembered that Robin Price was a highly intelligent, clear-sighted and deep-thinking man. And he had been there.

Mark Pottle

Gunner on the Somme

This account does not aim at being a description of the Battle [of the Somme], neither is it one of exciting deeds or horrors; the world has had enough of such writings. It endeavours merely to portray the day to day life of a Territorial Battery during the years 1915 to 1917 inclusive, and to be a statement describing events, and where these events and words spoken are reprehensible, or their mention unorthodox, they are nevertheless included if relevant.

William Robert 'Robin' Price, 1958

1

The Beginning

The First World War caught me at a convenient time. I had recently returned from a year's plant collecting in Formosa, was hardened by rough travel and anxious to continue my activities in that area. The outbreak of war put a stop to these ambitions, possibly forever.

I had no particular illusions about the war. It would obviously end an era, which might be a good thing, but why could not changes be effected by other means, and in any case what was it about? The invasion of Belgium settled it, so that argument became academic, but the situation we were in was the inevitable result of Balance of Power politics, and how far, I wondered, were these policies influenced by economic motives? How long would home life be denied us? I remembered while at school being told that the Boer War would be over by Christmas.

I had nothing else to do, and quite welcomed the exciting prospect, being free of dependents and commitments.

I wandered off on that day of August 4, 1914 into the county town [Gloucester] with a vague idea of joining the Artillery of which one Battery, the Third or 'C' Battery of the County Territorial Royal Field Artillery Brigade, had its headquarters at the Barracks there.

In the street I met an old family friend, a man of standing in the City. We discussed the War. He held forth, and listened perfunctorily. Suddenly I heard him say, 'The Germans were getting all our trade. It couldn't go on'. So that was it. When I could collect myself, I remarked that I had been afraid that that was the cause of the War, 'Now, now, don't talk like that', he rebuked me. I made an excuse and hurried away.

Walking the streets I watched the crowds all excitement and laughter.

I had met the Quartermaster when the Battery had spent a week-end in the country on field exercise, when I thought what a jolly lot they were.

His cheery 'Hullo Sir' at the Barracks made me feel that this was a good beginning. I was sworn in as a gunner, and then received, or had thrown at me, an old jacket, trousers and hat, which I heard later comprised the entire stock in store at the moment. Turning in late at the billet, which was a school, I found the only sleeping space available was a half-landing on concrete steps. There was no chance of digging in the hip bone here, and night was a torment. It would have been a relief, had I known, that as regards sleep discomfort, I would never again endure so painful a night.

After several chaotic days we entrained for Plymouth, where we spent a period in flea-ridden Raglan Barracks, later moving to Crown Hill under canvas. It was lovely weather and I always enjoyed camp life.

Our Brigade, now united, was composed of three four-gun batteries and an ammunition column. Each gun had a first line and a second line ammunition wagon, all with six-horse teams, which meant 18 horses to a gun and 72 for the battery, with in addition those for the column, N.C.O.s, signallers and officers, making a total of 140.

Our gun-park and horse-lines were soon a fine sight, as we all took a pride in the battery, as did the Major who had built it up, and the guns, wagons, and horses' coats and harness were made to shine.

It was all a great adventure, everyone was keen in his work, especially keen on gun-drill, shirking was non-existent and grumbling good natured. We were a mixed lot, mostly town-bred mechanics and farm workers, the latter becoming our very efficient drivers. Everyone came from the same area and knew everyone. We were in reality just a large family of noisy, high-spirited boys, on the whole well satisfied with our N.C.O.s and officers, and ruled over quietly, efficiently and benevolently by our popular, tall and handsome Sergeant-Major Parker. Our officers were a good lot; they had learnt their job in peace time and were efficient and fair and we respected them. We were probably a pretty good specimen of a Territorial unit of that time.

We did not bother much about what lay ahead, but we knew that excitement would be involved and that suited us. I ceased to think about the 'trade' we might be fighting for.

Looking back over the years, I feel impressed at the magnitude and genuineness of the morale and enthusiasm of those early days. But we had much to learn and much disillusionment to experience. We sang, 'When Irish Eyes are Smiling' and 'Nelly Dear', and were carefree and happy.

Our Saturday afternoons were spent mostly searching out the female sex in Plymouth, and on Sundays a surprising number of our men went to church, more especially to the smaller churches and non-conformist chapels which laid on services attractive to the Forces. I went to one such small church service with some of our N.C.O.s and men, and found the church full, almost exclusively with khaki. We behaved appropriately as on parade, and the whole service could only be described as enthusiastic, especially when we sang 'Onward Christian Soldiers' and 'God Save the King'. The sermon, preached by a most admirable and earnest young clergyman, left no doubt in anybody's mind that God was on our side, and we came out feeling immensely cheered and hopeful about the outcome of the War.

It did occur to me, however, on the way back to camp, that the Kaiser had said most definitely that God was, indeed had always been, on the side of the German Nation, but I noted that neither he nor our preacher had produced any definite evidence. Anyway God could not be on both sides, so one of us must be wrong.

I pined for some enlightenment on Life in the sphere of reasoned thought, which seemed to me at this time to be non-existent. I had not then discovered that any organized rationalist thought existed. Moreover, I could not discuss a reasoned outlook, as my companions were either unwilling or unable to do so, so in my free time I withdrew into myself when in a contemplative mood, which was a process I was well used to, but at the time unhelpful.

2

TRAINING

We soon learnt that horses came before men, they cost more, and that the harness was almost more important than the horse. We wondered whether the time would ever come when we would be too busy firing the guns and running ammunition to be able to clean harness. As a matter of fact, it did.

Horse-lines work and the usual guards and fatigues soon became automatic and soul destroying, but for the gunners there was a definite interest in the guns. I bought a pocket edition of Major Straubenzee's 'Manual of Artillery Drill and Procedure' and learnt it by heart. It was soon apparent that there could be no limit to the improvement of efficiency and, more especially, speed with which a gun could be served. The team of six must have their drill at their fingertips, have quick reaction and be able to jump to it, each man in any of the six positions that may be required of him.

Our guns were 15-pounders. We were pleased with them, knowing no better, though somewhat daunted when we heard that they had been through the Boer War. In those days the barrel was fixed, and numbers two and three must have had a rough time on their seats, if they had seats then. Since that time buffers have been fixed above the barrels, inside which was a coiled steel spring lying in a glycerine mixture. On firing, the barrel ran back on slides, compressing the spring, which expanding again, slid it back into position. We little knew what future trouble we should have from these springs.

A gun detachment consisted of six men: No. 1, the N.C.O. in charge, who gave orders and manipulated the trail handle; No. 2, who sat astride the right hand seat, dealt with the range wheel with his right hand and operated the breech lever with his left; No. 3 was the layer, who sat on the left hand seat facing forward, manipulated the sights and elevating wheel (and in the 18-pounders the traversing wheel), controlled the hand-brake and fired the gun; No. 4 was the loader, who stood on the left of the trail and 'yanked them in', taking care that his right pushing hand took a final upward course, so as not to be cut off by the closing breech block; Nos. 5 and 6 stood behind the first line limber drawn up close on the left of the gun, set the fuses and passed the rounds to the loader, No. 5 being also responsible for the corrector bar, a finely made brass bar with sliding centre, normally carried on the gun shield, having three rows of figures, the bottom being corrector numbers, which had reference to barometric pressure, the middle sliding scale being fuse numbers, and the top row range numbers.

The first order in battery practice was always the corrector number, usually 240. When the range was given, No. 5 read the fuse number and shouted it out.

All our practice was with imaginary ammunition. The position required for a shrapnel burst was at the beginning of its descent in its parabolic curve.

The four guns were equidistanced on a hundred-yard line, the two right ones, 'A' and 'B', being the right section, and the two left, 'C' and 'D', the left section, each with its N.C.O. behind.

The next order was aiming point, generally a church spire or an isolated tree; then so many degrees and minutes left or right, which the layer put on the dial sight, the gun being then quickly thrown onto line by No. 1 (final setting with traverse handle in 18-pounder). A useful rule was taught us in case of emergency: with hand outstretched, knuckles of first and second fingers give three degrees, and three knuckles five degrees. Layer then sets his sights at zero and a gunner runs out in front and plants two aiming rods in line with sights, guided by layer's hand. The layer should then or later pick out a convenient auxiliary aiming point in case anything happened to the original; he should note the angle of zero line to this and tell it to the others, who should write it down.

Angle of sight, which could be of elevation or depression, came next, the layer putting in on the clinometer and levelling the bubble.

Range when called was put on the range wheel by No. 2, this wheel moving the barrel automatically by an ingenious mechanism whereby his elevating screw worked inside that of the layer and did not affect the clinometer bubble.

No. 2 then reported 'set', layer 'ready', N.C.O. 'No. 1 ready', Section N.C.O. 'right section ready, sir'; then, when left section reports ready, came the order 'time load' or 'percussion load', then came the firing order, which could be one or more rounds' battery fire, three, or more, seconds (intervals between guns); or ditto for sections; or 'prepare for salvo', then 'salvo, fire!' or 'gun-fire', which to us meant fire like hell until we got the order 'stop'.

In reality it was a very quiet proceeding as we used no blank charges.

Taking up position practice was, however, our chief exercise on our bi-weekly days on Roborough Common. It was surprising how easily chaos resulted. The junior officers were then always in trouble. Our Colonel, a fine soldier, marvellous instructor and strict disciplinarian, had a fetish for pouring out his rage on the young officers. 'I'm not going to blame the men,' he would shout, 'when it's the fault of the officers'. He overdid it. He would hold up some wretched lieutenant to scorn before us all and make him repeat a movement again and again.

We galloped into action over the heather. 'Halt, action front' involved a gun and wagon stopping where indicated and the rest forming up in line on the left of it, guns swivelled round and teams away. 'Action rear' was similar but guns were not turned and 'A' gun became 'D' gun (significantly we never practised this). 'Halt action right' required 'A' gun to pull sharply to the right and the rest to line to its left. 'Action left' was the same, but 'A' gun became 'D' gun. But the movement which appealed to me most was 'right (or left) take ground'. There were special arm signals which the Major riding ahead could use so that everyone could see the order if he could not hear it. Right take ground was signalled by his shooting out his right arm horizontally a number of times. This was an order for an extreme emergency on the flank, and was executed more quickly than action right, as each gun turned simultaneously and took position where it was, the distance of guns in column of route being approximately the same as the distance between guns in position. The nuisance was that in 'right take ground', 'A' gun became 'D' gun, which we hated, though this was not so in left take ground. We could not avoid a thrill at the thought that we might some time be doing this in open action, which is the gunners' dream. From what we could learn, however, it seemed that open action days had finished after Mons, and that henceforth static action would be the order of the day, and indeed it was so.

3

To France

On March 28, 1915, in the dark of an early morning, 'C' Battery walk-marched out of a gateway into a country lane at Broomfield near Chelmsford, and on along the main road to Witham, where we entrained for Southampton.

We disembarked on the 30th at Le Havre and loaded into a long train, ourselves in vans, where according to notices five men equalled one horse, which we were glad to know.

It was night by the time we reached Hazebrouck and we were glad to end up in the early hours at a farm at Rouge Croix, where an abundance of hay to crawl into in the barns was an unexpected luxury.

In the morning we realized that the peculiar rumbling sound which never ceased was the war. 'Here's the war and we're in it' became our first gag.

The flat countryside, still in its winter garb, with rows of poplars, would have had its attraction, had it not been that every poplar was destined to die, the bark all round the trunk of all of them being eaten away for eight feet by horses which had been tethered to them, apparently Uhlan horses.

On April 5th we proceeded to the Lille main road, where very self-conscious and eyes-front we passed through Méteren into Bailleul, a fine old town. Few people were about and nobody was interested in us, and we realized we were not as important as we had come to think we were. In one roadside house I saw, and have always remembered, two small Belgian soldiers standing in the window watching us. They were in their original blue uniform with peculiar shaped kepi, remnants of the devastated Belgian Army. It was the only time I ever saw that uniform.

Following the Armentières road, here all *pavé*, we turned left into the little strip west of the Yser River and canal, which constituted what remained of unconquered Belgium, passing the abandoned customs post. Here we were in a troop billeting area, practically every farm and house being full of them.

It rained steadily. I had smuggled a mackintosh, which was not 'issue', and kept dry, but everyone else was soaked.

Our farm billet was full with a Regular Battery, a fine lot of men who had been through Mons. We had to lie down where we could. They were friendly and mildly amused at us, but ready to help, so it seemed that night. However, they had lost all their kit, literally all, and their main interest was rather naturally to acquire fresh. On our return from grooming for breakfast next day, consternation reigned. We were now without kit, nearly, and our friends had left for important business at Ypres. They had swiped everything out of our kit bags and haversacks that was easily portable, shaving kit, spare clothing, all badges and buttons torn off, in fact we were reduced to looking like a lot of tramps, and this just when we had prided ourselves over looking so smart, whether anyone noticed or not. The Quartermaster thought it funny, and when I found I still had two buttons on my forage cap, suggested I ask them to 'come back for them'. It was a long time before he contrived all the replacements that we required.

In spite of the rumble of gunfire it was evident that there was no activity at the moment on this front. The First Battle of Ypres had not altered the general course of the front lines, which ran from Nieuport on the coast along the River Yser and canal, round to the east of Ypres, then bending west of Messines on the ridge of that name and round again east of Ploegsteert and Armentières. Hazebrouck, Kemmel and Bailleul were situated on a western extension of this ridge. The small town of Neuve-Église (Belgian name Nieuwkerke), below which lay our wagon-lines, was the eastern limit for transport without observation by the enemy. Less than a mile beyond the ground rose up, very steeply for this country, into the formidable 233 ft. high north-south ridge of Messines, which was in the full possession of the enemy.

Our Battery went straight into position in a hedgerow just beyond the town.

Neuve-Église was our first sight of a shell shattered town, about half the houses being destroyed and the streets filled with shell holes full of stinking green water. Some civilians had stayed on, but shops were empty. Our Brigade H.Q. was in a nice little house on the outskirts on our side, and, to my annoyance, I was attached here on duty as Third Battery orderly for a fortnight.

I had with me my favourite old horse, Buttertub, who had seen better days, and he and I were very comfortably billeted at a small farm a short distance down the Nieppe road which belonged to a delightful Walloon family called Desiré. They spoke good French and they could not do too much for me. I slept in straw in a loft. The whole family, especially old grandmother, continually plied me with questions about England; they wanted news and had been unable so far to communicate with any of their billetees as none could speak French. I used to play sometimes with the children, and it was extraordinary how when a bombardment was in progress and the whole farm shook, these kiddies seemed not to notice it. What penalties knowledge brings. Their mother, Germaine, a pretty, fair young woman, worked hard on the farm. One day after heavy shelling, when the farm had been plastered, I returned to learn that the poor girl had almost gone berserk, running round the fields chased by the shell bursts.

I was glad when the order came for me to go to the guns. They had now moved a little forward into a small field with Messines ridge towering 250 ft close in front and Ploegsteert Wood on the right. The guns were in a hedge below a row of small elms. We hardly knew the word camouflage in those days and our efforts in that direction were limited to sticking a few branches in the ground in front of the guns.

We had now given up our Territorial nomenclature. Our Brigade had become the 240th and we belonged to the 48th Division and were in the 2nd Army, replacing the 4th Division. Our 'A' and 'B' Batteries were on our right in hedges, in fact every hedge here contained a Battery; 'A' Battery fired directly over 'B' Battery, an arrangement to which at that time no one took any objection. Behind were Regular 60-pounder batteries and shelling was fairly continuous and all heavy.

Our first impression was that it was difficult to tell whether shells were coming or going, but we soon got to know; also they seemed to travel at such a leisurely speed that we found it hard to believe that by careful watching we could not perceive them in flight. Actually the only shells we could see in flight were our own for an instant when we stood immediately behind the gun.

I was pleased to get the layer's position on 'A' gun. The range was 3,600 yards and the sweep angle 15 degrees, which gave our gun 900 yards of trench to cover. Unfortunately we could do very little firing owing to shortage of ammunition, our battery ration being 8 rounds per day. The Germans knew this, and, having plenty of ammunition, replied with interest (whenever we fired) upon our infantry, who did not thank us and sent back rude messages telling us to 'shut up'.

We now experienced a real worry, which later at odd times became unbearable. One day a round from our gun went off with a peculiar whining shriek which we had not heard before. Order came 'stop, examine gun'.

We then saw some cavalrymen billeted in a farm on the slope in front franticly waving sheets. It was our first premature, a time shell having burst on firing. The cause was of course some fault in the fuse and we could only hope it would not happen again. There was no re-occurrence till Somme days.

It was fortunate we had no complaints from infantry, because our guns proved to be what we feared, inaccurate. The whole dial sight unit wobbled in its seating, the elevation of the barrel was not in an absolutely vertical arc, so that the layer was supposed to 'correct for error' every time the range altered. They were heavy and unwieldy guns in spite of their small size, and we daily longed and enquired for the new 18-pounders which were promised and plied our officers with questions about them.

4

TRANQUIL DAYS

I adopt this heading with diffidence. This account purports to be a description of the day to day life of this battery, an account of what happened irrespective of any preconceived notions. In most parts of the line the situation was by no means tranquil, but with us it was so, the war seemed appreciably distant and our woes scarcely exceeded lamentations upon the scarcity of Fray Bentos. But we knew there were plenty of people not experiencing this kind of life.

My first sight of such people came one day when I happened to be on the main road near Nieppe and watched a battery file through a gate to horse-lines. It was a battery of Regular Divisional Artillery on trek to battles in the north.

Divisional Artillery were, I realized afterwards, the salt of the earth in our world. They were used continuously for, and existed for the purpose of, being thrown at a moment's notice into any position of extreme danger or crisis. Wherever shelling was worst, there went Divisional Artillery in support. How any survived, I do not know.

This battery had obviously only just pulled out from some hot spot further south; they were dirty and bedraggled, riding in silence with tired eyes; we were overawed. They filed into the field, a sergeant pointed to a gunner who slid off his limber, took a rifle, went to the gateway, shouldered and ordered in one movement, and, with an expression of utter, blank exhaustion, appeared to sleep where he stood. I never forgot his face; he seemed to be without hope. If so, he was right. They trekked on next day towards Ypres. How it was that they were allowed to take that road, I never discovered, as we all knew that the road from the north edge of Neuve-Église was under full observation by the enemy. They went along it, were caught near Kemmel, and, so report said, blown to bits.

Suddenly spring came. I had never experienced a continental spring before. There was no gradual growth and unfolding of leaves: one day it was winter and the next was spring, so it seemed. A little brook of surface water ran in a ditch by the cart track leading to our position. Its banks seemed to flower in a night with marsh marigolds, cuckoo-pint, primroses and quantities of golden saxifrage and moschatel. But the real feast for the eyes was the green of the grass, a green that you just do not see in England, a green of unbelievable intensity and brilliance, the green of the coloured pictures in old children's books, which I used to think exaggerated and unreal. It seemed a natural paradise in our little field. The weather became sunny and dry, the war had momentarily gone to sleep and we indulged in inter-battery cricket matches on the flat ground between the other two batteries.

However, soon our peace was disturbed. The range was good, but the shells were so small, probably 12-pounders, that they were greeted with hilarity and derisive shouts. But it was the first and the last time that we thought shelling funny. Later, one night was enlivened similarly when I was on guard. Small shrapnel burst with alarming accuracy round the elm trees. After reporting at the officers' dugout, I became very occupied in trying to decide on which side of my elm trunk to stand. Curiously, I was never troubled with 'small stuff' again until 2½ years later, when, after that period of 5.9 and 8-inch infliction, I treated another spell of the 'small stuff' with disdain at Ypres, which led to my undoing.

Another event quite shook us. On April 22 we aroused to find our eyes smarting and stinging. Of course we knew what it was, in view of the Germans' first use of gas recently at Ypres. Authority could not have been much impressed, or we would not now have been completely without protection. In due course thick flannel hoods with talc eye spaces, soaked in some solution, were issued. It seemed possible to breathe, work the gun and hear orders in them, but after a time one suffocated with carbon-dioxide which could not escape. Fortunately, proper gas masks arrived fairly soon afterwards.

There was a form of guard which I rather liked, telephone guard. Our signallers were fine fellows and had been so well trained that they could talk more quickly by Morse key than in words. Farm houses were made into exchange stations with complicated switchboards and the signallers' dugout on the position was a terminal.

Night work entailed waking the battery if a fire order came through from F.O.O. (Forward Observation Officer). I had to know the Morse call for the battery and nothing else; it would come from Joe at the exchange station called Dead Man's Farm. I could talk only to him, but he assured me he could put me through to all the other batteries, horse-lines and column, Brigade H.Q., Boulogne, Le Havre and England, which I doubted. However, I was sufficiently entertained merely listening in. There was a continuous babel of conversation all night. Joe explained: 'You see, you are tapped into the brigade batteries' line, which can be connected at brigade to anywhere, and if so connected you can hear over the whole system, the area increasing directly according to the cube of the number of connections,' so he said. He was a better mathematician than I.

On my first night I was on from 23.00 hours to 01.00 hours. The signallers slept all round, snored and talked in their sleep about wires. I had a candle and some literature.

Two calls, a loud and a soft one, went on persistently, but they were not mine. But there were also various conversations: 'I can't have this fooling on the phone, consider yourself under arrest'. 'All right old boy, but it isn't at all like the Adjutant's voice.' At last the loud call got through and an irate officer's voice shouted 'I'm the Adjutant of – Brigade; are you Forward?' 'No, I'm James.' 'Damn it, I said Forward, No. 5 dugout, brigade?' 'You want who, Forward, never heard of him, not in our lot.' 'Oh my stars, I said Forward, F.O.R.W.A.R.D., not a man's name.' 'Oh, Forward, I'm sorry, but you can't hear over these things. I can't think what would happen in case of an attack. I'll put you through.' Pause. 'Is that Forward No. 5 dugout – Brigade?' 'Yes, and the grub we get, well I bet it is worse than yours and never a drop of beer, and as for the officers …' 'Get off the line there, get off the line damn you, you've no business on the line at all this time of night. Is that Forward?' 'Yes, oh is that you Jimmy?'

When they had finished I hear again the fainter call speaking. It is a refined Scotch voice who also is having difficulties: 'I'm testing the wires at Centre. Are you – Brigade?' After endless difficulty he gets an answer: 'Oh, yes, our line's all right, thank you'. Then he starts another call and keeps at it persistently, so that whenever I take up the receiver, I hear his patient Scotch voice say, 'I'm testing the wires at Centre'.

I then hear two voices I know conversing, 'Yes, it's not a bad game, do you think he'd teach me'? 'I daresay, call him up and ask him'. Then my instrument buzzes the battery call. I snatch it in a frenzy thinking it is an attack, 'Say, Gunner, will you teach me poker tomorrow? Baldwin's mad on it'.

I never got down to teaching poker to the signallers, but I taught it to 'A' sub and they wallowed in it.

Our wagon-lines were now at a farm on the main Armentières road just outside Nieppe. We made ourselves shacks in a nice meadow full of buttercups by threading our ground sheets together. Two Gunners per sub-section took turns there. We had an easy time, but there was too much horse work for us gunners and we preferred being at the guns.

Every evening the whole battery would assemble on the roadside and sing songs. We sang well and they were good tunes, but the words of course were disgusting. In the later years of the war we would reminisce about those summer evenings 'on the Nieppe road'.

Towards the end of June rumour had it that we were going south. I was at the wagon-lines and had one day to go to H.Q. I took Buttertub and rode via Nieppe, as this road went past Desiré's farm. I felt I must say goodbye to my kind friends. I was hailed by Germaine, the pretty daughter, *Monsieur Preece, venez et dire bonjour à Maman*. They all seemed pleased to see me, especially dear old grandmother, who obviously had had no opportunity to talk about England to anyone since the last time I was there. I was given some *déjeuner*, plied with questions about England and myself and asked when I would *revenir*. I was quite sad to say goodbye to them.

On June 26 our guns came out and we all moved off from the wagon-lines on our move south, to the Somme we thought.

We were, henceforth, to be in the Third Army.

Getting the battery off is a long and hectic job and we did not pull in to 'lines' in a field west of Bailleul till 02.00 hours next morning. The next evening the trek was a short one to Strazeele. The next evening we had a long march through Merville and Calonne to Robecq, arriving at 01.00 hours.

Battery trek was a slow and monotonous business. Our starting order was 'walk-march' and the walk was indeed a slow one; such a thing as a trot behind the lines was unknown. Moreover, when further south we came to what might almost be called hills or gentle slopes, the immediate order was, 'Halt, gunners dismount'. The horses had to be relieved of unnecessary weight. In these days it was pleasant to get off the hard limbers and walk, and we were unaggrieved.

Road transportation of artillery in this war was definitely slower by half than walking pace. I estimated it at about two miles per hour.

Robecq was a pretty little place and there were cherry orchards, which we raided.

Next day we travelled on along our plodding course through Lillers to Ferfay, a village on an Arras road and some ten miles west of Béthune. Our camp was a pleasant place under large trees in the grounds of a *château*.

We were invisible from the air, but as it was the only wood for miles around, this was not very much comfort. Outside our park it was an ugly district with coal mines; St Nicolas on the cross roads ahead was a miserable place on a *pavé* road flanked with rows of empty miners' houses.

After three dull weeks we started off again, but in the reverse direction, back to Lillers, where we entrained. The men worked so swiftly here that the Major[1] gave out that he would time us on our disentraining, so as to be able to boast to the other batteries. Our train took us through Doullens, which was to be our Divisional Base, to Pas-en-Artois. Here at the word go we set to, and when Sergeant-Major Parker reported, 'All ready, sir', the Major announced the time to be 25 minutes and gave a word of praise. From an historical point of view, it is remarkable to realize that there was a time when men worked willingly and with a sense of pride in carrying out the orders from above.

After a five-mile trek south we came to a pretty valley at the bottom of a partially wooded slope of a chalk escarpment, and camped in a field at a little village called Thièvres.

It now transpired that we had been sent here temporarily to form part of an army corps to co-operate with the French further south, and that we would be under a French general.

Our first day, or rather night, here was somewhat disastrous. Our men had experienced literally no opportunities for *estaminet* crawling, and what beer they had come by was French beer of which they took a dim view. There was a little *estaminet* in the village anxious to welcome the Tommies, and this they did by offering unlimited quantities of *vin rouge* at five francs a bottle. Few of the men had ever drunk wine and they proceeded now to do so after the manner of beer. Towards lights out terrible scenes were witnessed, half the battery returning to the lines on the backs of the other half. The situation was deplorable and it seemed at the time that everyone, men, N.C.O.s and officers, were entirely anxious that all knowledge of the night's events should, as far as might be, be suppressed. I felt sorry for the Major; he was a fair-minded man and would be sure to feel a certain sympathy for the men. He dealt with the matter over the next week tactfully and quietly; half the battery were under open arrest for several weeks. As, however, we were from this time forward to be denied convivial evenings of any kind, being under arrest was no punishment at all and made not the slightest difference to our dull life.

---

1   Major Geoffrey Dennis Browne: see note in the Appendix: Artillerymen Mentioned.

While we were here, news at last came that our Mark II 18-pounders were
ready for collection. Our old guns and wagons were thankfully hitched up
and away went the teams to Pas, where we dumped them and transferred
joyfully to the beautiful new, slim, shining guns and wagons. These guns were
a joy to manhandle, being lighter than the old ones, easy to run forward or
switch round, in fact two men could do it. The ammunition of the old guns
had been laughable. The shell and the charge were separate, the former being
rammed up with a short rod. Now we had real rounds which were like huge
rifle cartridges, such things as we had never seen before. You 'yanked' them
in and slammed the breech. But they were heavy, and later, when we were
issued with canvas shoulder carriers which held four, together weighing one
hundredweight, we knew what hard work was when 'ammo thumping' was
in progress for any length of time.

We moved up the pretty valley eastwards. The fields on both sides were
crammed with infantry and artillery camps, gun-parks, wagon-lines, ammunition and ambulance parks, both French and British, in fact it seemed a mix up.

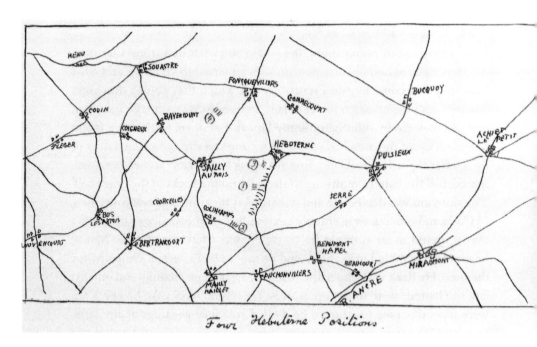

Four Hebuterne Positions

At Coigneux, a tiny village, we parked in a field under a wood, parked the wagons just off the road and made sleeping holes in the wood. The guns went on into position (First Hébuterne Position) but I was not with them. We expected to be here indefinitely, and our sojourn was indeed lengthy and also peaceful. Tranquil days continued. We made shacks in the wood and had our meals in a room in the farmhouse of Hirondelle Farm, a nice farm in the village. Broad-leaved campanula and periwinkle grew around, but flies tormented, and now for the first time that other war started, the one against crawling rather than hopping, things. Above the valley the land was entirely arable, the crops being light but growing at a great pace, wheat, oats, barley, beans, peas, vetches, sainfoin and lucerne.

In due course I went up. We were now on the extreme eastern point of the northern side of the salient which occupied the area of the valley of the River Somme. The gun position was on what we called the Hébuterne Plain, which was a wide flat expanse terminating to the east with a considerable escarpment, which we were lucky to hold, as it gave a fine, wide view over enemy territory. This plain had been fought over for so long that it had run wild, what crops there were being of the nature of forlorn remains.

Our position was close behind the edge of the escarpment about half-way between Hébuterne and Colincamps. It was an old French position. The French batteries were the famous Soixante Quinze, which fired minute shells at such a speed that they were as effective as machine guns or more so. The French artillerymen were jolly, friendly fellows, apparently without any discipline whatever, who certainly knew how to fire guns. The little guns themselves appeared while in action to be in danger of falling to pieces, all their parts appearing to be loose. Most of the French troops had pulled out and gone south, and soon they all went.

We were now at the beginning of our two years' sojourn on the Somme.

It was now that we were introduced to the extraordinary contraptions, which we had never even heard of before, called casemates. Whether or not we thought that we and the guns were going to sit out in the open day and night summer and winter, I cannot remember, though the time was not far distant when this was the case. The casemate was meant to protect the guns, ammunition and men, and most certainly they did so. We developed implicit faith in them for months, until it was borne in on us that the Germans were only waiting for enough ammunition before making the attempt to blow them all up. Anything more ridiculously conspicuous on this wide open plain could hardly be imagined.

The word camouflage had at this time never been heard of, at least I had never heard of it in connection with war. But after a few literally shattering experiences in casemates, we welcomed the issue of the large nets covered with painted rags and felt stupidly as safe under them as we had previously felt under casemates. Unfortunately, camouflaged positions soon became as easily recognisable by scouting planes as were the casemates, for this reason: all batteries had to be approached regularly by ammunition teams, and the tracks of these were bound to show from the air after a very short time, however much the drivers tried to vary their routes. Nets were no protection against shrapnel, but latterly we never experienced shrapnel, but when we were treated to 5.9 bombardment we tended to wish ourselves back in casemates. The point of course was that the enemy could soon spot us anyway and if he decided to blow us in the air he could do so any day, but there was an ameliorating factor in this argument, eventually, which was that in time our batteries numbered such thousands that no amount of ammunition in the world would suffice to blow all of them to bits. We rather dreaded therefore being given any special job by ourselves to harass some special German battery, for obvious reasons.

The French casemates were substantial, but the proportion of sandbags to timber was too high and the gunners' dugouts, which were placed a little in the rear, were nothing more than holes in the ground with earth roofs. Unfortunately, some wet weather caused most of the latter partly to disintegrate.

Three of 'A' sub crew were allotted the worst hole. On arriving at the position in a downpour, I had a shock. I was used to hard ground and dirt, but not yet to lying in water. Water dripped through the sodden earth and a ground-sheet pegged up over my bunk barely succeeded in pouring its contents into the central trench which was our standing space. Our dugout never quite collapsed, but it was a tremendous incentive to work, when, as soon happened, it was decided to build a new position just in front of the existing one.

It is curious at a distance of time to try and estimate one's reactions at the time to unpleasant situations. Thinking now of that dugout, which gave no protection except against splinters, it is obvious that any near hit would have resulted in our being both buried and drowned at the same time, but I do not remember thinking this at the time. The fact was, we lived for the day, and the future fortunately had little part in our thoughts. But I confess that when my mind did turn to it, it was with an ever increasing dull foreboding.

We worked like furies. Supply did wonders; huge baulks of timber arrived and we fixed them as side walls and roof for each casemate. We then filled sandbags for weeks and made endless processions to build up the roof and make it up to a six feet depth. Two dugouts, one on each side, with interior passages to the gun chamber, constituted an ammunition store and crew's quarters. The whole gave the appearance of a long mound some twelve feet high. Our gun crews consisted now of four men, numbers one to four, this being ample with ammunition close at hand.

Our new guns were a joy. Their best feature was their No. 7 dial sight fixed on the shield with a short periscope projecting above. There was also a traversing mechanism by which the layer could adjust his line by 4° left and right without having to call for the trail to be moved.

To my delight I became layer of 'A' gun.

For night firing, a small lamp was fixed on a post which was placed on the right front; I was always in agony as to what would happen if a shell blew the post away. Our pair of aiming posts was our O.L., or original line, which was fixed by careful ranging.

Layer's instructions, which had to be learnt by heart and were pinned on the wall and written down in each gunner's notebook, were as follows:

Original Line – zero on aiming posts.
Night Line – 24°, 40' R.
Angle of Sight – 20' depression.
Range – 2,875 yards.
Extreme left switch – 37°, plus 4° traverse.
Extreme right switch – 24°.
Half Zone – 6° right of O.L.
S.O.S. on Half Zone – angle to lamp 30°, 40' R. Range 3000, sweep 45'.
Retaliation on Puisieux, when enemy shelling Sailly-au-Bois: Battery Action Puisieux 4°R of O.L., A.S. 10/ depr. Range 5,900. Angle to lamp 28°, 35' R.
Retaliation on Puisieux, when enemy shelling Hébuterne: Right (or Left) Section Action Serre – 22°R of O.L.A.S.O. Range 3850. Angle to lamp 45° R.

I had the misfortune to develop a complex about alterations to angles, that is, on adding or deducting degrees and minutes. If I had, say, 2°, 10' right on the sights, and was suddenly ordered in a bombardment to add 45' more left, I feared a sudden inability to do this simple sum. There was a right screw which, turned away from you, added, and a left screw which deducted. I took

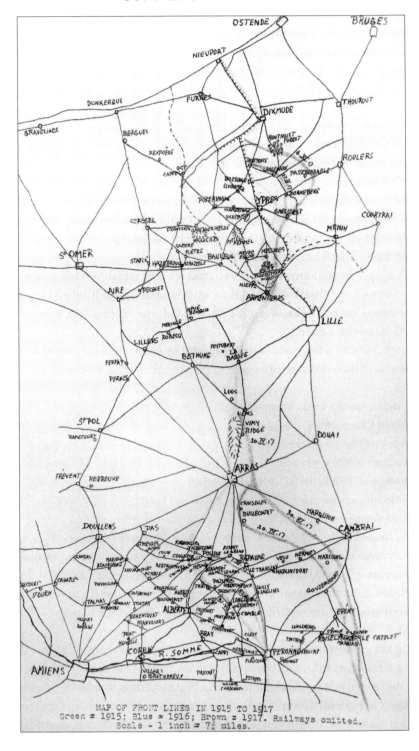

MAP OF FRONT LINES IN 1915 TO 1917
Green = 1915; Blue = 1916; Brown = 1917. Railways omitted.
Scale - 1 inch = 7¼ miles.

to turning the left screw over 9 strokes of 5 minutes, which would mean 45' taken off, but I feared interruption to my counting. I felt ashamed of my anxiety over such simple sums, but gradually developed confidence and never got into trouble. But the fear of the shouted order, which I once heard, 'What reading has the layer of – gun got on his sights?', and, after the reply, 'Layer of gun is under arrest', was always with me.

Ammunition was still short and the ordinary ration was five rounds per day per gun and that generally for [the purpose of] registering.

This front was at the time entirely one of artillery duels, that is duels between 'the heavies'. Throughout the war it was perhaps not realized that quiet times were rarely quiet for the batteries, so much so that there came a time when we literally welcomed an offensive, because then we found the enemy had no time to attend to us. Great shells of size anything up to 8-inch rumbled leisurely over Hébuterne in both directions nearly all day. We soon got used to it, as they were not directed at us but to lines of communication, and we ceased to listen to the distant crashes; probably 200 a day passed over.

The noise of firing inside the confined space of the gun-chamber was pretty bad, but we found it bearable provided we never stood immediately behind the gun. Sometimes a man would go temporarily deaf. I had luckily provided myself with a pair of Mallock-Armstrong ear-defenders which, screwed into the ears, completely deadened the shock whilst enabling one to hear orders clearly. Eventually rubber ones were issued to all gunners.

Our O.P. (Observation Post) was in a French trench on the actual ridge a short distance in front, and consisted of two splinter-proof huts, one for an officer and one for the signallers, and a deep dugout for the telephonist.

The signallers had their own headquarters in a minute cottage, almost the only one with an entire roof, in Hébuterne, where they made themselves very comfortable, though it was a noisy and unhealthy place. They were independent people and took orders from no one except their own officer, but they did a wonderful job and were a jolly, friendly lot. They had been able to take over the French wires, which were of different colours and bore names. Ours was called 'Rossignol', and it ran from O.P. to the billet and on to F.O.P. (Forward Observation Post) in the trenches.

O.P. was always manned by an officer, 3 gunners and a telephonist signaller.

My first turn on observation was from 22.00 hours to midnight. It was a warm summer night and things were quiet except for bursts of rifle fire down the slope. Orders were to report S.O.S. (three red lights); danger (red and green); excessive rifle fire; and note the direction of all gun flashes by their angles from the magnetic north with an illuminated compass; also to watch for Morse signalling from our signallers in the trenches.

There was a bright moon and I tried to make out the features of the landscape. I knew roughly where the villages of Serre and Puisieux were, and their woods, but the light was insufficient.

The men seemed to find guards irksome, and so they were in winter, but on a summer night I quite enjoyed them. In the ordinary routine there was so little time I had to myself, that I welcomed the opportunity to bring my thoughts together in quietude.

At midnight I called Mr Todd, a really nice young officer. I had not had an ordinary conversation with an officer since we left England, and, as he seemed glad of my company, I lingered on and we talked. Somehow the conversation got onto the subject of Free Trade, and I held forth rather ignorantly in its favour. If he had been a less nice person he would have been annoyed, as he knew something about commerce and I did not. I dare now to wonder whether my arguments after all may not have been nearer the truth. We also discussed and disagreed upon theories of war. By the time we had finished it was 02.00 hours and I turned in till 04.00 hours.

The dawn always fascinates me. There was a slight morning mist, but it cleared gradually and the landscape seemed to extend and open out on all sides. There was a tower of some sort in Serre, which the Germans undoubtedly used as an observation point. One day we had a go at it but it still stood. Gradually I made out more villages and scattered farms and unnatural-looking hedgerows, sure signs of enemy batteries; there were long poplar-lined roads, but no sign of life anywhere, not a living thing, in spite of the fact that armies were facing one another. Suddenly there is a burst of rifle fire below and later a regular covey of bullets come over; they seem to sing along quite leisurely and you can hear them coming.

Orders came that gunners were to be familiarized with the infantry trenches, which was wise, as we were in danger of becoming exclusive in our isolation. Each day a gunner went to Hébuterne, dumped his kit at the signaller's billet and went out with the signaller patrolling 'Rossignol', which was liable to be cut or buried by a shell at any time. At night the signaller patrolled with a stick having a ring at the end through which the wire ran.

On my first day we began operations by apple hunting and actually found some Russets.

Hébuterne had been taken by the French in June at the cost of several thousand men. The Germans had retired merely to the low land just east of the town, where their trenches now were. The whole town was wrecked and the church was a pitiful sight with the pulpit alone standing. It was impossible to walk along the main road of the town, but there was no need to do so as trenches ran everywhere, and where a house stood in the way, the trench burrowed under it; houses were loopholed and many of the streets were blocked with barricades.

The signallers were well supplied with food, as the battery cookhouse was with them, no fires being allowed on the position. They had a very cosy time when off duty, and they deserved it; they played cards and gossiped, and were the source of all information which came over the wire, mostly via infantry.

My first night was rather disturbed. A slight whistling gradually increased in intensity till a tremendous bang made the house shake. It was one of our 6-inch howitzer shells on the German trenches nearby. Soon some of our heavies were at work and some field batteries. Then the Germans began. Some of their shells you could hear coming, some not, and before long I learnt that the ones you do not hear are the ones that may get you, and that it is better this way than the other if the matter can be considered dispassionately. It was my first experience of heavy shelling, and it was disconcerting not knowing where the shells were bursting. They always sounded nearer than they really were; the big bursts made a noise like 'bwank'.

The next morning I accompanied a signaller to O.P., from where we followed 'Rossignol' along an old trench, scratching it out where buried and pulling it out of pools of water, back to the village and into the communication trench to the trenches. Here the going was easy on duckboards and the wire was pinned to the trench side. After many zigzags we came to the firing trench and called in at the F.O.P. dugout. This was close to the infantry commander's dug out, in fact the two communicated. Here calls for firing support were passed instantaneously to the battery, so many rounds on a certain map reference, or S.O.S., meaning gunfire, on some section or on the whole sector, and it would only be a matter of seconds before our guns were firing.

The infantry, this lot being Worcesters, had confidence in us, I heard on all sides, and it was pleasant to hear. When I was introduced to a sergeant, we were received with friendly smiles and remarks such as, 'Yes, you blokes stopped them all right last week'. He was in charge of a machine gun and took us along to see it. The German trenches were only fifty yards away, but there was an impenetrable line of wire entanglement in between; they appeared as rough lines of turned up earth. I felt we owed these fellows pretty well everything, and only hoped they continued to have confidence in us.

The sergeant then offered to take us into some old German trenches, now unoccupied. They were situated in front of part of our firing line. We followed along the firing trench through innumerable twists and turns, past dugouts, bomb magazines, snipers perched up behind iron shields, artillery F.O. officers watching their sectors through periscopes, graves of French and British soldiers with little wooden crosses, often consisting simply of the poor fellow's own dugout knocked in over him. At last we came to a bit of low parapet over which we slithered with some haste, the knowledge that the German trenches were now only thirty yards distant being enough to make me feel inclined to do the rest of the scramble on hands and knees. We then found ourselves in a trench utterly smashed to pieces by artillery, an extraordinary sight. It was just a mass of debris, the parapet only being intact here and there, and what had been dugouts had all collapsed with their timbers either lying about or sticking up on end in chaos. We scrambled along talking only in whispers, darting across places where the parapet had been blown away, and sat down to inspect the view in a safer spot. We then became aware of an odour, my first experience of the smell of the dead.

There were plenty of souvenirs if I had wanted any, bits of German newspapers and letters, tins of rations, bits of bandoliers, a pair of boots; I picked up the latter, but dropped them quickly enough for there were feet in them. A skull and some bones lay about and some bodies partly protruded through the earth.

I picked up a German letter encrusted with mud, but I could read it. It was a pretty fancy little sheet of notepaper printed at the top with blue doves and the words 'Aus Liebe'. I prepared to have my heart wrung and was not disappointed: 'Your friend Adler has been wounded in the head and Ernst is dead'. *Am letzten Sontag war Ich in Waltershausen, das war schoen, Viel schoener wurde es gewesen wenn Du auch konnen Urteil nehmen. Wie lange kann der traurige Krieg lange dauern. Deine treue Anna.*

Back in the firing trench I took some photographs. The Worcesters were delighted and we parted with many cheerios.

I had brought out with me a marvellous little pocket camera which had a Goerz lens the like of which I have never had since. The definition on the tiny films was quite beautiful. After the first month in France the order had come that all cameras were to be handed in. It was sent home, but in due course my faithful factotum, on my instructions, returned it to me in one of her food tins, and I carried on, but with much circumspection. I continued to take photographs till we had been some time on the Somme, after which photography no longer appealed to me, apart from the danger of being wounded and having the camera found on me, I got rid of it and never grieved the loss of anything more, as of course I never saw it again. I managed, however, to take enough photographs to illustrate my first year on the Western Front.

Towards the end of September we sensed there was something in the air. Bread ceased and dog biscuits were substituted, ammunition supply was for the first time abundant and included H.E. (High Explosive). Drivers seemed disinclined to linger and chat, and drove off quickly with 'Bye-bye chaps in case we don't see you again'.

Then on 22 September it came: 'An attack which will last three days will commence tomorrow at 15.00 hours'.

Next morning we got ready. I was No. 5 fuse-setter. It was disappointing, but our bombardier had precedence over me for layer. At the appointed time our 4.7s at Colincamps loosed off a salvo with a crash. This was the signal. Our orders were Battery Fire Five Seconds. There were five other 18-pounder batteries behind us and on the flanks. Our little gun had on nearly his full range at 6,100 yards, evidently ranged on some battery position, and looked comical with its nose sticking up in the air. Then we drop to 2,775 yards and we hear we are wire cutting, the usual prelude to infantry attack.

All the batteries on this front are firing, the Territorial 18-pounders and 4.5-inch howitzers, the Regular 4.5-inch long-barrelled gun, replacing the 60-pounder, and the Kitchener's 6-inch howitzers, and the resulting roar is only short of what could be called an intense bombardment in that you can distinguish each bang but can hardly count them.

No. 4 [the loader] has most of the work to do and hardly appreciates Sergeant's remark to 'stop dripping perspiration on the trail'. I make the discovery that fuses vary, as this is the first time anyone has had more than eight to set running. The fuse key turns some of them easily, others are stiff and it is wrist-straining work to turn some at all. The fuse number is 8.6, and some packer has smeared them all with such a thick layer of grease that it obscures the number. I use a wiper to remove the grease, but soon find I do it quicker with my hands; soon my breeches and face are black with grease, and Sergeant Williams, putting his head in to inspect, refers to me as 'that dirty-looking ruffian'. I have a worrying job to be sure that each fuse is correct and to hand rounds across fast enough.

Suddenly we hear the whistle of an approaching shell and bang it goes some yards ahead, then the same happens a few yards behind. This we know is ranging, and 'Now look out' says somebody, and we wait. It comes but passes well over. We were at this time unused to the strain of 'waiting for the third one', but it became in due course a refined form of torture, one of the worst that war could devise. Then they began to let us have it back and we were aware that the noise was now considerable.

Everyone seemed to be yelling orders, the telephonist to the battery commander, from him to section commanders and from them to sub-section number ones, always with added imprecations to 'get a move on for God's sake'. Suddenly there is a rush like an express train and the whole position shakes. A glance behind shows a large cloud of black smoke hanging low, and soon the smell of nitric acid pervades everything. There is now a veritable cannonade and you cannot hear anyone speak. Shells burst in front, behind and apparently just over our heads and some pitch by the officers' dugout. We can hardly speak for dust. Bits of stone and shrapnel strike the gun shield. This is our baptism, and we get so excited that we yell 'Go it, let them have it back'. (War is still a game.) I, however, have to concentrate absolutely on my 8.6.

Then comes our first casualty and a stretcher is called for. Bombardier 'B' of 'D' gun has had it in the form of many small splinters all over himself.

Then suddenly everything stops and 'Cookie', who marvellously has had our hot tea hidden away, brings it out. We are all pleased with ourselves and it has been fun. We have fired 150 rounds per gun.

It is a comical fact that it was not until 45 years later that I took the trouble to look up and see what happened on 23 September 1915. It was the start of the Battle of Loos. At the time we had no idea what was happening.

The next day we began again at the same time; Battery Fire Ten Seconds, Section Fire and Salvos, all came in various orders. The reply shelling was not so heavy.

After a time the Bombardier complained of a headache, which was not to be wondered at in the confined space. 'Let Price have a go, Sergeant,' and I jumped into the layer's seat. It is easy work. She is bedded in firmly now and hardly moves at all, but I must keep my eye on the aiming posts and clinometer bubble. 'One – Fire!' bang, and so it goes on, the sights jump and vibrate, grit falls from the roof on our heads and dust flies. I am beginning to enjoy it.

Then, 'One, Fire'; I had my hand on the firing lever and in a fraction of a second would have pulled, when there was a tremendous bang; I catch a glimpse through the shield of logs flying through the air, the baulks of the wall seem to come in and all becomes unaccountably dark in front and the air is full of dust and pieces. My hand is still on the lever. I think, what the devil has happened? Then I remember I have had the order to fire and have not done so. I have never been a person who could make up his mind in an emergency quickly, which is a considerable disability, but perhaps this time it saved us all. All this mental struggle on my part may have occupied the space of 1½ seconds, I do not know. But a voice behind me said, 'Stop'. I realized then that what froze my muscles was the fact that I had seen a baulk of timber fall from the roof and lodge exactly across the front of the muzzle of the gun. It was a relief to feel that I had done the right thing, but I hardly expected praise for not obeying an order, nor did I receive any. A shell, probably a 5.9, had struck the outside of the casemate just on the outer side of the timber, and, exploding there, blew the front ends of all the logs onto the gun. One ten-inch log was split in half. If I had fired the shell, the shell and log in front of it might have carried away, but the gun shield could hardly have stood up to the explosion. A couple of yards more left, and it would have come in at the entrance.

We were out of action though the gun was undamaged.

'Anyone hurt?' 'No.' No. 2 had his arm bruised by a spanner which flew off the wall. 'Number one gun out of action, Sir.'

By 01.00 hours we had got the logs back in position and were all tidy again and gun in action. That was my first 'near one'.

We made several clear ways through the wire, much to the delight of the infantry. A general came round next day and congratulated us and inspected our casemate.

When we were well settled in our new position, work became purely routine, and the tail end of 1915's summer made life on the position quite pleasant. There was a good deal of time on our hands. We always preferred being at the guns rather than at the wagon-lines, because at the latter there was always work, grooming, harness, cleaning and making new lines, whereas at the guns our officers were very reasonable, and when there definitely was nothing to do, work was not invented, and we could sit around, play cards or sleep.

An intriguing occupation for a time, until it became boring, was to watch our anti-aircraft guns pursuing German planes. On a bright still day there was generally a German plane high up stooging around observing. We noted his oblique cut, fish tail and black Maltese cross. Occasionally a white puff emerged from one side or he would make a slight dip, bank or swerve to indicate something he had seen.

There were two anti-aircraft guns, one at Hébuterne and one at Colincamps. You would see high up little round white clouds of shell bursts, then after an interval came the faint popping sounds of their bursts. The procedure was always the same, the gun ranged with single shells creeping up at the same intervals; when the bursts came apparently quite close, firing ceased, recommencing on a different lay to furiously build a wall of bursts in front of the plane in order to divert him. This caused him to change his course, but as he had every other direction to choose from, we could not see that much was achieved. It was some time before we realized that the chance of a hit was so remote that all efforts were concentrated on heading off. I only once heard report of a plane being hit and brought down.

Each gunner had a spell at the wagon-lines at Coigneux exchanging with another gunner coming up. It was a change, and while the lovely weather lasted, it was pleasant there. The men had shacks made of ground sheets on the steep side of a cut wood, a nice place to be in. Life was dull and there were the usual fatigues and guards. Our watering place was at long troughs down the valley at Couin. There were enough of us for each man to take a couple of horses and we rode bareback and became quite used to it.

One lovely evening, it was 16 October, I took my camera and took a photo of the horses at the troughs. It was a warm autumnal evening, everything was bone dry and life seemed an easy and comfortable business.

I do not remember being particularly conscious at this time of our tranquil days, or of speculating much as to their probable duration, but we surely knew that they could not go on, that, after all, this was war, though its horrors had so far not assailed us. There certainly was a presentiment at the back of our minds that bad times must come, the question was when.

The answer came next day. On 17 October the weather broke and it rained from then on most days for the rest of the winter. At this date we merely cursed and thought no more about it.

We moved at once from our shacks into the cowsheds and barns of Hirondelle Farm in the village. It was a well built farm consisting of a good living house facing a quadrangle of stone-built cowsheds and barns. The whole battery were found billets here, right section in a long, low cowshed with a rough stone-cobbled floor. The men set to work to make bunks, which they made with stakes cut from the wood and fixed together to make small bed frames on legs, the bed base being of stretched sacking, which in spite of its sagging made a very comfortable bunk with a couple of blankets and a greatcoat. I was kindly given help in my amateur efforts and soon had a bunk ready, which I shared alternately with my friend Gunner Dan Smith.

We had our meals in a room in the farmhouse and were on good terms with the farmer and his family.

By 3 November the horse-lines were in an indescribable state. They were in a sloping field below the wood and soon the lower end of the lines was a sea of liquid mud in which the poor horses stood up to their fetlocks. We moved the lower ones higher up, but even so the mud was so deep that the hay we put down for them got churned up in it by their frantic stamping at the sight of it. It was marvellous how the drivers worked to save their horses, continually shovelling mud and trying to protect the hay and the feeding bags. So many of the latter were torn to pieces that there were soon not enough to go round and many horses had to have their oats poured onto sacking, which they immediately stamped upon. Though the horses received their proper ration, they only succeeded in eating about half of it, and became so permanently hungry that it was quite dangerous to be too near them at feeding time. But worse was to come, for at present it was warm.

As time went on the condition of the men's feet became chronic, the ordinary issue ankle-boots being quite inadequate under these conditions. I had a good pair of field boots made by Manfield, and when these were worn out, I just ordered another pair. Even so, I was no better off, because when leather is soaked in water all day and every day it absorbs it like a sponge, and it was like having one's feet permanently in a wet, cold compress. The skin of our feet turned white and dead and peeled off. Trench boots were not available for the artillery, except two pairs for the piquet. As the weather became colder our hands and wrists became cracked and the cracks became permanently filled with dirt, one just washed to get the surface dirt off. I got myself an oilskin and sou'wester, and my ability to provide to some extent for myself caused me embarrassment, but I never heard a word of reproach. I used to ponder whether there was anything I could do for the fellows without making myself conspicuous, because I liked them all so very much and I never had a cross word from any of them. Eventually I did manage something.

In one corner of the yard we made a small canteen, but it contained little but tinned salmon and tobacco, and the men required neither of these. It also contained a gramophone which I had brought out with the help of the Quartermaster. The corporal in charge seemed to spend most of the day winding it. The tune 'When Irish Eyes are Smiling' haunted me ever afterwards and is for me still always associated with Coigneux.

One day in conversation with the corporal, I ascertained that there was an unlimited supply of tinned food at Divisional Stores canteen, so we arranged for a supply of Oxford sausages sufficient for a breakfast for all. I paid over a bundle of five franc notes and in due course they arrived. News had gone round and everyone practically ran back from early grooming. Dixie lids of steaming sausages were rushed into our eating room. Suddenly I thought of the sergeants' mess. I had no idea what to do, however corporal settled it for me and rushed them over. All went very well and it was a lovely breakfast. A senior gunner proposed a vote of thanks to 'Gunner', and I responded to the effect that if and when I had any more 'arps, we would have some more. A message of thanks came from the sergeants. But I felt the whole thing was improper and subversive to discipline.

I became aware about now that my name was 'Gunner'. I always liked the name and appreciated being called by it. It was obvious to me that to live for a long period with the same people and be on good terms, it was primarily necessary to be natural, secondly, not to criticize, and thirdly to adapt. I think I succeeded in this and was, consequently, I thought, repaid all the time by real affection.

I used to fear sometimes that, in this existence rather than life, my mind would atrophy through lack of stimulus, but I contrived to maintain myself on the 'Weekly Times' and 'The Nation', the latter, under the editorship of Massingham, proving a depressing influence with which I failed to disagree. The time came when Massingham's office was raided by the Censors, unsuccessfully, for supposed incriminating evidence, the only result being that the paper was ordered not to send itself abroad in future. This was a nuisance and meant that my factotum had to pack it into my weekly food tins.

No politics were discussed, and of course all knowledge and opinions emanated from the 'Daily Mail'. It has been said that this war was very much 'run by newspapers'.

The cause of this war, and the likelihood of future wars, did not interest the men, this one being amply sufficient for their consideration; they accepted all wars as inevitable, and this would have depressed me more at the time, had I known what future wars would have in store.

One gunner had opinions like mine, only more so. He would burst out, even in front of an officer, about 'bloody capitalists', and appeared to think that Socialism would end all wars; he was optimistic.

I often longed to discuss the subject with an officer, but only managed to do so once with Mr Todd on night observation.

It was fortunately obvious to me that politics at this time was irrelevant. The only exception I took was to the view that if we did not beat the Germans, we would have to 'fight it out all over again', because this implied that, if we did beat them, there would be no more war <u>because</u> we had beaten them.

To me, unfortunately, the problem of wars had become almost an obsession, and a definite obstacle to any reasonable and at all hopeful outlook on life. The subject seemed to me to be a hopeless and insoluble one, and it rankled so continuously in my mind that the immediacy and overwhelming nature of the present war never succeeded in driving it out. Whatever the nature of the catastrophe towards which we all seemed to be heading in this war, it seemed obvious that the apparent inevitability of wars in the future, and <u>for all time</u>, was a far greater and quite unlimited one.

I would doubtless still feel oppressed by the same hopelessness now, had it not been for a fantastic event which took place thirty years later.

Things were too well run in the battery for the existence of any real discontent, in fact we did not at this time realize how well off we were. We grumbled frantically. I often thought back in later months on this grumbling, when I discovered that, when things really were bad, there was no grumbling because we had no time for it.

One incessant habit, peculiar in its most extreme form to the Ranks in wartime, was of course swearing. It was distinguished from what the officers indulged in occasionally by complete absence of restraint. 'Bloody' qualified every noun and most verbs and was often interposed inside compound words, also it gradually became of the many words the least used.

When completely enraged, the practice was to string adjectives together and continue doing so as long as possible without using any one word twice, an extra-long string generally receiving applause.

Swearing resulted from boredom and from not having enough to do, or at any rate not enough to think about. But it developed as time went on and conditions deteriorated into at times a continuous shouting outpouring by everyone at the same time, a non-stop flow, each of us concentrating upon finding words and each completely aware that nobody else was listening to what the others were saying, for the simple reason that we were all, in fact, saying nothing intelligible. It was unedifying and just a habit carried to extremes, and we all partook of it under the impression that it relieved our feelings of aggravation. Possibly it did; I cannot say.

Unfairness, naturally, caused the quickest outburst, having it 'swung on me', more fatigues than one's share, not being relieved on guard punctually and being imposed upon by an N.C.O. who has 'got me in line'.

The fact was that there were few cases of any such unfairness in the running of our battery; it was too well run, and I say so advisedly.

In these early days, when we had nothing – literally – to think about, grievances were thought up. A very satisfactory one was of course that a man was of no importance as he cost 'a bob a day', and that it took five of us to equal in importance one horse, as the railway van notices implied. More specifically, horse-lines life was a horse's life, they alone counted, they, whether in permanent lines or on trek, had to be fed, groomed and watered before we could eat. But we didn't make too much of this argument because we knew it cut no ice.

During the Somme Offensive in 1916 we swore most, but on a slightly higher level, the adjectives being chosen to apply more to top military and political individuals.

Imperceptibly it died out. The first six months of 1917 proved to be a temporary reversion to easy times, and we became tired of swearing. From the time Third Ypres first loomed up ahead till the end, we swore no more, there was too much else to think about, grievances were too great for any words of ours to have impact. We were cured of the habit.

Our officers were strictly fair. Our Major was a great disciplinarian for a young man, but he carried it off, and it was his enthusiasm that made us a good battery that could be relied upon and that made the men dependable and non-shirking. We owed a lot to the officers, who all had a personal interest in the battery, which was not the case later on when, owing to casualties, their places were taken mostly by strangers.

One great grumble became chronic and there was substance in it. It was in the matter of our food, not in its quality, which was good, but in its quantity. Our breakfast consisted of a fair-sized hunk of bread and a smallish, thick piece of bacon, and tea. Dinner was stew and cheese and never varied, except when on trek or in action, when we had bully and biscuits, which personally I rather liked, because they took a long time to eat, and eating was our only pleasure. For some reason the stew, which consisted of bits of meat swimming in greasy water, could really only be drunk, the bits being chewed and spat out, being unbiteable. I could never make out why the meat must always be uneatable; it was not as if occasionally it was eatable, it never was. We rarely ate the cheese because it required bread to eat with it, and if we wanted bread for dinner, we had to save some from breakfast, which we could never do. I discovered that, however hungry you are, you cannot eat cheese by itself. Tea was really the most important event in the day, when we received our second slice of bread, some butter or jam and a wonderful billy-full of hot, strong, sweet tea. After tea, which was at 16.00 hours, there was nothing more that day.

This was not enough for healthy young men living a strenuous outdoor life. If we could have supplemented a little from a canteen, other than our useless one, we should have had enough, but we were literally never near a canteen because we were never near a town. The infantry in their rest billets were further back and within reach of canteens and we did not grudge them anything, but we did not count in that way.

But the ration described was the proper ration scientifically worked out in calories, and if the meat had been eatable we should have been all right, provided we got the ration. That was the trouble; we never quite got it, the ration was on paper. We got it pretty well in summer, but fairly seldom in winter. We were underfed, and the reason was that the ration, adequate in itself, made no allowance for wastage on the way up. There were bound to be items that tumbled off G.S. wagons, were pinched, lost or damaged during the long journey, often in many stages. There was no official imagination. Bread was the worst shortage. Often our precious slices were half size, and Cookie's excuses of damaged loaves were genuine enough. The bread came in sacks. Our brigade had a dump by the road down the valley, where our G.S. wagon collected from the A.S.C. It was a rough board platform by the roadside and there was no guard. If it rained there was a tarpaulin of sorts to cover the heap, but a sack of loaves easily rolls down into the water where it sucks it up like a sponge, all the bottom loaves becoming a sodden pulp which Cookie could do nothing with; he had no oven; his stock of utensils consisted of dixies and lids, the lids were frying pans and the dixies were divided into greasy for stew and non-greasy for tea. The shortage was not bad at Coigneux, but it became awful the following winter.

After the war I was talking to an ex-officer about this. His reply was that of course there was plenty of food at all times for the troops. I was glad to know that I had been suffering from a delusion; however, it was curious that all my companions should have suffered from the same delusion.

I rarely spoke to an officer and could form no opinion as to their way of life. Looking back now, however, it seems to me that the paramount difference in living between them and us was in the matter of food, more especially drink. They could eat in their mess whatever they cared to pay for, and the same with drink, which was whisky. I have a note that we had on a certain day an issue of beer. No doubt we had, but I remember nothing of beer issues either then or thereafter. Our drink issue was, in the winter, in the form of rum at night for the guard and picquet. I could never make up my mind on this matter, as it seemed to me that the after-effect when on guard in the early hours of freezing or pouring mornings, the reaction, had a more depressing effect than there would have been without the stimulus.

Early in November, as conditions worsened, a site for the horse-lines was chosen, on slightly higher ground, for permanent lines which were to be roofed. This required a number of corrugated iron sheets. The A.S.C. did all they could and driblets continued to come in. Fatigue parties cut poles for building the framework. There were plenty of handy carpenters and the lines gradually grew. Meanwhile the rain deluged and on the 29th I wrote that the mud was such that if you got well into it in a deep place, you stuck and had to call to be pulled out. The poor horses, except at feeding time, stood motionless. Fortunately, there were no really hard frosts or they would, so I wrote, 'be frozen in and die'.

Grooming was useless on their mud-soaked backs and legs and harness cleaning equally so as we had used up all rags and could only rub the bits in the mud to clean them. Mud shovelling became our chief occupation, often leading to altercations about not chucking one's muck onto your neighbour's horse's stand.

On one despairing day, when we, all of us, stood hopelessly surveying the scene, squelching the muddy, icy water in our boots, we saw to our surprise a smart looking young staff Major passing up our lines. We had never seen H.Q. people at our horse-lines before. Coming to our group he stopped and talked to us in such an informal friendly manner that we were astounded. He seemed genuinely distressed at our condition and in fact said as much, intimating that he would do all he could to help us, especially in the way of iron sheets for getting us dry stables. He congratulated us on having our horses and harness so clean, which we could not agree about, said that the mud was 'awful', adding, 'Anyway you will never have it worse'. We thought this a happy phrase and one likely to prove true. We were immensely cheered and grateful because we realized now that the top people had not forgotten our existence, as had seemed to be the case. He could not possibly have known how much his visit cheered us.

Eventually we got into our winter lines. We carted chalk from a quarry and gradually made firm stands for each horse, and at last we had them all and ourselves standing under cover in the dry.

Our chief stable builder was a popular little Corporal called 'Benny' Cove. He was almost the most popular man in the battery because he was always cheery and singing. He always sang while he worked, and our winter lines were always associated in my mind with his then favourite, which he sang quietly over and over again. It was in its words ruthless and scandalous and was called 'Again, Again and Again'. It included the lines:

And when I was single my pockets did jingle,
And I wish I was single again.

We would have felt awkward about it, had we not known that he was a devoted husband and father.

We were original over our songs, no 'Tipperary' for us. Our first, the never-to-be-forgotten 'Three German Officers crossed the Rhine' had been out-sung. Our undoubted favourite throughout – that is during the time when we sang, for the time came when we no longer did so – was 'Fred Karno's Army':

We are Fred Karno's Army,
The **** R.F.A.
We cannot fight, we cannot ***
No bloody good are we,
And when we come to Berlin,
The Kaiser he will say,
Hoch, hoch, mein Gott,
What a bloody rotten lot
Is the **** R.F.A.

We never tired of this, especially when on trek and passing through a village, when we seemed determined to broadcast our disabilities to the world.

But when grooming, to pass the weary hours, it was some relief to sing our third popular, which was appropriately called 'Grooming':

Grooming, grooming, grooming,
Always bloody well grooming,
From reveille to lights out,
It's grooming all the time.
Grooming, grooming, grooming,

Always bloody well grooming,
Shan't I be glad when my time's up,
I'll groom no bloody more.

One of our gags, for which I was said to have been responsible, was appropriately addressed by any group standing up to their knees in mud to any other
passing group. It was improper and caused more pleasure than anything I ever
did or said before or after. It was short:

Here's the shit,
(pointing, and two seconds pause)
And we're in it.

It spread all over the battery and to the other batteries, and it reached a point
when men would come and stand and wait for it, and all shout the second
sentence in unison. There was a technique about it, which I explained with
care and success. The first line was to be shouted, but the second should,
according to my rendering, be enunciated slowly and deliberately. When they
did it properly, it became difficult for the Sergeant-Major not to laugh, and
the officers had been known to turn their heads away.

Christmas Day was uproarious and great fun and the A.S.C. did us well.
We sang and ate till the early hours and the officers looked in and healths
were drunk.

Our little village was too small and isolated to attract much heavy shelling,
but just after Christmas one of our teams was hit, the wagon smashed and a
horse killed, the men luckily escaping.

We were not entirely cut off from social life. Those of us not on fatigues
or ammunition running were free after tea. If we felt sufficiently energetic
we would walk to the nearest *estaminet*. There were plenty of these down
the valley, but they were some way off and the nearest one was, curiously
enough, two miles up the valley at the little village of Sailly-au-Bois. Very few
inhabitants remained here, as the village was on the edge of the Hébuterne
plain, and was the last outpost of civilization; it might have been a dangerous
place to be in, as it was the meeting place of four roads, but up to this time it
had for some reason not been too badly shelled.

There was one little *estaminet* there in the little village street of the
Hébuterne road, and its owners had so far succeeded in clinging on to it.

Here on winter evenings we would push ourselves in from the pitchy darkness outside to a bright, tiny room packed with a solid mass of bodies and drink French beer. It was a relief to be for a short time in a warm, dry atmosphere, where everybody talked loudly and continuously without listening to what anyone else said.

I remember once speaking to the nice young woman at the bar when she was momentarily resting, and asking her, '*Quand pars-tu?*', and her answer that they had been under orders to evacuate for some time and were afraid that they would soon be fetched.

Soon afterwards they went and Sailly became uninhabited, and I at any rate never saw the inside of an *estaminet* again for another nine months.

A flu epidemic, quite a mild one, and the only one I remember, caught us, and I was only too thankful when my turn came to go back to the guns.

Here on the high ground there was no mud or water to speak of, and our new casemates were bone dry and we could laugh at the weather.

A wonderful new 'issue' had come along, one of the best things that was ever thought of. They were thick leather goatskins with long black and white hair, sleeveless and reaching to the waist. Some of the men started wearing them with the fur inside. I should like to think it was I who said, 'Turn 'em round; animals don't wear their fur inside,' but I am afraid it was someone else. The difference was incredible, as the long hair broke the force of the wind, and so prevented it from penetrating. We kept beautifully warm in them, and especially now, as a new stunt had started which involved standing all day out on the open plain.

The Wandering Gun was a scheme to deceive the Germans as to the positions of our batteries and the numbers of them. Apparently it is possible to fix the direction of approaching shells.

Every few days a team came up, pulled out 'A' gun and walked off with it, its detachment and a signaller uncoiling a wire, and proceeded about half a mile to a flank. The idea was that, as the Germans knew the exact position of all our batteries, shells coming from an unusual angle would bother them and perhaps make them think there were more batteries on the plain than there actually were.

We stood about all day without bothering about camouflage and it would have been precious cold sometimes if we had not had our lovely skins. We did not do very much firing, but one day after much supplication we were allowed to try what we could do in the matter of speed at gunfire. We wanted to try for 25 rounds to the minute, but such an expenditure of ammunition not being permitted, it was settled that we could try it out for a quarter of a minute and calculate from that. We did it properly. When given our line and range, we were told to start when we liked. No.1, with watch in hand, rapped out his orders in a quick stream: 'Time load', from 2 'set', from 3 'ready', 'fire – time load, set, ready, fire, time load' etc. We got off six, which was 24 to the minute, and we were very pleased and also warmed up.

About now we had been conscious after dark on some evenings of commotion away in front, not gun or rifle fire, but faint poppings and warning rockets which were not ours. It eventually transpired as follows: the battalion then in the trenches consisted of an energetic lot of fellows who were irked. Nothing 'was doing' and they apparently felt they ought to be doing something about the war and so decided to stir it up and make trouble. The time was not far distant when there was trouble enough without any need to look for it. Squads formed themselves and their leaders on a voluntary basis, obtained permission from their C.O.s, armed themselves with handy weapons such as revolvers, grenades and clubs, blackened their faces, and, when the night was dark enough, sauntered out over the top. They must have looked an appalling pack of thugs. They could not have expected a great deal of opposition, as it was believed that the Germans very sensibly left their front line trenches empty except for machine gun posts. However, there were plenty of dugouts and these were all visited in swift and stealthy silence and presented with a grenade or two each, everyone became gloriously trigger-happy and pandemonium was soon worked up. The idea appealed to all and we overflowed with admiration. I can remember no definite account as to a night's bag, but they took one or two prisoners and suffered no casualties. But of course these goings on resulted in reprisals, as the Germans must have taken a poor view, and our nights began to be disturbed more often than not by yells of 'S.O.S. Gunfire, poop 'em off, like Hell'.

Our first S.O.S. was hilarious, in fact we welcomed such a bit of fun as a break in the monotony. During these easy days at the guns in our dry quarters, the detachment's dugout being connected by a side passage with the inside of the gun chamber, I had been in the habit, strictly against orders, of retiring to bed in civilized manner in pyjamas. So I was properly caught the first time.

We were up in one rush, I in pyjamas and bare feet and finding the layer's seat decidedly cold, but ribald remarks from the others were soon drowned in laughter, when Sergeant Williams convulsed us with the news that the Major was standing by the signallers' dugout giving orders dressed only in a shirt. This was the kind of Army life we liked, a life you could laugh at.

'All guns 14 degrees right of night-line; angle of sight 26 minutes depression; range 2,775 yards; corrector 168; time load; report when ready'. A short pause with cursings, then 'set', 'ready', 'No.1 ready, sir'; ditto the others; 'battery ready sir'. Then the Major, 'Prepare for salvo', pause, 'battery salvo – FIRE'. The whole position shakes with the roar of the four guns, the shells shriek away into the night and the sound of them dies away. In about six seconds comes a faint dr-r-rrruw of the four bursts in the distance, then the same again. Then, 'Cease fire, stand down'. We puff and giggle and wait. 'Go and ask the telephonist what the report was', says Sergeant. 'Anything through, Joe?' 'Yes, Major chap at infantry says we stopped 'em, right on and thanks a lot.'

Now came news that we were to become used to. Having laboured endlessly to make a good position, we were to leave it and move to one near Hébuterne. It was maddening because the position we were going to was another old, dilapidated French one and we would have to rebuild that as well. Fatigue parties went there every day from both guns and wagon-lines and during the whole of February we were working on it. We built the usual great casemates for subsections 'B', 'C' and 'D', but 'A' gun was to go into a little shack of a place at extreme shouting distance on the right. We took a dim view of it, but it turned out to our advantage in the end.

All January [1916] the weather continued awful with wind, rain and frost, guards were no joke and guns froze up and had to be thawed out with boiling water. On February 25 came snow; also whiffs of gas which enabled us to practise firing in masks.

Then, unaccountably we came out early in March and went off to the south-west edge of the plain to a position (Second Hébuterne position) on a track just south of the little village of Colincamps. A Regular battery had been there, unfortunately a dirty lot and the place was a pigsty. We were less isolated, there being several villages in sight and also an occasional railway train. The casemates were weird, being built up with logs so high that any hit would have tumbled them over. I wrote, 'There's more to see here than the two hawthorn bushes at our last position.'

Now the country became snow covered and our dugouts, being on ground level and completely draughty, I wondered how we would react. Fortunately, a spell of still, sunny weather intervened, and we felt fine, but as usual half-starved and also completely unwashed, as all water had to be carried a mile from the village. It was so much easier to be dirty, that is for a limited time.

We could see our old position far away across the plain. One day I saw our men pointing agitatedly towards it, and sure enough a large white cloud was seen covering the left section dugout. News came soon by the usual bush-telegraph method: a 6-inch direct hit and five Warwick gunners killed. We were subdued all day.

One day there was a crash of such sharpness that it hit you. We had never heard one like it. It is curious to relate, but this seems to have been the first aeroplane bomb we ever heard. We saw the German plane away over the village.

On the 18th and 19th [March] we barraged and were barraged, mostly by night; a bit of white-hot metal hit the casemate and a dud fell in a hole just in front of the gun. Getting up early the morning after one barrage, a platoon of infantry with their officer came out along the path behind the guns. I was shaving and it was most embarrassing; I saw them waving as they approached and then heard them calling out, 'Good old –, you didn't half stop 'em', I was the only man awake, so I had to be the recipient of their thanks on behalf of the battery; there was nothing I could do but wave my shaving brush at them, much to their officer's amusement.

On the 20th while we slumbered in our rat-infested shack, a small shell exploded against some logs laid against the front of the shack, the resulting cloud of cordite fumes inside nearly suffocating us. As all seemed well and it was cold outside, we just went to sleep again; when you are really tired you don't worry about such things. Next morning I investigated and found that of the row of small pine logs laid vertically, two had been removed probably for firewood and the resulting open space was partly filled by a post which had fallen diagonally across it. The shell had hit this small post in the middle, and I had been exactly in line with it inside.

This was, I decided, my 'near one number two'.

The two events of the last few days were unsettling. The men could not put into words what was oppressing us, which was a sense of apprehension.

One evening, with Gunner Frank, I was detailed to proceed on night fatigue to infantry lines to work on the repair of our O.P. Neither of us had been up forward before in this sector. We were ordered to report to an R.E. corporal, but I don't think either of us understood the directions given us for finding him. With the dark came rain. We got into the trenches and slopped along, seemingly for miles, never meeting a soul, until the nearness of occasional rifle shots made us think it best to stop. We waited and listened and heard no sign of life, wandered on, stood and wandered on. We then turned back so as not to get lost altogether. We did not know where to go and assumed that if we went back to the battery we would have been put under arrest.

There was nothing for it but to try and find somewhere to sleep. This meant finding a dry place, and such a thing on a pouring wet night in a practically unused and disintegrating trench system, was obviously non-existent. At last we found a small complete and undamaged dug-out about five feet high inside on trench floor level. We thought here was our place for the night. Unfortunately, the roof was not thick and the earth of it saturated, and, although nothing much dripped through on us, the floor was a wet and slimy one. We searched for bits of wood or duck-board, a sack or anything to sit on, but there was nothing. We decided to try and sleep the night out squatting in the dug-out on our heels. I had had some practice in this in Formosa and Japan, but had never been able to keep it up long without utter paralysis, much to the amusement of the Japanese. I got myself into a corner so as to be supported on two sides and squatted. Gunner Frank was opposite. We were too tired to talk and we had nothing we wanted to talk about, and we had six hours of darkness to go – in here.

My thoughts ran in the following vein: anyway we're quiet; now how to get to sleep; is it possible? Seems not; listen to odd sounds, water dripping, rats scurrying; how about stiffness? How long without changing position? Change position. To my surprise I find it possible, not to sleep, but to stay put if I change position every so often. Can I sleep? Perhaps. No. Can I think myself into sleep? Start thinking about what to think about, 'Henry Esmond', the war, food. Only the last bears thinking about, and that not for long. What is Gunner Frank thinking about? Gunner Frank gives periodic groans from stiffness, or rheumatism or dreams; anyway he seems in a torpor bordering on sleep and I wish I was too. Try counting, humming, thinking of new places to lean my head, which is really the most vital problem of all. Then a problem arises which proves at last to be interesting for pondering over on numerous occasions for at least a quarter of an hour each – this is passing the time beautifully. What is this new problem? It is, have I been to sleep, and if so for how long? Yes, that really is a very interesting problem, because the question arises as to whether it is to be solved in any way at all. Is it just, then, a matter of opinion, my opinion, and, if so, what value does my opinion on this very vital problem have? My spirits go up a point because I feel, surely this is passing the time. But they fall again. My wrist watch with its fluorescent dial is not encouraging; hours to go yet. Gunner F. groans. Start up suddenly at some sudden shots near; doesn't matter where they are; what does matter is that the devils have woken me up.

Start now to consider the really vital question of position; this is serious; I am getting stiff in position 'A,' also in positions 'B' and 'C', and I can't think of any other position; I can stay for shorter and shorter periods in the same position; so what hope of sleep now? Also rheumatic pains coming along; shall I watch the minute hand of my watch? It is 02.30 hours; try, but fall straight into a raging state of mind; I don't mind the mud, the wet, the cold, but I do mind being condemned to sit in it for hours for no purpose or good that it can be to anyone. If only we could find the O.P. and dig and dig all night, we could keep warm and to some extent awake, and digging is something positive to think about, such as the way the spade goes in, the anticipation of the size of the dollop of mud that comes up, the decision as to the optimum size for the spade, and many other absorbing subjects that I had by now been able, when digging, to conjure up. Frightful scream from Gunner having a nightmare. Think nothing of it one way or another, because at the moment only problems, not screams, are of interest; but what was I thinking about? I can't remember the problems; I was thinking about nothing and what it is, absorbedly, and that is not thinking at all, or is it? Or am I asleep, or going to be, or what? ...

Good Lord, there's some light in the trench; it's morning of a sort. Yes, but I'm stuck and it doesn't feel as if I can get up; so I have been asleep, perhaps for hours, yes, about an hour by my watch I should think. So one can think oneself to sleep and success approaches when one's thoughts tend towards nonsense.

The question now is, do I get up, if I can, or, if I'm stuck and sleepy, why not stay so. Gunner snores hard. Am amazed that I am comfortable on my heels, but I am; what I failed to do in Japan, I have done here. I evidently have been asleep again, as I wake again to see more light outside and shout out, 'Wake up you, hi, Gunner, stop snoring, untwist'. Roll over on the slime and walk out into the trench on my knees; gradually straighten out, but it takes time; surprised that joints function so well, in fact quite well.

Better get back now; there'll be breakfast soon and hot tea, come on.

We plod out and along the trench discussing what to tell Sergeant. Well, it wasn't our fault; it was his fault, and we'll tell him so.

On the 27th, after three months with the guns, I went down to Coigneux again. I found lovely warm weather and a cloudless sky, a jump into Spring, just as had happened a year ago in Belgium.

It was the end of the awful winter which had lasted continuously for five months since that day in October when we were watering at Couin. Out of the grey slough of mud had sprung brilliantly green grass again, and this time there were sheets of wild daffodils by the streamside under the poplar trees by the wagon-lines. I took my first chance to wander off among them and think of the 'daffodil country' at home.

On 14 April we were suitably depressed by being told that all leave was off. It was hard on the men as they pined to see their families and never ceased talking about them. They longed for leave so pathetically that I sometimes thought that I would be willing to forego my turn, as I had no particular need for it and, eventually, for a certain reason to do with what I saw at Victoria Station platform on my own return from leave later on, I wished I had done so.[2]

On the 17th we went into our new Hébuterne position (Third Hébuterne Position), which was now rebuilt. The weather was lovely, there were no fatigues and little firing. We lay about. I had carried Vol. I of a small edition of 'Gibbon' in my haversack since leaving England, and now started on it for the first time when I could get away to a quiet place. But I did not progress; it takes some time to become historically minded to the point of remembering about the antecedents of the period about which you are reading; also the wars seemed unreal; David Copperfield would have been a better choice.

It was now that I made my best friend in Sergeant Gore. He had been transferred from one of the other batteries to be in charge of 'A' Sub, Sergeant Williams having been appointed Quartermaster. Gore was a young man and good tempered and tactful with everyone, treating us when off duty all alike and as pals; moreover, he was intelligent and could talk; he was a Godsend. He knew his drill and worked quickly. His job in civilian life had been on the Executive of the L.M.S. Railway. We all of us in 'A' Sub from now on were a happy lot, we liked each other and helped each other to the extent that my chief fear in becoming a casualty would be losing their company. Unfortunately, our little casemate away on the flank made us rather sufficient unto ourselves, whereby we earned for ourselves the name 'Jam Battery', or 'that cushy lot that never does any work'. We were much taunted, but not ill naturedly, and on the whole we deserved it.

Somehow on explorations, which were forbidden and rare, I had discovered a house at Sailly-au-Bois, the village just behind us, where a woman sold *vin rouge* at five francs a bottle: I used to drop in and buy a couple at a time, and became very popular in 'A' Sub and ever less so in the other Subs.

2   See below, p. 61.

After a time, we continued being more and more casemate conscious. The main position was enormous, and was visible for miles and from any plane. Thank goodness, we thought, and with reason, our little casemate removed some way on the flank is inconspicuous in comparison with the main position.

On the 25th [April] after some firing, the Germans started on us, and with 5.9s. After this it always happened so, and we knew what to expect. We also knew we were there for firing purposes, which would be in the main counter-battery work. We had to do the job.

The job resolved itself in detail as follows: we heard their guns fire, then silence, then the shells on the way. I do not believe in taboos, whether religious or otherwise, and fear is as much a subject for ordinary discussion as any other. It can be said that there is nothing new to be said on this subject. Still it was new to me and probably to most of us, since in civilian life fear of physical violence is fairly rare, certainly (in those days) of sudden annihilation. I had never experienced it nor thought about it, as we tend to submerge unpleasant thoughts in the subconscious.

After the first few times, it came upon us all, when we heard the shells on the way, and was, of course, in the form of shaking knees. One did not think coherently at the time, but afterwards my reaction was: what an extraordinary sensation; I have never felt anything like it before. We seemed not to have proper control of our legs, but No. 2 and I were lucky in that we had seats!

I wrote in my diary: 'I think we all held on to something, I to the elevator wheel, trying to concentrate my thoughts on the sights and their structure. The first on our line fell short, the next went over us, this was it, they were ranging, if we are going to be hit, it will be the next one, come on let's get it over." "Bwank" in the distance, here it comes, someone says "Now for it chaps", hold on, gosh it's coming at us (we learnt to keep quiet after a time), no, over some way behind, so they weren't ranging, we are too inconspicuous.'

Then an extraordinary thing happened, a cannonade of 5.9s fell for quite ten minutes on our left, the German battery firing full out. We were firing as fast ourselves and had no time to look-see, but we were terrified for the other subs. It sounded as if they must all have gone west, and we almost dared not look when action was over. When we peered in trepidation through the smoke, the sight was extraordinary. There was a narrow band of churned earth, almost a trench had been dug, extending from just behind 'C' Sub's casemate back nearly to the Sailly–Hébuterne road. 'C' Sub had been hit and some of its fitments knocked about, but the men were unhurt, just smothered with dust. Their range was a few yards too long and they were unimaginative in not 'sweeping'.

I was often aggravated at the apparent unimaginativeness of firing orders in cases when 'A' gun had to fire all day at set intervals on the same point, and felt an urge to make slight variations both in line, range and time, to catch people unawares who perhaps were counting on each burst being at the same time and place as the last, but fortunately I did not give way to this urge.

As time went on we began to dislike our position, our first experience of such dislike; nearly all our subsequent positions became quickly the objects of our dislike, and more than dislike.

Early in May my first leave came, the first for thirteen months, and to be the first and last of my two and a half years in France. I had no feelings about it either way, as I had lost touch with friends through being abroad so much, and my relations in England consisted only of three very kind aunts. I enjoyed eating asparagus.

After ten days I was on Victoria Station platform and then sitting in the crowded embarkation train, feeling thankful that I had nobody with me to see me off. As I sat there, I watched the scene. What I saw of wives saying goodbye to husbands made me wish I had never come on leave, so that I would never have seen it. The memory of it still haunts me.

5

THE SOMME

24 June 1916

The Somme Offensive was not a British idea. The interest of Britain lay further north in Belgium, where Haig from the beginning of his command wished to concentrate his strength and stage his main and, he hoped, his decisive attack which would end the war. Strategy would be involved here, namely the safeguarding of the Channel ports. But Fate decreed otherwise.

Falkenhayn, in spite of his stated belief that there could now be no decisive military decision, concluded that his only route to victory lay in the cracking of the morale of his weakest enemy, namely France, who would give in if only one strong point of famous name could be taken. Such was Verdun, in spite of the fact that there was no strategic advantage to be gained, as a German success here would actually result in a shortened French line.

He attacked in February and failed in the attack; moreover, his armies, being the attackers, became the first to undergo the 'bleeding to death' process and to suffer a 'decline in morale', from which they never recovered.

The other side of the picture, however, was, firstly, that the French armies' casualties, though less than the Germans', were sufficient to set up on their side such a deterioration in will to resist, that only one more slaughter, albeit the smaller one of Nivelle's [Offensive] in 1917, was necessary to reduce them to a state in which, in the words of the historians, 'they could thereafter do no more.' Secondly, Falkenhayn could afford his casualties, which the Allies could not; German man-power was unlimited and continued so right into 1918.

After Verdun, the Western Front and the war itself depended upon the British armies alone. From 1915 onwards it was always to Britain that her Allies appealed for help. The first appeal came from the Russians in that year, that we should attack the enemy's 'under-belly' at the Dardanelles, and by so doing strengthen the morale of their stalemated armies. As always, we responded, but with forces so inadequate as to lead to a costly failure and the jeopardizing of the Western Front; 'Any further dilution of the military effort was absurd and dangerous.'

In June 1916 came the French appeal after Verdun, that we should attack at once on the Somme, not for any strategic purpose, because an advance there would merely shorten the German line, as eventually happened, but because such an attack would be located in physical contact with the French armies, i.e. on their left flank, and any success on our part could be calculated to encourage the French at least to continue in the war.

In 1917 came an appeal from our third Ally, Italy. Always the appeals for help were to us; always the appeals were accompanied with under-cover threats, savouring of blackmail, that a refusal would mean surrender; nobody ever helped us until American troops became operative in effective numbers in 1918.

If we, as individuals, were assailed with dull foreboding in contemplating the future, and our morale suffered, it was hardly to be wondered at; fortunately, the effects showed themselves in words rather than in deeds.

So all Haig's plans were upset, and 'the great attack which would win the war' was transferred from Belgium to the valley of the Somme. The largest Army Britain had ever had, comprising 22 divisions and some three million men, all volunteers, no conscripts having yet arrived, was concentrated round the Somme Salient by the end of June 1916, '*pour encourager les autres*'. Unfortunately, before the battle started its purpose was out of date as the French were by now effectively discouraged. No tactics were involved and no particular objectives were in view. It was, nevertheless, the most amazing, the most colossal and greatest mass attack that the British, or any other army, had ever undertaken. There was never anything comparable with it in the history of War, nor is there ever likely to be.

This account does not aim at being a description of the Battle, neither is it one of exciting deeds or horrors; the world has had enough of such writings. It endeavours merely to portray the day-to-day life of a Territorial Battery during the years 1915 to 1917 inclusive, and to be a statement describing events, and where these events and words spoken are reprehensible, or their mention unorthodox, they are never the less included if relevant.

The account from now on is given with diffidence, as C/240 Battery took an average part in the 'Somme', and later in 'Third Ypres', and no more, and we were on the whole lucky as regards casualties. Where my account appears unrestrained, it is because it is in places taken word for word from my diary.

It is inherent in our outlook on life that this should always change, and our outlook upon the war was no exception to the rule. In the months that followed, this change in opinion and feelings, though not, I think, in our actions, was for the worse. It must have been the same everywhere, and it is time somebody said so.

Our good young Major must have sensed something of this later, as he occasionally gave us a pep talk. I remember his words on one occasion, 'We've got to see this war through; we've got to win it; if we don't beat the Germans, we shall have to do the whole thing over again in future.' I thought much about this, but, as it seemed to me that permanent peace was the only worth-while objective, I failed to see how anyone being beaten could help the world towards this objective. It was therefore, it seemed to me, just a war for our survival as a nation and no more.

The Somme Offensive started with us still in the Hébuterne position which, it transpired, was at the extreme eastern tip of the northern limb of the great sideways U enclosing the Somme Valley.

We were now in Rawlinson's 4th Army, in which we formed General Hunter-Weston's 8th Corps, which extended actually from our position south to the River Ancre. Our guns covered a sector just north of the river at Beaumont-Hamel.

I returned to the position on 12 June and found things not the same. Tranquil days were definitely over. Our plain was no longer the quiet place it had been, all the positions on it having been well registered by the enemy. It could be understood that what happened to us from now on depended upon whether the Germans had the ammunition and the time to deal with an appreciable proportion of the quantities of our batteries now deployed.

The first thing I noticed was that our porch had disappeared. The French had made a rough porch over the entrance to our dugout and it had vanished. I sensed an unwillingness on the part of the detachment to discuss the matter, so refrained from questions, as it was obvious that the dugout had been as near to a direct hit as makes no odds. To make things worse, the rest of the battery thought it funny and kept on saying so. After a time I thought it funny too and that really made them angry.

There were now a lot of shell holes about.

Sergeant Gore and the other sergeants had been to the Major's dugout for a briefing. He returned with papers and a preoccupied look. We sat round him in silence. 'Tomorrow, chaps, there is going to be the greatest boost the world has ever known. It's a great thing to be in and you want to be careful with the laying (with a look at me), and above all, the Major says, you must get in all the sleep you possibly can'. I thought what a sensible man our Major was.

The next day, 24 June, the artillery bombardment of our great offensive was to begin, the date of the actual offensive being 1 July. The bombardment was to last a week, and then the infantry was to 'go over'. We were to work in eight-hour shifts of three, and would be firing practically continuously day and night, with occasional rests of not more than an hour. Every day as many gunners as possible would be sent up from the wagon-lines as reliefs, but we had only three spare gunners in our sub.

We were up at 04.00 hours, or rather Sergeant Gore, Gunner Wiggin and I were, getting the casemate straight, the rounds sorted and a certain number of fuses set. It is with the ammunition where the gunner finds his work. Each round weighs 22 lbs, and when the hateful order 'replenish dump' is given, it means lugging nearly a hundredweight at a time in canvas carriers over one's shoulders, and continuing to do so until told to stop.

The ammunition had to be stacked round the gun to the maximum amount for which space could be found, but this process was made difficult because there had to be four different dumps for four different kinds of rounds: shrapnel fuse 80, shrapnel fuse 85, H.E. (high explosive) cordite and ditto N.C.T. (nitro-cellulose tubular). There were even dates of filling, which were supposed to be kept separate. We were expected to cram into the casemate 300 rounds. We worked for an hour stacking and managed to fix 200 but no more. Even so, unless the bottom layers were firmly wedged, the whole pile would slip with deafening clatter.

We lost all fear of rounds exploding. Apparently they never did, and that satisfied us. We understood that they could not do so without the revolving motion imparted to them by the gun. Once our drivers had been seen throwing H.E. rounds to each other to catch and dropping an occasional one fuse downwards on a hard road, and of this we did take rather a poor view.

The gun was laid and loaded and Sergeant, Wiggin and I waited quietly and excitedly for the order to commence firing, which was to come at 05.00 hours.

At this time exactly the great bombardment began. We fired at Section Fire H.E. all morning, about 140 rounds per gun. Left section fired in the afternoon. A casemate was blown up in 'B' Battery in front of us and five men wounded, and there were many high shrapnel bursts. Several other 18-pounder batteries were doing section fire ten seconds, which means that the two sections fire independently, the second gun ten seconds after the first. Almost immediately the 'heavies' behind us opened up. They began with the great boost of a 12-inch, the great shell of which seemed to plough its leisurely way along over our heads, its burst reaching us much later as a distant roar. In a few minutes the bombardment became intense. Eighteen-pounders and 4.5 guns made the most noise, their concussion seeming to hit the air everywhere with a ripping, tearing noise as of sharp blows which hit everything besides one's ears, till you felt as if you were being knocked sharply but painlessly about.

The rhythm of the firing, if so it could be called, combined it all together. At a distance it would have sounded like a long dull roar, as did the firing miles away to the south, but on the spot there were intervals between each gun from a fraction of a second to three or four seconds; an interval of five seconds was rare. And so it went on, section fire with its regular and leisurely firing; battery fire one second, a continual and persistent bang, bang, bang, bang, salvos which seemed to tear the air, brrrip, brrrip; 4.5 and 6-inch howitzers, which barked shortly and severely, 8-inch howitzers, 6-inch naval guns and 15-inch monsters which boosted.

Inside the casemate we were less aware of the din and too busy to listen. Section fire ten seconds for three men, one of whom must be standing near the entrance most of the time listening for orders bawled through a mega-phone, is all very well for a time, especially while the stock of set fuses lasts. The layer can give his mate practically no assistance, though he can work the breech with his right hand, but very awkwardly.

More fuses must be set whenever there is a second to spare, as we changed periodically to shrapnel, and it is surprising how soon twenty rounds disap-pear when one is struggling to keep the unset rounds from rolling down onto those already set, or when one has a tight fuse which moves partly round and then sticks, or when, worst of all, a new range is unexpectedly given, requiring a resetting of all the set fuses.

Our first day's firing was mostly wire-cutting using both shrapnel and H.E. Later on we find ourselves searching for various suspected machine-gun emplacements. This entails continually altering switch angles, ranges and fuses, but the rate of fire is slower, each battery round being separately ordered. From big corrections we come to small ones: No. 1 gun, 5 minutes more left, drop 12½ yards. 'This ought to get him', we say, as I pull the lever. The burst must have been practically right, as the next order is, H.E. 3 rounds gunfire, and off go three rounds as fast as the loader can bang them in. Later on we hear, 'No. 1 gun detachment will be glad to hear that they have had a direct hit on a machine gun emplacement, from the Major.' We appreciate it when our officers find time to send such messages.

As the hours pass, we fire slower, section fire 30 seconds, becoming later one minute. Then comes the order, 'replenish ammunition when you can', and two of us set to work on the hateful job. We have fired sixty rounds and the empty cartridge cases are entirely blocking up the entrance to the casemate, and these have to be cleared away first.

As our eight hours draw to a close, we have a chance of looking at the view behind, and of listening to the din which has somewhat abated. The novelty is wearing off a little, and we begin to feel tired and hungry. Our breakfast has been brought up and put in a lean-to behind, but we are only able to bite at dusty bread and bacon and sip tea long since cold.

We discover we are really weary, and remembering the Major's orders, turn in as soon as the relief arrives and we have handed over. We eat some dinner, kick off our boots and fall down on other people's blankets in the dugout, and, in spite of the gun firing within a few yards of us, fall asleep at once.

At night we come on again, but firing now is easy at a slow rate of section fire.

What we thought then to be remarkable was that all day there had been no reply from the Germans at all. We became so used to this in future, that, after many long supposedly quiet periods when we were pasted irregularly at any time for weeks on end, being never really free of it, we literally greeted the news that there was going to be an attack next day with enthusiasm. The point was, of course, that while an attack was on, the Germans had no time for counter-battery work.

Section fire one minute is really only a one-man job, so Sergeant Gore sends Wiggin off to come on again in the early morning, and he and I sit down with our pipes and bang off the gun every two minutes.

Having plenty of fuses set and time on our hands, we fall to discussing the importance of the attack. It seems ridiculous now to think that we felt able to form conclusions about it, but we did, and the one which came as rather a shock was, that 'everything' hangs on whether we can assume the offensive successfully, or with some success, all along the line. When once that has been accomplished, the war, we say, would almost seem to be won. Verdun would be safe, and afterwards the slow general advance all along the line to Loos, the Ypres sector would then be cut off by the taking of Lille, and then, why, we would experience a wonderful feeling of confidence, mingled with surprise, that we should have been able so soon to show ourselves superior to the greatest of military countries, against whom in old days a war was regarded secretly as an impossible nightmare.

'Ah, well, Sergeant, but it hasn't been done yet', I venture. 'No, Gunner, but we're going through all right now, sooner or later. Look at our artillery superiority to begin with; the world has never before heard anything like what we have heard today.' I think he was right there.

We begin to get sleepy after midnight, and the monotonous bang of the slow battery fire conduced to sleep rather than otherwise. At last Sergeant intimated that he would turn in for two hours, if I would carry on alone, after which he would relieve me; in a case of a jam or alteration in line or rate of fire, I was to call all of them. So I took over and made myself a comfortable seat 3 [layer] in a niche upon some ammunition. Bang went No. 3 and the shell whistled away into the night and all was quiet again except for distant batteries also doing section fire. It was not going to be very safe for the Germans to mend wire that night.

I always enjoyed being alone with 'A' gun. A sensation seemed to come over me as I sat there and I no longer felt sleepy. It was the weird unnaturalness of the situation which was now able to make itself felt. The siege candle gutted slightly in the draught, and light and shadows flickered on the gun and casemate walls, showing up the rows of ammunition and accessories, such as fuse-bar, fuse keys, tools for removing jammed cases, pull-throughs, a tin of tobacco and a letter stuck in a niche by some gunner.

'Bang' went No. 4 and I look at my watch. Yes, quite likely I had, or would, kill some Germans by pulling that lever, an easy way of doing it compared with the infantryman's job. I had never thought of this before, and was glad to find that the thought did not interest me. What did interest me was to find a rational explanation of things that certainly were not rational.

The next day I went down to the wagon-lines for two days, where there was complete peace and rest, but the sound of an increasing cannonade in the distance was ominous.

On the 27th I went back in the evening. The position had been shelled with 5.9s, and a shell had hit up 'C' sub's dump and Gunner Clements had been wounded. Sergeant, Wiggin and I were on firing all night.

On the 28th we were firing and ammunition thumping all day, firing over 300 rounds, with a stint at night and a burst close to the dugout and in front of gun.

On the 29th we did wire-cutting on and off all day at section fire, our gun firing 300 rounds, our heaviest firing yet.

Sergeant and I took on all-night firing salvoes and frequent three rounds gunfire. My diary says, 'good fun'. On the 30th it was the same.

July 1st. was the fatal day and zero hour was 06.30 hours. We started with section fire 30 seconds. The infantry went over at 07.30 hours. We fired for six hours, the gun getting very hot and the breech later started sticking. It is terrible at such times when a defect develops in a gun and there is fear of being out of action. We were out of action twice for short periods, but the other guns more often, 'B' having its oil boiling and 'C''s casemate caught fire. However, we were told afterwards that rate of fire was 'sustained very well'. This just meant that our fellows had worked like hell.

Reports began to come in. They said that the 31st Division had taken Serre and German third line trenches, but were out of touch; London Scottish on the left had taken Gommecourt with heavy casualties and had taken 300 prisoners, some of whom we saw walking along the road behind us, the first Germans we had seen. A large number of our casualties passed by all day. While teams were up we had some 4.2 shrapnel over and a horse was hit in the leg. My notes say, 'whacked to the world'.

The next day, apart from two half-hour section fire stints, things were easier. But now developed our first intimation of gun trouble which was to plague us so desperately later, buffer springs. We did not then know why it was that the barrel started to hang back on its recoil after firing, and run up again slowly, and later not at all and have to be pushed. This turned action into a terrible labour and worry, and at the time we understood that there was nothing we could do but let the gun cool, when the springs would in some unaccountable way recover.

Tear gas shells came over all night, and as I was on guard from 00.00 to 03.00 hours, I had a bad time, my mask for some reason not keeping out much of it, my eyes and nose streaming all the time. The place stank of ether.

Next day I went down to the wagon-lines where I remained for a week, being allowed to lie in all mornings and only do one watering parade. The Major was always considerate.

Papers from home were all enthusiastic with big headings, 'Battle of Somme Valley', and statements that gains were being consolidated.

On the 10th I returned to the guns and found that much damage had been done there, the large 'C' casemate dugout being partly blown in and four signallers slightly wounded in the dugout by shrapnel. The next day I was out of sorts and dizzy, possibly from effects of gas, and it was some time before I recovered.

One day Sergeant Gore came in and said calmly, 'All our troops are back in their own trenches.' We sat struck dumb. This was, however, only partly true, and referred only to the northern side of the salient from Thiepval through Beaumont-Hamel north.

I thought of Sergeant's optimistic prophecy of a great advance that was to break the German lines and of my doubts. If this, 'the greatest boost the world had ever known', was going to result in a negligible advance and thousands of casualties, what hope for the war, what chance of any decision, when two apparently immovable forces face each other. A slice of the salient had been cut off on the south about two miles deep, but the salient remained and the offensive was now twelve days old. We did not know then that our casualties on 1 July were 60,000. Again I felt that dark cloud that seemed to loom in my vision of the future, the cloud of dull apprehension.

On 20 July orders came to move out, to leave after nearly a year what my diary called 'this cursed plain'. The time was near when we would willingly have come back. We handed over our guns to a Welsh Battery of the 27th Division, and went singing down to the wagon-lines.

South

The next day, July 21, reveille was at 02.30 hours, and in lovely summer weather we moved off and left little Coigneux, which I had really become quite fond of, forever.

We knew what we were in for. We knew that so far we had been only on the edge of the Somme Battle, and that now we were definitely going south into it; it would be a case of, 'Here's the war, and we're in it.' But the welcome change, the peacefulness and the warm weather made our trek seem like a picnic, and moreover we were once more tidy, smart and polished up and felt all the better for it.

Having no guns, the gunners travelled by lorry. Our route was south through Bertrancourt, Acheux-en-Amiénois, Forceville, Hédauville and Bouzincourt to Albert. Enormous quantities of troops were everywhere. Albert was a shambles, the figure of the Virgin on the top of the cathedral hanging over at right angles. From here we walked to our new position which turned out to be unexpectedly attractive in Authuille Wood close to the River Ancre and opposite Aveluy. It was a good position and had been very little shelled, but was supposed to be dangerous at the moment on account of what was thought to be a new kind of gas shell, which was rather alarming; also there was a new type of gun which put in occasional shells with the sound of a violent 'whack-smack', a high velocity type which made no shell hole. The battery we took over was a six-gun battery, so we were made up by the addition of a section from 'B' Battery. All our batteries were now being made into six-gun batteries.

We learnt that a new Army, the Fifth, had now been formed under Sir Hubert Gough for the purpose of holding and attacking on this left flank of our salient. Its tenth Corps included three Australian Divisions, of which the First was now holding the slope close to the village of Pozières. On the left and immediately in front of us was our own 48th Division, which was holding a line from Ovillers running north through the tip of our wood. We fired on Pozières.

The next day, 22 July, was a terrific one for the infantry.

Half our detachments were on for eight-hour spells, I having been on with Sergeant and Wiggin the previous night. There was an intense bombardment and a terrific infantry attack at midnight. I noted that I had never heard anything like it and that thousands of guns must have been concentrating on the Pozières sector. News came that the 6th Glosters and Anzacs attacked through gas and liquid fire, the former surrounding the Leipzig Redoubt, and the latter taking Pozières and its crest, thus giving a clear view of Courcelette and Martinpuich. The bombardment continued all day and, at a slow rate, all that night.

On the 24th I went to the wagon-lines near Bouzincourt on a wide open plain among corn. There were no bivouacs and we slept in the open, the weather being lovely. We did not worry at being in the open, as the Germans had at the moment no time to attend to rear areas, besides which the numbers of men and horses were so enormous and spread out over such a wide area that we never bothered about being bombed.

We heard while here that an H.Q. Captain and our popular Corporal Stanley and some other signallers were casualties while on observation, the officer being killed.

On the 25th the Germans counter-attacked at Pozières, but the attack was completely broken up by our barrage, and a second attack was again scattered by 'the dominant all-observing guns'.

I do not remember at the time being given any intimation that the work of the batteries covering Pozières had been so effective.

On the 29th a surprising thing happened. Just when we thought that Armageddon was near, we went out for a rest; presumably it was our turn.

We were glad, but there were to be times in future when we were really tired and near breaking point, when we would long for the rest that we were now to have, and would see no likelihood of ever getting it.

We had a long walk-march in very hot weather. Our route was through Acheux, Doullens, Hem-Hardinval, where we watered, Fienvillers, Berneuil, Domart-en-Ponthieu to Saint-Ouen. Here we camped in a lovely park under tall black poplars. The whole 48th Division was there and the Artillery was a fine sight.

We were often out of action in future, but then always on trek with little rest to enjoy. During the remaining sixteen months during which the battery was in France we never after this had another battery rest.

We were here for ten days in perfect summer weather. We made no shacks, just covered our kit with ground sheets and slept in the open. There was naturally routine work to be done; in fact complete idleness, even if possible, could not have been borne; we should not have known what to do with ourselves. No one could switch to 'Gibbon' to order for ten days. There were exercising, watering and a little taking up position practice, but the extraordinary thing was that there now occurred a perfect fever of grooming and harness, gun and wagon cleaning and polishing such as the battery had never known before. It was of course initiated by the drivers, but even the grumbling gunners joined in not unwillingly. I think what started it was that a few drivers having good horses started vying with each other, especially over the horses' coats, and some of them literally could not stop grooming. Soon all the horses shone with lovely sleek coats, also the harness, bits, leathers; then of course limber gunners got to work and polished and oiled the guns and then the limbers and wagons. Soon our officers came, stood, admired and were not ungenerous in their praise; then the Colonel came, and, as was his unvarying habit with the men, was completely generous in his remarks and praised the work of each driver individually. Officers from other batteries also came and also staff officers from Brigade and Division.

Plenty of good food was obtainable in the little town, nicely served on tables with tablecloths at all the little cottages, there were *oeufs*, *bifteks* and French beer. Diversions were a Divisional Band, the 'Curios' concert party, tug-of-war and boxing.

I always remember a corporal one late evening in the twilight of a lovely summer day playing on a cornet quite beautifully 'There's a long, long trail a-winding to the land of my dreams'. It was wonderful to hear something beautiful, for our senses were so starved of all beauty; it encouraged me to think that perhaps the trail would some day have an end. I have hated it ever since if I heard that song being hackneyed or made to seem commonplace.

On 9 August we moved off refreshed. We took our time as it was now very hot and dusty. On the 12th we came back to Bouzincourt to practically the same lines.

Crucifix Corner

On the 13th we marched to our new position where we took over a six-gun battery from the 12th Division. It was a good position on a steep chalk bank at a junction of the Arras and Bapaume roads near Aveluy, and we called it Crucifix Corner because there was, or had been, a crucifix there. The position and trenches round were all dug in solid chalk, which gave immense protection. Ammunition was a difficulty as it had to be carried fifty yards up a trench.

Sergeant Gore, Gunner Haydon and I were on No. 3 gun from midnight till 08.00 hours and fired 150 rounds section fire. Ammunition coming up all night gave no one any chance to sleep. We now for the first time began to be conscious of what was coming to us out of England; obviously munitions production had been stepped up to a stupendous degree, as the supply now seemed unlimited, and it seemed as if our teams wanted to dump it on us day and night irrespective of whether we could possibly carry, stack and deal with such quantities. It was a nice feeling to have, though, after so many months of scarcity.

We fired on a trench on a crest south of Thiepval. The Germans attacked and took it off the Oxford & Bucks, but the latter retook it.

Next day was a strain, as our dumps were empty, a gunners' horror, and ammo thumping became continuous.

Next day another division took our guns off us and went into open action at Ovillers just in front. I wrote: 'We know we are in for this ourselves soon,' but the words open action now did not mean anything much, because after our next position we were hardly ever in action otherwise than in the open under a net.

There followed two days of rest, when we bathed in the Ancre and hunted rats.

On the 18th the 7th Warwicks went over near Thiepval and took trenches with the Anzacs and 1,800 prisoners. Saw several lots of these come down all looking starved and white-faced. The different types were curiously mixed up. One of them said quite rude things about the Kaiser, which I had the satisfaction of hearing and being able to translate to the men. I noticed a vile little lieutenant with a small detachment who stood apart from them and would speak to no one.

On this day I heard that I would be receiving from a grateful country the sum of 6*d.* a day extra pay for 'first class proficiency as gun-layer'. I was overjoyed and put up my layer's badge, which I had scrounged and kept ready in my pocket. This was my complete and ultimate military ambition and I felt that the Army had now nothing more for me that I could want.

We now started to dig positions a few yards to the left of the existing ones, which did not please us as digging here was identical with quarrying.

On the 21st the 4th and 6th Glosters went over again near Leipzig Redoubt and took a lot of prisoners. Changed detachments and I went down to the lines walking part of the way with the prisoners.

Next evening after tea I was sitting in our shack when Gunner Gardiner more or less fell into it. He was obviously all in, so I waited. When he had recovered slightly, he gave me the following account:

'Well, Gunner, I reckon you were lucky being out of it. I'm all of a shake still and when I do get to sleep I see things flying about all round me in smoke and fire. I've never seen anything like it and don't want to again. It was awful. Thursday afternoon it began, shells every minute or so, mostly 5.9s pitching all about over us and the 4.7 battery and the bomb store. In the evening they got to work and we all got under cover. At times they came over in couples at about ten second intervals, and the first thing they hit was the roof of one of the 4.7 casemates. Then they started with 8-inch and, well you know what they are like. They put two of the 4.7s out of action, one of them was chucked right up in the air. Then they put one in their dump and 200 of their gas shells went up bang. It was a hellish noise. As luck had it, the wind was blowing away from us or we should have been fairly smothered. By this time they had dropped a good few all round the bomb store and there were regular fireworks going off there, lemon bombs, Stokes bombs, rifle grenades, star lights and trench mortar bombs all blowing up in the air and scattering about all over the position, and such a row you couldn't hear a word anyone said. What with 8-inch bursting about and shaking the trenches and dugouts half in, the position wasn't a place to stay in, but we crowded down into our ammunition dump as being the strongest place handy. I'd hardly got there, when we heard somebody crying out for a stretcher. A piece of one of our bombs had hit Sergeant Price in the chest. He was up by No. 1 gun at the time with Bombardier James. They got him onto a stretcher, when a whole lot of bombs went up at the dump and the concussion blew the poor fellow off the stretcher. As Bombardier James put him back on, he turned his head and gave him a look and died. James went quite frantic, poor kid, and came to us crying.

'Well, we were all crammed into the dump, which fairly rocked every time anything big went off, and only one or two chaps ventured out to see what was going on. After a bit I went back to our gun casemate to see if any of the chaps were still there, and while there I saw someone standing over by the bomb dump with what I took to be a bucket in his hand. I couldn't see clearly as the air was so full of dust and smoke. There was a fire on the dump in one place, and I took it that the chap, who turned out to be Lieutenant –, was trying to put it out, and I thought at the time it was a damned risky thing to be doing. Then I saw Gunner Hughes go up to him with a full bucket, which he took, and poured onto the fire. I saw him standing there then watching it. The fire seemed to go out, but then flared up a bit.

'Then, there was the MOST AWFUL EXPLOSION I HAVE EVER HEARD.

'I really cannot describe it. A huge mass of flame went up – oh, more than three hundred feet, and I was blown straight into the A casemate and fell over the trail of the gun onto Leach and Roddick all in a heap. Fellows were blown off their feet, down dugout steps and off their bunks. Wiggin, who was in his bunk reading a paper, was blown up against the roof and the paper was all torn to shreds. I scrambled out of the casemate and looked out. Up in the air was a huge black cloud with black specks all about it; I should think it must have been up there almost a minute. Then I knew it would be falling down on us and I yelled, screamed, "It's coming down". The other two threw themselves down under the gun as the only place likely to give any protection, and I crouched down by the sandbag wall. Then the pieces began to fall on the corrugated iron roof, first in a pitter-patter, and then in a roar – earth, sticks, stones and bits of iron poured down and covered the ground for yards round. When we got out again the chaps were running about looking for people, but we could see practically nothing, because the smoke and dust were so thick that you couldn't see half a dozen yards and you literally had to grope your way. Fires were burning everywhere, wood and sandbags were blazing, bombs were still exploding and shells still coming over. We were all dazed. Then the Major gave the order to clear out everywhere. I dashed down to the road and down the opposite slope; I hardly knew what I was doing nor where I was going, except that I must get away from such a hell on earth;

my knees shook under me so that I kept on falling down. Other chaps came reeling along just exactly as if they were dead drunk, falling down slopes and scrambling over everything in the way. All the time the air seemed thick with falling stuff – first a bomb came shrieking over and the pieces flew all round me, then a 5.9 whistled over my head, then an iron bar off a mortar bomb came whrrr – whrrr – whrrr spinning in the air, and I could feel the draught it made as it passed me; then I heard an 8-inch coming and threw myself flat, but it burst with a roar near Aveluy village. Then I got to the infantry dugouts on the lower road. They were crammed with infantry, R.F.A., R.G.A. and R.E. Somehow I got into one and pretty well collapsed.

'When I went back as it began to get light, the chaps were searching for Mr –. He must have been right on top of the dump when it went up.

'Well, I tell you, I'm all of a shake still, Gunner, and keep on seeing those iron bars and things whrrr – whrrring through the air.'

I was appalled at the story and wished I had had a spot of brandy to offer the poor chap.

On the 25th I went back to the guns and found the men very tired and nervy. There was an attack at night and we barraged all night at two minute section fire. There was a heavy German attack by the 5th Prussian Guards, which failed.

On the 27th there was another attack for which we put up a heavy barrage, lifting after three minutes. It was said to have been very successful, and several hundred prisoners came along past us.

The next day we came out of action with our guns, and a 25th Division Battery took over. At midnight the battery left the wagon-lines and moved off to a new position.

Mesnil

The position was rather high up under a wood on a ridge just west of the village of Mesnil-Martinsart on the west side of the Ancre Valley and directly opposite Thiepval. As we reached it, some drivers fetching away kit felt they had to indulge in the usual banter, 'Oy, you're for it, 'ell of a place it is'. It was to me unaccountable why relieved batteries always had to do this kind of thing with relieving batteries. It was always the same and it was cruel and unnecessary. The result was we made up our minds that the place was sinister, and as soon as we saw it, we were confirmed in the opinion, and made up our minds that the place should prove to be an abominable, evil place, which would hand out death to us all. It was an unfortunate and stupid state of mind to be in, but we hated the sight of the position as soon as we saw it. As we drove up and unlimbered we certainly felt it to be an uncanny place. It had huge strong casemates, which would have been conspicuous had they not been covered by long green sheets of camouflage netting, which blew eerily in the wind. There was no sound and no sign of life, the only movement being the blowing canvas. It was a complete example of how a pre-conceived idea can fix itself firmly as one's conception of a place.

To start with, all seemed well. The position had not been much shelled after all, and when we were settled in we had an easy time.

September 3rd was the first day of the Battle of Thiepval.

We started firing at 05.00 hours with a suddenness that was incredible, so terrific was the bombardment. We fired on three barrages at section fire and kept on for eight hours. We and other batteries near were shelled.

A West Riding Battery nearby happened to have all its men out unloading a limber when a shell made a direct hit on the limber, killing six, wounding twenty, only three men being left. The teams bolted and most of the horses were killed. It was an awful sight. We helped to bury the horses. The next day at midnight gas shells poured over accompanied by some 4.2s. Our casemate opening was large and the ammunition stacked at the sides was exposed. Cecil Bevan went to 'B' casemate to call guard relief, and just as he was leaving, a 4.2 struck the shield of 'B' gun, blowing off the top and bottom flaps. Four of the men were wounded and Bevan ran back with his forearm pouring with blood. Sergeant Gibbs and I dashed off to see to them. Bombardier Phipps was half buried and his head was covered with blood, and Gunner Baker was in poor shape. After a long wait owing to the shelling, we took the two on stretchers to the dressing station, Corporal Hawling, Bombardier Baldwin and Gunner Bevan being walking cases. We had to wait there in a dump feet down with respirators on during more shelling for hours, while the poor chaps groaned with their wounds, but we got them all off before dawn. We then went back and managed to get a short sleep.

In the morning we inspected 'B' casemate, finding it in an awful mess and the gun out of action. Gunners Wright and Morris were the only men left, and we had them into our casemate. Later on Gunner Dan Smith developed delayed gas symptoms and became unconscious and we carried him off. He got over it later, but eventually was invalided out entirely on account of this gas.

I took a photograph of 'B' gun and its damage with Gunners Wright and Roddick, and as I did so I said to myself that this should be the end of my photography, which seemed to me a pastime belonging to another world, one different from this, and that things like this, and the hit up limber which I also photographed, did not need photographing by me. So I contrived soon after to get rid of my little camera, and this was the end of my attempt to illustrate my life during this war. This account will therefore carry no more photographs.

On the top of all this came news of the failure of our infantry attack with enormous losses. Better news, however, came from the south; we took Combles and Guillemont and the French made a big advance.

In the afternoon there was more heavy shelling and we took refuge in the dump for two hours, shells bursting just outside and shaking the position.

Then 'D' gun had a direct hit inside the casemate, the gun shields, buffer and a wheel smashed, the detachment fortunately being in the dump. The ammunition caught fire and the fire was put out by Lieutenant Ryan.

Lieutenant Ryan was, I always thought, our best officer. I admired him immensely without admitting it. I admired him most because he put common-sense before King's Regulations. I can hear him now, when some question came up in an emergency or when we were stuck in the mud, as to whether we should do this or that, and he was appealed to as to what to do. 'What to do?' he would yell. 'Use your bloody common-sense, get on with it, don't stand there looking at me.' He didn't look for somebody else to put out that fire in the casemate, he didn't waste time shouting to get us out of our holes, he did it himself.

Much has been written about courage, and about fear. The appreciation of the courage which prompts incredible acts of bravery done on the spur of the moment seems nowadays to have become secondary to the appreciation of the capacity to endure. But is passive endurance without prospective alternative necessarily the highest form of bravery? There must be an alternative choice, and passive endurance implies no such alternative. One cannot just walk home out of it, although apparently that is exactly what thousands of French soldiers did nine months later, and later still all the Russians. It seems to me bravery is best defined by such terms as continuing under impossible conditions to function in act and word without depreciation of normal efficiency, to do which indefinitely must imply character above the ordinary.

Our morale was now appreciably lowered. We would argue endlessly about which of two shelled routes to take; we would, when we felt particularly bad, shout out to each other about the 'bloody war' and 'This bloody country, look at it, who wants it? We don't want it, let the Germans have it'. Such times occurred, and such things were said by us, and it is humbug at this distance in time to pretend otherwise.

Mr Ryan never let things get him down, at any rate not in our presence, as we did; if he had to get to a trouble spot, he just went there without arguing about the route, and he seemed to be in all the trouble spots. He had no time for grumbles, and I remember one occasion when we were hard at it, no doubt to the hindrance of our work, when he came up and said quite calmly, 'Be quiet, and remember this: "Wealth lost, something lost, honour lost, much lost, courage lost, all lost"', and walked away. It was not until years later that I discovered that the words were Goethe's:

Gut verloren, etwas verloren;
Ehre verloren, viel verloren;
Mut verloren, alles verloren.

I thought to myself, there is more to that than in all the sermons there have ever been.

He had resource, he had the ability to make quick decisions, he had courage, he had all the qualities I wanted to have and hadn't. He was a brave man.

I do not know whether he ever received a medal, but he was the man in our battery who ought to have had one. He came through the war, and I met him once in Piccadilly in 1919.

We had now only two guns in action, and the obvious speculation was whether it was 'A' or 'C' gun's turn next. We came out later that evening, but it was only for re-forming.

On the 13th we went back as a five-gun battery, consisting of our 'A' and 'C' guns and three second battery guns. For some reason I was not with them. News came down that new emplacements had to be made for the five guns in the open in front of the casemates, as a new Thiepval attack, requiring a wider switch to the right than the casemates allowed, was to start the next day. So we were to have the worst of both worlds; the casemate world left us unprotected when the Germans had us spotted; the camouflage world would not function for the same reason, and we would not have put any on if we had had it, which we had not.

I received orders late that day to go up with the ammunition, as I was to be layer on 'A' gun.

On arrival I was told to go and look at 'the crater'. While we had been away something like an 8-inch had fallen exactly on the left of 'D' casemate. It was the first really big one we had ever had on our position and it had missed 'D' casemate by inches, no damage being done. I noted here for the first time how damage from big bursts did not appear to extend on the ground beyond the lips of the crater, the force of the explosion apparently all going upwards. The men had decided that it was as good a shelter hole as any, and we used it when being shelled, arguing fatuously that a second one would hardly fall exactly in it, an argument which unaccountably seemed to give much reassurance. A bus inside it would not have been seen above the surface.

Then we were told that the attack had been postponed.

Next day we learnt that it would commence the following morning at 06.20 hours, and that it would be in conjunction with the French on the River Somme, an all-out offensive over the sector from Thiepval opposite us, to break what was called the 'Third Line', which had resulted from the July battles, and which had been established through Pozières, Bazentin, Longueval and Guillemont to the river.

The next day, 15 September, the Battle [Flers-Courcelette] opened, the second greatest bombardment since 1 July. Unaccountably we stood to all morning without orders or action. We were nonplussed. Then about noon the teams came up, guns were hooked up, we threw our kitbags on the limbers and we were off, thankful to be out of the place that we had been warned was sinister, and it was. But what now?

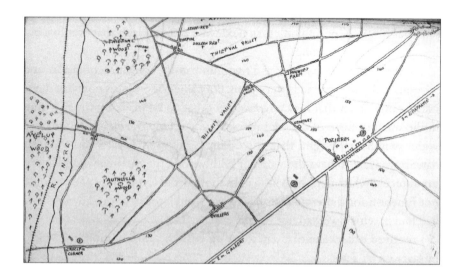

Pozières

We walk-marched to Crucifix Corner along roads crowded with troops and transport, and halted there for a breather. We were to have need of it.

We knew then where we were going, up close to Pozières on the open slope. This really was it; we had got to the war. We would be by the side of the straight main Albert to Bapaume road.

The roar of the guns had continued all morning, and, as we turned off up a track past our old position and dump of evil memory, it seemed to intensify. With the Major leading and all gunners on limbers and wagons, we sped up a steepish slope, and, passing the celebrated mine crater near non-existent La Boiselle, came onto the main road and dashed along up it. It was not a 'healthy' road to be on.

Never shall I forget that ride. On both sides of the road were batteries strung out in lines, first heavies and huge 8-inch howitzers, and naval guns, then further up our own 4.5 howitzers and beyond them batteries after batteries of 18-pounders in line or echeloned. In a sense batteries were wheel to wheel along the whole Somme front, each in its own category covering independently the whole enemy trench system, our battery's share of trench being likely to be equal to the width of the battery position, 100 yards.

The roar of the bombardment surpassed the capacity of words to describe. No bang of any individual gun could possibly be heard in such an Armageddon, which is perhaps a sufficient statement. It was a complex roar of rushing, whooshing, whooping mixed with cracking, ripping, smacking sounds.

Our sergeants rode alongside us shouting orders, but I could not hear a word anyone said. Only by putting my face up to the man beside me and shouting into his ear could I make myself heard.

I have thought about this ride into action many times and always felt that, even though we had more guns at Third Ypres, it must have been the greatest and most shattering bombardment which has ever been in history, or of its kind, ever will be. I have listened to accounts of bombardments in the Second War, accounts by Americans of the bombardments of Tarawa and Guadalcanal, and I can never satisfy myself that these can have exceeded in roar this bombardment of the second Somme Offensive.

Halfway along the road we thought we were dreaming. We had heard rumours, so we knew what it was. It was the well-kept secret, the tank, our first sight of it. It was enormous and unwieldy and had a broken track, but it was an exciting sight and we somehow felt that it might win the war for us.

On the left at a distance was an area of stones which was Ovillers, but we passed on between what remained of poplar rows till we actually saw the outskirts of Pozières just ahead. Then suddenly, to our relief, the Major waved us to the left off the road onto what had been arable fields, then almost immediately he signalled 'action right'. So the signals we had learnt at Roborough Common had come in useful, even though this was no action right at all, but merely a taking up of position.

There was no order for action, so we merely hastened to get the guns in position with firm trails and, with the help of the frantic drivers, who just threw the rounds down, to get the ammunition stacked. The teams departed at speed and we started at once by instinct to dig in. We then saw that our whole brigade was spread out in line, 'A' and 'B' Batteries being on our left and we, the right-hand one, were next to the road, that vital road. At the moment there were no other batteries in front of us, so we were well up this time and in a position which could give cause for thought, about as important a position as could be, it seemed to me.

We covered the guns and dumps with nets and did some section fire, made sandbag walls round the guns and started on our own funk holes, dumps and lean-to shacks. Firing all round was continuous, but we were not shelled, though the ground in front consisted of shell holes and nothing else, which was a disconcerting sight. Then it came on to rain as it got dark.

It is depressing to be dumped in a field in the rain on an open windswept slope at night, with the knowledge that you may have to make the spot of earth your home for an indefinite period. It also is surprising how one jumps to it when one realizes that, if one wants shelter, warmth and food at a time like this, one must work madly for these things. The true philosophy that the satisfaction of man's requirements results from his own efforts and from no other source.

By the time 'A' sub had nearly made themselves comfortable, I noticed that all our officers had gone down to the wagon-lines except for one junior second lieutenant in charge. He was a new man, whose name we did not know, a business man type. He walked miserably up and down in the rain all night. He never spoke to us or interfered with our efforts to make ourselves comfortable. In the morning someone commented on the fact, adding that he must be wet through, and saying further that the Major had given orders that the men were to get themselves dug into the dry before any work was done on officers' quarters. I thought to myself, in what army but the British could a thing like this happen? Mr Blank still walked up and down.

For the first time in my life I came to a decision about what to do without any hesitation. I did an unpardonable thing. Without a word to corporal I got up, went over to the back of the position and waited for Mr B to come along. I went up to him and said, 'Can't we make a dugout for you, sir?' He smiled and said, 'Oh, thank you, Gunner Price'. I went back, for some reason to left section, and asked sergeant there, a forceful person, well able to ask me who the hell I thought I was, 'Say Sergeant, it's a shame; we must start on an officers' dugout. Poor Mr B is wet through.' I don't remember what Sergeant said, but two gunners came along and we had a large enough hole dug by night to be able to put a bit of roof on it.

On our fourth day here it rained all day, the driving rain on this exposed slope and our shortage of rubber and iron sheets made conditions as miserable as they could possibly be. However, some mad scrounging produced enough iron sheets to partially roof our shacks, and by evening we were able to lie down in the dry. A few 'willies' fell round us in the evening, but obviously we ourselves were not receiving enemy attention.

Late that day I went down to the wagon-lines, which were by a lake outside Albert. Here too conditions were miserable, there being few shacks.

The next day, 19 September, we had appalling news. Our Major, the Adjutant of brigade, a Captain of brigade and a young second lieutenant of brigade were all in an elephant hut, that is, a hut made by bolting together curved iron sheets, behind our position, which was Brigade Forward H.Q. While they were holding a conference a 5.9 came in through the entrance and burst inside. The Lieutenant alone survived, with appalling injuries.

The Major was a fine man, young for his job. The Battery had traditions before the war, and he helped to develop and maintain them. He was strict, but fair and we felt he had a permanent interest in the Battery and its efficiency. He was not popular but was immensely respected. We never had his like again, as he belonged to us as from the beginning. None of his successors were the same. We all went to the funeral of the three men at the huge Aveluy Wood Cemetery.

Next day a 5.9 burst between the wagon-lines and 'B' sub horse-lines, showering our bivouac with dirt. Though the intervening space was only about ten yards, nothing was damaged at all. It seemed inexplicable, and we could only put it down to the soft condition of the wet earth.

The next day I returned to the guns in lovely weather. I noted, 'It is this sort of thing that makes existence possible.' There was now an enormously increased number of batteries around us and in front of us.

Things were quiet now, the big attack being apparently over. The history books say, '… it was without any doubt the greatest British victory, though not the most important, which had been gained up to date in the War. July 1 was the most important, and all subsequent ones arose from it, since it was then that the Chinese wall of Germany was breached … the Battle of Loos had taught us that the infantry must not outrun the guns, but this pre-ordained limit was attained at almost every spot. Martinpuich, High Wood, Flers, Delville, and Leuze Wood, all passed permanently within the British lines, and the trophies of victory amounted to 5,000 prisoners and a dozen guns. At this stage no less than 21,000 prisoners had been taken by the British and 34,000 by the French since the great series of battles was commenced upon July 1.' We heard reports to this effect and were tremendously inspired; we seemed to be on the road to victory; it was magnificent and the R.F.A. had helped. It was glorious.

It was as well that we could not then read another account, published years later, also describing the Battles of the Somme. 'They [the British] lost 60,000 men the first day alone; and when the offensive had dragged to its weary end in November 1916 only a few square miles of worthless tortured ground had been captured, while the losses of 538,000 troops on the part of the Central Powers compared to 794,000 of the Allied attackers. After this blood-bath a plaintive cry went up, "No more Sommes!"'

I do not comment. The Censor had to do its work, but equally the truth had to come out, and the longer it was in doing so, the greater the reaction when it did.

In the evening of the 24th [September] I was detailed with two others to go up to our F.O.P. to do repairs to it, as it had been blown in. It was situated about half a mile forward on the left flank and was on the eastward point of a low spur, from which in daytime there was good observation of the front lines from Thiepval south to Pozières. The way there was along one of the tracks made by infantry and teams, and there were roughly two, so that choice could be made of the one being at the moment least shelled, for both were known to the enemy and were shelled fairly continuously. It was always a dangerous job going to and being at F.O.P.

We nearly ran into two 5.9s soon after starting, and in the dark we lost the track and were ages finding the place. When we found it, it appeared to be completely exposed on the top of a slope and without a single sandbag. Shells burst all round us all night and we were covered with dirt by them twice. It was a case of concentrating on digging and getting too tired to think, but that did not really work. We were damned frightened. We started back when it was just getting light. When we were back in the shallow valley on one of the tracks, a barrage of 5.9s started, which was evidently meant for this track, but was about 50 yards wide on our right. We were walking in line as fast as we could and then broke into a run, hoping to get out of the shelled area, but they seemed to keep up with us always close on our right. We ran faster and faster sometimes throwing ourselves flat simultaneously with some terrific whoosh-bang; we thought of breaking to the left onto the other track, but we were in a trench of sorts and felt it best to stay in it; it seemed that the faster we ran, the nearer the bursts came; we were down and up and down again; I remember feeling, how long can I keep this up, with a dry mouth and bursting lungs I thought always how much farther to the battery; it seemed endless and the frightful crashes came closer and kept relentlessly on. At last the ground seemed a little familiar, and with thankfulness we saw our position in the dim morning light and found we had left the bursts behind; we slowed again to a walk and still panting came back to the battery where, thank goodness, all was quiet and the men asleep. We tumbled into our shacks and fell asleep exhausted, the worst fatigue ever.

The Artillery were subjected to two kinds of shelling, one, counter-battery work, and, two, indiscriminate. Our reactions to the first depended upon whether we were in action or not; if not, we did what we called 'a nip', a clear off to a flank, by order or without. If in action, then it was just too bad, but we had done nicely so far in such cases inside our strong casemates, but now under a net, it was somewhat different.

Our reactions to the second type of shelling, the indiscriminate, was different, and this was another problem altogether for our minds to turn over ceaselessly. Here at present for us, and for all the hundreds of other 18-pounder batteries, all shelling was indiscriminate, and this was obviously due to our nets and careful camouflage, not even a piece of paper being allowed to blow about the position, making our batteries practically invisible to overhead spotting and counter-battery work apparently impossible with enemy fire the intensest we had known. We rejoiced now under our nets and were thankful that no one had built up huge casemates here for us to go into. The result of this upon us was at first a burst of light-heartedness, we shouted off our apprehension, and apparently we had reason for doing so, for so far we had had no shells on the position at all.

Our argument was that every shell had such an immense area into which to drop, that with indeterminate targets the chance of any one of them falling upon our few square yards was comparatively small. But this outlook could not last, because the time factor intervened; it was a question of time, and the alternative argument eventually loomed up and prevailed, the 'if we stay here long enough, one has got to fall here some time' argument. Nevertheless, we continued to be thankful for and put our trust in our nets and be grateful to the inventor of camouflage.

When this subject of 'chances' was openly argued and too frequently, it drew from others the retort, 'You windy bastards', a retort which flew both ways and was not edifying.

All this is very boring now to write about and, because the subject involved is fear and nothing else, it is not a proper subject to discuss, or was not, but to omit this subject from a factual account of our lives would be to imply that there was no such subject, which is humbug.

The fact remained that from now onwards when in position, as we nearly always were, our chances of survival, on the whole seldom spoken about openly, became an ever-present complex that was with us at all times day and night and in our dreams, from which we were never free while at the guns, and which we knew could eventually 'get us down'.

I have no notes on the next three days, the 25th to 27th [September], and in view of what followed, I hope they were easy ones.

The troops disposition on this 'Breaking of the Third Line' on our sector of the front was as follows: we now had the 5th Army, Gough's, in front of us; starting on the left at Thiepval were the 18th and then the 11th Divisions, and on their right, immediately in front of us, the Canadian Corps, dug in over the crest which we could see just on the far side of Pozières rubble a mile ahead. We had never been so close. On their immediate right was our 4th Army; first came the Third Corps covering Martinpuich and in High Wood, next on their right the Fifteenth Corps in the trenches opposite Flers, and on its right the Fourteenth Corps joining up with the French on the Somme. What was holding things up on this whole front was the Germans' terrific bastion on the extreme left at Thiepval. We had not taken it, and there could be no advance until we had done so. However, on the 21st the Canadians fought down the slope and took Courcelette. For some reason we knew nothing about this, although we were where we were specifically to support them.

At 12.35 hours on the 26th the attack on Thiepval opened, but being nearly two miles away at an angle of nearly 50 degrees on our left, we were unable to give support. I regretted this, as the battle was an epic for all time. Thiepval, except for its north-east corner, was taken.

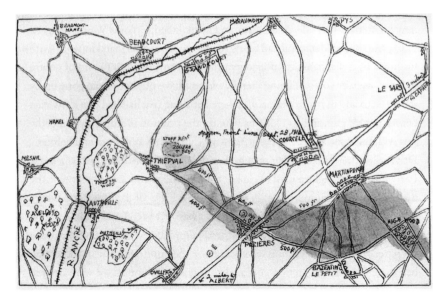

First and Second Positions of C Battery at Pozières.
Scale 1 mile = 1 inch

The next day we were not surprised to hear that we were to be ready to go forward the following morning. This really was it; to be going forward meant being just under the open height of land just outside Pozières on the far side, exactly a mile from the present trenches at Courcelette. We would be firing at shorter range than ever before, a lot shorter.

September 28 was a lovely day. Lieutenant Ryan and a new young officer came up with the teams, which included a G.S. wagon carrying a trench bridge, as we would have to cross a trench.

Shelling was becoming intense over the whole slope and much damage had already been done, including direct hits on two guns of a battery near and many dugouts blown in.

My diary is incoherent for this day and the next, but I give an emended edition of it:

All our teams up taking out guns and ammunition. Just before we started shells began bursting between the position and the road, just where we had to go; one pitched within three yards of 'B' gun team, wounding Drivers Price and Gardner; up on the road speed didn't matter much to us gunners, but the drivers weren't anxious to spin the time out; made the short distance to Pozières in short time;

new Lieutenant hit badly in the back and horse killed; Colonel West of Brigade H.Q., who had ridden on ahead to spy for obstructions, was killed instantly with his horse by a direct hit; cannonade working up to a maximum and of course the road we were on was being literally plastered; we ought to have gone up by the track; to add to it, our prematures were appalling (we had had one a few days before, not 'A' gun, and had killed a man on the position in front; my sympathy was with the layer; a dreadful event; message came, 'Shot at in front and behind'); Driver Shurmer broke his leg on a limber pole when horses swerved at a burst; Pozières an awful sight, a mass of rubble, rubbish and abandoned equipment, the pathways made of ammunition in carriers; a few sticks of fruit trees and where one walked seemed to have been former pathways between houses; came out on the far edge with the crest less than 50 yards ahead; here was the position, but a deep trench ran across, cutting what was to be the position in half; right section had to get over it; left section could take up position at once; we were delayed while gunners on the G.S. wagon were struggling with the trench bridge; got 'A' and 'B' guns across bridge and manhandled them into position; drivers flung ammunition down on ground and made off like scalded cats, this time by the track; shelling all round never let up and of course we knew that the Germans, though they couldn't see us, air-spotting then being nil, knew perfectly well that the ground just behind the crest would now be lousy with guns and that if they plastered it indiscriminately, they would be bound to knock a lot out; a deep German dugout near was a relief; we realized properly this time the inevitability of the time factor and got stuck into it sandbagging.

As soon as we were in position Mr Ryan and a signaller left unnoticed to go to F.O.P., some shell hole, we imagined, right in the open over the crest in full view of the enemy; we only hoped he took a net with him. It was the most dangerous place of all and, of course, he was in it. Signaller Levison, the popular 'Levy', stayed with us at the end of his wire in a shell hole.

Our A.P. was a shattered tree on the right, and we then looked for an A.A.P. nearer at hand. Close in front was a quite suitable one, a rifle stuck upright in the ground by its bayonet, which later on investigation proved to be marking the spot where its owner, a British soldier, lay dead beside it.

We were too busy to look about, but I realized one thing, that 'A' gun was not more than 50 yards from the main road where it issued from the village, the road which surely must have been the route for countless invading armies throughout history passing from northern France into Belgium, or the reverse. Oddly it appeared that the Germans considered the strategic route to be through the Ancre Valley, which was the reason they had fortified so tremendously and held on so stubbornly to Thiepval. 'A' gun, so it seemed to me, was closest to, and would be the first to fire over open sights on the point where a counter-attack would come into view, that is, in conjunction with some 'F' sub gun of a battery on the other side of the road. The thought thrilled me in a way nothing before had done; after all the months of preparation we had really got there this day.

Another thought added to the excitement, which was in relation to the line on our left. I assumed that the front ran at right angles to the direction of attack, which was the Albert–Bapaume road. If my sense of direction was at all correct, Thiepval lay definitely behind this line on the left, by a matter of some 15 degrees, which meant that we were well in front of Thiepval, which had only just been taken, and from which the enemy had not yet entirely withdrawn.

Though far too busy to spend time scanning the road to the right, the crest in front, or the left flank, it did also occur to me that it was literally comic that, after all these months of guard duty, gas guard and aeroplane guard, it was not considered necessary for anyone to be detailed as a look-out, presumably because there is no such category in King's Regulations. The Germans could have walked up to the position and we should all have been too busy sandbagging to have seen them. Further, if we had seen any on our flanks we could have done exactly nothing to protect ourselves from a machine gun or grenades, as we had no rifles, machine gun or grenades, only our officers having revolvers, and guns cannot be used as rifles and switched about and fired along the line. One German on our flank could have picked us all off with a machine gun before we could have got 'A' gun on him. Our lack of small arms made me mad,[3] but I found that the subject was taboo. But the time did come, months later, when we were given one machine gun.

When it was dark the order came for all gunners except two per gun to go back to the old position. Gunner Gardiner and I remained, I probably because I was the only first-class proficiency layer in the sub.

As we now had the gun adequately protected and covered with a net, the next immediate job as always was a dugout for our two selves. Here Gunner Gardiner proved a genius; he became confidential and explained he would do the digging, it would be a one-man job and 'you go and have a bit of shut-eye in the German dugout'. I liked Gunner Gardiner, nothing excited or worried

---

3   Struck through at this point was written: 'none the less so when I understood that gun duty was to serve the gun as long as we were alive'.

him, he almost put the war from him and became aloof from it, he was always calm, deliberate, of few words and with a friendly smile. When I returned to do my stint, I could not find him; I called and a head appeared out of the earth; he had almost finished, having dug a slit trench just wide enough to take a body and now over six feet deep; there was just room for the two of us squatting, at the bottom and I never felt so safe. We sat facing each other and slept.

The next day, the 29th, we expected the ammunition wagons and gunners at 05.00 hours. However, being paralyzed with cramp, we crawled out of our hole before light and went on sandbagging, which at a time like this was a job without end because you could not have too many sandbags.

Suddenly 4.2s started bursting near and over the trench across the middle of the position, and this soon developed into a barrage. We crouched in our trench until a burst nearly got us, when we scrambled out and made for the German dugout faster than either of us had ever run before. We sat there for a time keeping halfway up the steps so that we could hear orders if any came.

They came. I heard a yell. It was Levy racing along the position regardless of the barrage; he was literally shrieking 'S.O.S. – Range 1,800 – GUNFIRE – GUNFIRE – GUNFIRE'. We dashed along to the gun; she was on line; we put on the range which meant a target exactly in Courcelette; it could only mean a counter-attack: this was it.

It was gunfire for a detachment of two; we had never thought this out; our 25 rounds a minute at Hébuterne had been with six men. I fell into the layer's seat, Gardiner put on the range and we started, fortunately it was 'Percussion. Load H.E.' We shouted to each other 'come on do 25'; I yelled that I would work the breech to save him, as it all depended on him if we did it or not, and whether he could get the rounds up in loading position fast enough. At gun drill, No. 4 stands on the left of the trail and receives the rounds on his right from No. 5 in loading position, which is left arm forward and right hand to push up, all in one movement. Here for some reason all our H.E. were stacked on the right of the emplacement, consequently he had to stand on the right of the trail, swing the rounds behind the gun and load by pushing up with the left hand, making two movements.

This really was IT. It was what I had joined the Artillery for. It had taken two years of preparation, drill, grooming and harness cleaning, and at last we had worked forward and were right up. It was what we had dreamt of; there was no officer; there was no N.C.O.; we were on our own, Gunner Gardiner and I; it was terrific; it was our gun and our war, and it was GUNFIRE WITH JUST THE TWO OF US.

The gun jumped and shook but kept on line and with a steady bubble, the trail was firm and the traverse nearly on centre. Gardiner managed to watch the range drum, which I could not see, and we went at it: bang – click – up click – bang – click – up click – and the intervals between the bangs should be 2½ seconds. I don't think we did it, but good old Gardiner went at it till he sweated streams, so that at the end of a minute I yelled 'change over', he leapt into my seat and I threw them in. The gun behaved perfectly and the buffer ran the barrel back properly all the time.

There never was such an action for me before or ever again.

Gradually I became conscious of the roar and of the fact that it was resolving itself out into that of (1) our four guns, (2) our guns behind, (3) the barrage overhead, which we couldn't look at, having no time, but supposed it was there, and (4) a new noise which most of us had never heard before, the chatter of machine guns – whose, we did not know.

I always felt as a gunner in a position of inferiority vis-a-vis the infantry, and rightly so, as we were often a long way back, but this time we were up, really up.

Then, just as we finished gunfire, we heard voices behind us and Sergeant Gore and three gunners came to relieve us. There was cease fire and we never knew what happened, but if it was an attack it petered out. Later some of us went into the dugout to eat bully and biscuits and drink water, the supply of which in our water bottles was running out. The others went down to the 'room' at the bottom, but I for the first time had a twinge of imagination. This deep dugout had only one entrance and a hit would bury anyone below; on the other hand, to sit at the entrance was no protection, so, I argued, the chances were best if one sat halfway down the entrance, which I did. It seems that in those days we did not know the meaning of the word claustrophobia; we did not dwell on or spend time imagining horrific situations, as there were too many of them. I continued having no feelings on the subject of being buried until I was in hospital a year later, when I asked an elderly pioneer corps man in the bed next to me what had happened to him. He replied that he had been buried, adding, 'Don't talk to me about it, Gunner.' Ever since, I have had slight feelings of claustrophobia, but not enough to trouble me. It seems that when young I had comparatively little imagination and that as the years pass, imagination grows and recollections of the past not only crowd upon one, but do so vividly, and I assume this is generally the case. This means that distance in time may produce not only forgetfulness, but in some cases an intensity of view.

In the afternoon we had section fire, after which news came that we were to be relieved by the 25th Division, the left section to go out in the evening and the right section the next day, guns to be left behind and all gunners to return to wagon-lines. We had been amazingly lucky having had no casualties.

For some reason Sergeant Gore and I left in the afternoon, he for wagon-lines and I for the old position; I wondered why.

I shall always remember that walk, the relief at getting away made us light-headed, and we laughed and sang as we trailed along through the rubble of awful Pozières, paying no regard to bursts which continued everywhere. I felt sure I should find all quiet at the old position and be able to relax and have a sleep, for I was weary after two such days without any.

Meanwhile we found that we were both parched with thirst, our bottles being long empty, and at Sergeant's suggestion we looked everywhere for anything resembling a cook-house where we could beg some 'cha'. This seemed hopeless, but suddenly we saw a tiny wisp of smoke coming out of a trench and looking down we saw an elderly cook or officer's servant squatting by a tiny fire on which was a billycan containing what looked like ink. It was 'cha' and had evidently been stewing all day, but we cried out together 'Give us a drink, chum.' The old chap smiled good naturedly and handed it up to us without a word. Sergeant and I years afterwards agreed that that drink was nectar.

Then on we went across the desolation talking about the day; what a wonderful experience it was.

It was quiet at the old position and the only people there were Corporal Jennings, our good cook, and two signallers, one being 'Levy'. Jennings brought us tea, we rested, then Sergeant left for the lines. I then noticed the others looking at me and sensed something was up. 'Gunner Price, on at 0.5 Observation Post tonight'. Such a thing had not occurred to me, and I wondered whether I would be able to keep awake. The signallers were sympathetic but said they had to have one more man for the night, and that there had been so many casualties lately that I was the only gunner available. I then realized, when on the point of a flow of language, that, if the O.P. was a quiet one, I might well be better off there than on the noisy old position, and also that I probably would not be able to sleep at all anyway. Jennings cooked a good supper with more strong tea, and when the time came, I went off with the two signallers, 'Levy' and a 'B' Battery man, feeling quite spry.

The place proved to be on a crest near Blighty Wood, quite a long way back and facing Thiepval on its south-west side. It was in an old German trench and was, on this night, completely quiet. I was on from 20.00 to 22.00 hours. It was pitch dark with not even a gun flash to plot. I turned in down in a small dugout and slept intermittently, coming up again at 02.00 hours. I asked specially for this time as the early hours fascinate me. 'Levy' had given me the direction of Thiepval, which I was anxious to see, and had fixed a pointer on the parapet along which I could look, indeed had to look as it was the chief point for observation. 'Levy' brought me out some tea and I settled down alone with my gaze along the pointer. A kind of peace of mind came over me, a reaction brought about by the quietness and the tea. I wrote in my diary how glad I was to be here; I ought to have written how thankful I was to have come through Pozières, but I didn't. To express thanks for good fortune is a natural instinct; it is also a primitive and childish instinct: it may well be comforting, but it is an irrational thing to do. You cannot thank events, they are Life, and Life can be conceived as some kind of Flow, caused by physical impulses, actuated partly by chance and partly by the effects of Man's mind. Insofar as results for the individual are good or bad, the individual has his minute share of responsibility, and the rest is chance.

I strained to get my first thrilling view of the terrible fortress of Thiepval, the position we had just stormed with such losses. Gradually I made out a wide, open, bare, scooped out and devastated plain below me to the north-east, with in the middle a small steep-sided hill standing isolated, appearing in the dim light in the form of some medieval, pinnacled, craggy castle. Apparently I was right, there had been a castle there and it had been called the Thiepval Château. Spellbound, I watched the great amphitheatre unfold in the morning light, a devastation of churned yellowish earth, and never a living thing moved, not a bird.

The relieving party was as usual late, and we did not get back to the old position till noon. A dead weariness came over me and I turned in and slept. But I started to have fits of jumpiness, and kept dreaming and waking. Suddenly I was scrambling up sweating; my dream was of 5.9s falling on the tennis lawn at home; the war had come to my home and its lovely garden. I had seen plenty of devastated French gardens, but when I saw these things happening to my own garden, it was a very different thing; I did not associate this war with my home. I must have called out because kind Jennings was standing by me saying, 'Come on Gunner and I'll cook you some cha.' Kindly people they all were. It was ridiculous to let a dream get one down.

In the afternoon right section came down and we all packed onto a wagon and went down to the wagon-lines, singing crazily.

My last comment about it all in my diary was, 'I am proud the Battery has been here in action in the open in front of Pozières.'

On Trek

We left the Albert front on 30 September and were allotted for the rest of the year 1916 the duties of relieving batteries in sectors first to the north of the original salient, then to the south. The Battle of the Somme was wearing itself out as winter approached, and fighting seemed to be dying down. Consequently, our various positions were fairly quiet ones, a fact for which we were supremely grateful. A good part of this time was spent at rear wagon-lines in between treks, where, to our intense aggravation but not unexpectedly, the regime of grooming, harness cleaning and spit and polish, over the absence of which we gunners had so much congratulated ourselves, was reimposed. But after all it was the Army and this sort of thing was the price of peace, as dirt and a certain laxity were the rewards of stress and strain; anyway, it was a change. Also we were much on the road or, as we called it, on trek.

On 2 October we walk-marched from the dismal wagon-lines by the lake at Albert with some sense of relief. However, on this day luck in the form of the weather served us ill, as it began to rain and continued to do so the whole day and all the next night. We went back to Louvencourt where we watered, then on through Authie and Pas [-en-Artois] to Warlincourt [-lès-Pas], where there was a complete and appalling box-up in narrow roads in the dark. We seemed to have no instructions as to the whereabouts of our lines for the night, not a soul was to be found and frantic N.C.O.s galloped about in all directions vainly trying to contact someone. We stood in the same place for two hours, the rain never ceasing and the men were soaked to the skin.

I always went off into a kind of stupor at such times, my mind ceasing to function. Years later the Sergeant-Major remarked to me that the spirit of the men that night was something that he personally had always been proud to recall. The men sang, sang solidly all the time and all the songs they knew, 'Nelly Dear', 'Irish Eyes', 'Three German Officers', and the favourite, 'Fred Karno's Army'. They not only sang but laughed, and continued to do so, when, after the lines had been found, horse-lines made and horses fed, they were told that there was nowhere for them to go under cover, as the nearby huts were locked and the whereabouts of the keys was unknown. We stood round a fire and still sang. As usual I was dry in a mackintosh. I made up my mind I must somehow do something about it, whatever the consequences might be. It was the lower part of the drivers' bodies which became sodden, not only with water but with mud, they sat on their saddles in mud; they could tie their ground sheets round their shoulders. Eventually the keys were found and we dropped onto dry boards and went to sleep. Some time later I wrote to a firm of oilskin makers in the north of England, with whom I had dealt before the war, and ordered thirty pairs of black oilskin slacks, sufficient for all the men in 'A' sub. I wondered vaguely what would happen, and, as nothing did, forgot about it.[4] For the next four days my diary says, 'Rotten time, rain and mud, horse-lines on ploughed field, reveille at 04.30 hours, at it often thirteen hours a day'.

Orders then came that all batteries were to be made up to six guns and complications were endless.

On the 7th we moved to 'made-up' horse-lines at Gaudiempré, which was an improvement. Next day right section gunners went up to 'A' Battery's position on the left of the Sailly–Hébuterne road, where we met two guns and made open positions for them on the right of the position, thus forming a six-gun battery. We had a good cook among us, Bert Nash, a prize scrounger of Quaker oats, and for once fed ourselves amply. After four days we, the gunners, moved again and took over the guns of a section of West Ridings on the left of Foncquevillers, a wet place but with good dugouts. Two days later a Warwick Battery took over and we walked to a position between Sailly and Château de la Haye (Fourth Hébuterne Position), and took over from C.243, joining up with our left section and the left section of C.243 to make six guns.

It was a miserable position, right section having no dugouts, only two small elephant huts. Later two of us acquired a small alpine tent in which we were dry and comfortable.

Unfortunately, there was an 8-inch battery immediately on the right of us. It was fascinating to watch them in action, and they seemed to be in action most of the time. The R.G.A. gunners were hefty men and I have never seen men work harder. It seemed to be action all day for them and it was marvellous how they kept it up, heaving up their huge shells and ramming them in. The obvious result was that they annoyed the Germans,

4   See p. 97.

who soon found them out, as they were either unable to, or could not be bothered to put a net over themselves. We wished they were anywhere else than where they were. However, we spent a fairly quiet fortnight and then on 1 November the heavies received a proper shelling of both time [shells] and 5.9s, and of course many of them fell round us. No damage was done, but by some extraordinary chance the Germans spotted our water-cart which for some reason was parked a couple of hundred yards away, in the open. They took an unaccountable interest in it and were always trying to get it; perhaps they were training their gun-layers. They were so persistent that fetching water for the cook house and for washing became a matter for serious consideration. We noted the frequencies of and intervals between bursts, and timed our hasty trips with buckets accordingly, with a view to getting there, filling buckets and getting back before the next one. This seemed to work all right. However, when my turn came, I acted with all speed, and, as I reached about halfway on my return journey, heard a burst and looking back saw poor old water-cart with wheels spinning in the air, a direct hit at last. As some eighty yards separated me from it, I decided not to count this as one of my 'near ones'. We really did suffer as a result of this, and in an unexpected way. Water had now to be brought up in petrol cans. Cans that had shortly before contained petrol were filled with water and brought up; it was as simple as that. Unfortunately, the water was thoroughly impregnated with petrol, so that for the rest of our time here all our meals, and worst of all our lovely tea tasted and stank of petrol. It was heartrending and awful and we had to force our food down. Curiously enough it did not affect us in any way.

A fortnight later in a mist a German plane came over us only 500 feet up and carefully inspected us and the heavies, who were as usual completely uncamouflaged. Anti-aircraft guns and machine guns opened up from all around and some twenty of our planes were soon in hot pursuit. It was reported to have been shot down, but that it came down in the German lines. He was a brave pilot.

We prepared ourselves for what we felt was sure to come, but nothing happened except for morning and evening gas shelling, which gave us an opportunity for practising action in gas masks.

We made a fine right section dugout, and then, of course, when we were comfortably in it, we were taken over on the 27th by a 49th Division battery. We rode down to the frightful mud again at Warlincourt lines.

1 Gunner W.R. Price 825366: C Battery, 240 Brigade R.F.A. (T), 48th Division. Photographed in January 1917, presumably in a professional studio in France; he has mud on his boots, to which spurs are attached.

2, 3 The field botanist in Formosa, 1911, collecting plant specimens for the Royal Botanic Gardens herbarium at Kew. *Above:* WRP (extreme left) and fellow botanist Henry Elwes (extreme right), and between them the Japanese Commandant and Regional Administrator (Formosa then being under Japanese control). *Below:* With Japanese soldier and group of aboriginals. In both shots WRP wears Japanese waraji straw rope sandals.

4 Formosa 1911. Henry Elwes and WRP flanked by Japanese administrators, local soldiers and aboriginals at an outpost in the north of the island; they were shown generous hospitality and given much support during their specimen gathering expedition there.

5, 6, 7 Training in southern England. *Above:* Volunteer soldiers, some still wearing their civilian clothes, marching to their first camp. *Left:* Learning to dig trenches. *Below:* WRP's fellow gunners of the 240th with a 15-pounder: 'Our guns were 15-pounders. We were pleased with them, knowing no better, though somewhat daunted when we heard that they had been through the Boer War.'

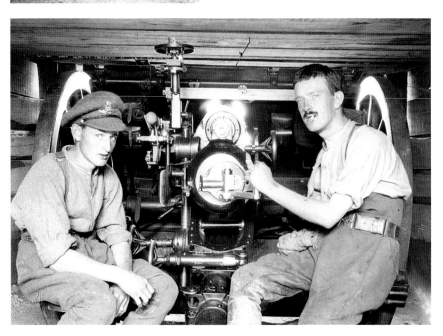

8, 9 Training in southern England: moving the trail of the 15-pounder (*above*), and loading (*below*), with WRP on the far right.

10, 11 In transit to the Western Front. *Above:* At Southampton docks, bound for Le Havre: 'the Brigade was split up among seven transports – the principle being that, should enemy submarines sink a ship, it would not wipe out a unit organisation but only a part of it, which could, with reinforcements, be made up again' (*240th Brigade*, 6). *Below:* En route to the front through a village in northern France.

12, 13, 14 At the front. *Above:* WRP outside casemate. *Left:* Signallers Bennet, Fleming, Levison and Iles laying wire in communication trench below Hébuterne. *Below:* 'I never got down to teaching poker to the signallers, but I taught it to "A" sub and they wallowed in it.'

15, 16 *Above:* WRP (with pipe) relaxing outside casemate with his fellow gunners. *Below:* 'Make do and mend' – WRP was deft with needle and thread, and was an excellent darner.

17, 18 *Above:* 15-pounder crew out in the open as a 'wandering' gun. *Below:* A well-constructed casemate near Hébuterne.

19, 20 Casemates. *Above:* front view of 'A' Gun with Gunners Wiggin, Haines and Murray. *Below:* 'A' Gun in a solid and superior casemate constructed by French gunners at Colincamps.

21, 22 *Above:* 'Ammo lumping': shells were often transported by hand to the front in special carriers, a gruelling and unpopular task, WRP second from left. *Below:* 'B' Sub as 'Wandering Gun', placed in open ground to attract counter-battery fire and confuse the enemy – dangerous work, and a risky occupation.

23, 24 *Above:* Hébuterne: machine gun of the 7th Worcesters, mounted on parapet. *Below:* Blown-up German trenches.

25 Horses lines with harness shacks in mud near Coigneux. Gunners were told in training 'that horses came before men, they cost more, and that harness was almost more important than the horse'.

26 WRP on Buttertub – a 'poor ride', and later replaced by Marcus, a superior horse 'acquired' from an unwitting Australian Brigade.

27 Building winter shelters for the horses near Coigneux in 1917.

28, 29 *Above:* Up to their ankles at the horse-lines at Coigneux: the deep mud here (and elsewhere) spawned a running joke, shared with many a passer-by: 'Here's the shit (pointing, and two seconds pause). And we're in it.' *Below:* 'D' Sub 'Wandering gun', Hébuterne.

30, 31 'B' Gun, after suffering a direct hit at Mesnil. Pictured (*above*) are Gunners Wright and Roddick. *Below:* WRP on leave in winter 1916 with his maternal aunt and 'faithful factotum', Miss Anna Philips, on the left.

I am quite well.

I have been admitted into hospital
{ sick } and am going on well.
{ wounded } and hope to be discharged soon

I am being sent down to the base.

I have received your { letter dated
{ telegram „
{ parcel „

Letter follows at first opportunity.

I have received no letter from you
{ lately
{ for a long time.

Signature } W. R. Price
only }

Date 26. IX. 17

[Postage must be prepaid on any letter or post card addressed to the sender of this card.]

A.F.A. 2042.
114/Gen.No./5248.

FIELD SERVICE POST CARD.

ARMY POST OFFICE
A
30 SP
17
S.63

The address only to be written on this side. If anything else is added the post card will be destroyed.

Mrs Philips
The Park
Prestwich
Manchester
Eng

32, 33 *Left:* A Field Service Post Card or 'Buzz Card' sent by WRP to his aunt Anna Philips reporting his injury, which he sustained at 3rd Ypres, 22 September 1917, and which ended his war. *Below:* WRP in 1973, two years before his death, about to give a talk at Kew which, to widespread amazement, he delivered without a trace of his lifelong speech impediment.

While we were in this position, though we did not know it, we took on the 13th Beaumont-Hamel, our target on the first day of the offensive over four months before, when we thought we were blasting the way for a great and permanent advance, an advance which came to nothing. With this successful attack, so the history books say, the Great Somme Offensive came to an end.

Two days later we started off again on trek. My diary notes, 'Everything very easy now and almost slack compared with what it was in our late Major's time.' We went through Pas, Famechon, Thièvres, Amplier, Doullens to Frohen-le-Grand, one of the prettiest little villages we had been in. Wagon-lines were in a field where there was no mud, and we slept in good barns. The people here were friendly and I had a delightful evening with three others in a little cottage, where we played cards and ate chips, the old couple, our hosts, being refugees from Arras.

After two days we moved off in the dark one morning and proceeded through Candás to Talmas on the Doullens–Amiens road. We made our lines in the dark on an open plain in a cold wind and several men became ill with the cold, and to make things worse supper consisted of cold maconochie without tea. A day like this without life-giving tea at the end of it was nothing short of a disaster. However, there was plenty of straw in our barns and we slept well.

The next day we went south to Béhencourt on the Amiens–Albert road. This road was flanked all the way on both sides by continuous camps and parking grounds of every branch of the Army, and one realized what an immense military population there was here.

Béhencourt became a frequent back area line for us in future, and we became friendly with the inhabitants, whose houses we could visit for coffee.

The day after we arrived was a busy one, as the battery was united and had several days for tidying up, cleaning and kit renewal. I happened to be near the Quartermaster's stores after stables one day, when I heard the latter's loud shout from inside: 'Fall in for your slacks'. My mind gave a jump and I felt paralyzed and I knew I must act quickly. They were evidently the slacks I had ordered for 'A' sub. 'Quarter' naturally took them to be 'issue' for the whole battery. I thought now for it. Quartermaster Williams had been our 'A' sub Sergeant, and I got on quite all right with him, but he was dreadfully moody and often silent for days, and we never quite knew where we were with him. I was prepared for, and indeed expected, a 'Who the hell d'you think you are?' I dashed into the stores and gasped out, 'Hi, Quarter, look, those slacks are for "A" sub. I ordered them.' I stood panting. Quarter was adding up figures and went on doing it. When he had finished, he looked up and said, as if it was the most ordinary thing in the world, 'Oh, thanks, Gunner,' and going to the entrance, bawled, '"A" sub fall in for your slacks.' I fled and went for a walk. I had said nothing to anyone about it, but of course 'A' sub suspected and found out. I refused to discuss it.

Next day was pouring wet as usual and the teams were out all day at our new position. I was in the village in the evening and heard them coming back; they were singing. I looked, and there were 'A' sub's three teams in front with all nine drivers wearing their slacks. They caught sight of me, waved their whips, and all of them together shouted, 'Hi, Gunner, look, we're all dry.' I felt so glad. But now I was tormented. I felt sure I should be the recipient of reproachful looks from the other five subs.

What could I do? But there was never a word or a look. I struggled with myself; I could easily order slacks for all the rest of the battery; I could keep them all dry during this awful winter just by writing one letter. But what would the Major think; might it embarrass him if other battery O.O.s asked how he came by 'that issue'; would Quarter stand for it again; he might or he might not. I failed to make up my mind and did nothing. During Martinpuich days, now imminent, when the poor drivers had to walk their horses with panniers through knee-deep mud, I cursed myself for not ordering for the battery, or at any rate for the rest of the drivers.

In the winter months keeping warm was obsession number two out of our three obsessions, which, in order of intensity, were: 1. shells, 2. cold and 3. food. Military training subsequently, if not at this time, taught, in the matter of sleeping out, that the first fold of a blanket must be back over the feet with whatever spare was available, because 'sleep is impossible while feet are cold', or perhaps the word was 'difficult'. We had not had this instruction, but experience seemed to have taught me something. My teaching would have been: 'sleep is impossible if you are really cold below the waist', and of course in the winter, to be wet was to be cold. My further advice would have been: 'keep warm below the waist, and above it the body will take care of itself – by shivering'. Shivering warms you, that is why you do it, but you cannot shiver below the waist. I always had the feeling that, if I could keep my extremities dry and warm, the rest of me did not matter. That was why I laid such store by these waterproof slacks.

When the time of mud came the Major and the Quarter would assuredly have said nothing over a further order turning up unannounced, but I was haunted persistently by the fear that someone might imagine I had ulterior motives.

I don't think now that anyone would have thought this.
I funked it and did nothing, and the opportunity was lost.

Martinpuich

On 5 December we moved off for Martinpuich, where we were to experience the worst conditions yet.

My diary says:

Walk-marched to Albert, cold and rain. Took Fricourt road and there turned left to Contalmaison. Road narrow, traffic tremendous, blocks awful. Arrived wagon-lines in dark. Managed to get some tea and marched on to Bazentin rail-head. No trolly transport for us, but managed to get five trollies and piled kits on them and pushed several miles up hill. Country terrible. Open plain, torn to pieces with shell holes; mud dangerous in places, so deep; position on ridge on right of Martinpuich, of which we saw no sign; relieved 15 Division battery; most awful conditions we have struck. We were on a completely open and exposed hillside sloping to the west near the top of a ridge; everything had to be carried up the sticky, slimy mud slope from the track in the valley; the mud on these higher slopes was not deep, owing to the thin soil overlying chalk, but, the surface being sloping, it was like walking on oiled glass and we were continually slipping and falling flat; if we had had to put guns in, it would have been impossible; ammunition came in panniers on battery horses, each driver leading two, and they dumped the rounds in the valley and we had the endless task of carrying them up to the position in fours in canvas carriers; N.C.O.s carried revolvers to shoot any horse that became bogged; casemates were non-existent and dugouts mere apologies; however position had not been much shelled and there was no firing to do; the view north and south along the slope consisted entirely of mud and a few blasted woods with their skeleton trees.

We were in this miserable place for three weeks, during which it rained most of the time. We spent all our time trying to drain water away from our dugouts, many of which had fallen in and become deep pools; we could not do anything at first to protect the guns, as we could not fill sandbags with slime.

After a few days Sergeant Gore came to me and asked me to come in with him and Bombardier Roberts in a tiny dugout on the flank, which had probably been built for the N.C.O. in charge. He had appropriated it and tidied it up. It was a surface dugout with low sandbag walls and roofed with two iron sheets; in front of the entrance inside was a small trench, on one side of which was an earth platform wide enough for two people and on the other side one for one person. You took off and left your boots in the trench, so that the bunks and blankets kept clean and dry. But the great joy was the fireplace, which consisted of a biscuit tin with half the front cut out and with a hole in the top into which was fitted a tin tube which projected through the roof as a chimney. This little fireplace burnt better than any fire I have ever known owing to the good draught, a few small pieces of wood making a blazing fire in less than a minute. We kept it continually stoked with quantities of small pieces of wood, and with a couple of candles and our combined blankets we could not have been warmer or more comfortable when we turned in at night. It was lovely lying there at night hearing the wind and rain raging outside, keeping as warm as toast, reading, yarning and stoking. I always felt completely safe here when we were being shelled, entirely because of the dugout's small size. This dugout alone transformed the position for us and made its miseries much more bearable.

I think at this time I never appreciated my pipe more. I had settled for Waverley Mixture, which was an issue, and as Sergeant and I were literally the only pipe smokers in the battery, there was never any difficulty over supply. I cannot imagine my getting through the war without my pipe. I had no continual craving for it, but only after tea, or when sitting waiting endlessly somewhere in the cold and wind, when the sudden thought 'pipe' transformed the miserable present into what amounted to a joyous ceremonial, of which the initial movements, that is the filling carefully and slowly, performed a little bit at a time, were almost as enjoyable as the actual smoking. During the boredom of day-long treks, sitting on an ammunition wagon I would secretly light up, and by doing so find myself transported at once into as complete a state of luxury and happiness as I could desire. It was a state in which my mind seemed (only seemed) to be free of my body and of the war and to be able to range over the understandings and misunderstandings of life, of life's meaning, and more especially as to why there need be this idea of meaning and purpose, and to free itself temporarily from the problems of the hard seat, the chances of scrounging grub and of keeping warm, more especially dry, which ordinarily monopolized exactly all our waking hours.

After the war I tried in vain, but the magic of my old pipe had gone; it merely made me feel sick. But now there is rather a depressing, if not disgraceful, story to tell, which reflects no credit on anyone, and least of all on me. There was deterioration of morale. It was with us before we came to Martinpuich, but it seems that I inadvertently triggered it off.

Our fire was the cause. It required wood. The only wood obtainable was in a small blasted wood some way off, and a daily trip there was necessary to provide the evening supply. I took on this job only too willingly, only vaguely aware that there was an order that no one should leave the position without permission.

The wood was a chaos of dead shattered trees but, there being neither axe nor saw on the position, I had to break off what splinters I could. It was not a place to walk about in, as unexploded shells and grenades were everywhere. All went well for a time. Then one day left section sergeant caught me at it and blew up: didn't I know I must not go off the position; it would be better if I did more work and less scrounging. 'If I see you going off again, I'll put you under arrest, bloody Gunner,' he shouted.

At school I learnt some Greek, but the only words I eventually remembered were Ἔπεα πτεροεντα.

These 'winged words' now proceeded to fly across the position both ways. I was disgruntled and reckless: 'You can't put me under arrest, I'm not in your section, and it makes no difference if you do because in a place like this being under arrest is the same as not being; I'll go off after dark and you won't see me.' 'Oh, can't I? You wait, I'll report you to the Major.' 'He won't do anything, he never comes near us.' 'You bloody Gunner, you lazy old bastard, you, you old b----'. The controversy degenerated into a swearing match to the enormous delight of all. I retreated into our dugout, where I found Sergeant Gore quiet and embarrassed. I felt bad about it.

After that my visits to the wood were in the dark, and it was an eerie business, and there could have been a chance of being taken for a spy.

We had two casualties about now, drivers Nash and Bannister being wounded by shrapnel in the valley.

Wherever we dug, the hole filled with water; we sat and swore and no improvement in the drainage and sandbagging was apparent. Then one day we became aware of officer figures coming up the slope. They were our Major, accompanied to our horror by Colonel Lord Wynford, our new O.C. Brigade. We had seen the latter a few times and were impressed by him, a small, smart looking man, obviously efficient, but quiet and restrained in manner, a man not out to terrify or bully, just the right type. All the same we were apprehensive and had reason to be.

He surveyed the scene in silence for some time. Then the Major called us together. Lord Wynford then spoke as follows: 'You have quite obviously done no work at all to improve the position while you have been here. You have done nothing to protect your guns and your ammunition; you have done nothing to drain the position and build up your dugouts; your guns are disgracefully dirty and you yourselves are disgracefully unshaven and dirty. All you have done has been to complain and ask me for this, that and the other; you want help for this and help for that. Now listen to me. There is such a thing as Self-Help. I see no sign of it here. When I do, I will help you. Until then [and he raised his voice] I won't help you at all, no, not at all, in fact I'll hinder you.' He turned and walked away. We were struck dumb because we knew we deserved it, and, as for myself, I did not feel too good.

That night Sergeant Gore said, 'We'd better give left section some help tomorrow.' We all felt ashamed and work went forward and we got the guns protected. Tempers cooled and I kept very quiet.

Discipline had apparently been sinking down considerably on this position, and I seemed to have hastened the process. But so small a matter as a fire could hardly in itself have been responsible.

The fact was there was a feeling of disillusionment abroad. The enthusiasms of July 1 at Hébuterne, and of September 29 at Pozières had suffered much cooling with the news that we had only recently taken Beaumont-Hamel, with the rumours of the magnitude of our casualties, which were said to exceed those of the Germans, and with the observable fact that our average advance on the Somme since September had hardly exceeded one mile. We had captured a mile depth of 'worthless tortured earth'.

For the last month I had felt a return of my earlier sense of dull foreboding. I argued, to myself only, that two immovable forces faced each other; there seemed no reason to believe that either could drive the other back, unless one side cracked, and there seemed no reason at all why the Germans should crack, and of course the possibility of our cracking was not to be entertained. The obvious answer to that question, it seemed to me, was that the side whose manpower lasts longest will win. Germany's population is greater than ours, so what? It was well that we had at this time no inkling of what was to happen later away to the south, and later still in the east.

During the last week of December, and so that we should spend a really happy Christmas, we were suddenly moved to another position not far off, nearer to Martinpuich. It was about equal to the last position from the point of view of misery. My chief recollection of it is of huge shell holes filled with water and of enormous piles eight feet high of cartridge cases. The battery we took over must have fired thousands of rounds into Martinpuich. I was appalled one day when I heard our officer angrily telling a gunner, who had been ordered to stack these cases for collection, and had been amusing himself instead by throwing them into the water, that they cost probably £1 each. It was an impressive thought.

A few days after we settled here, something very new and quite alarming happened. We were shelled with quantities of small gas shells. We put on our masks, but they did not keep the gas out. It was a new kind of gas. We had heard rumours that our masks could not be expected to protect us from any gas that could be invented. Fortunately, this gas apparently did us no harm. In fact it smelt quite pleasant and did not affect one at all as long as you sat quite still. But with the slightest movement we were subjected to paroxysms of coughing; it was a coughing gas. We were in action at the time, but had to stop because we could not work the guns for coughing. The gas could not have been more effective or more humane. We sat and chatted and waited for it to blow away. The thought occurred to me that if both sides could use this gas continually, the war would, of necessity and without need for further argument, come to an end. However, we never experienced it or heard of it again, probably because the Germans had not found out how to keep it out of their own gas masks.

Apparently Christmas Day came and went unnoticed on this occasion as I have no recollection of it.

On 30 December we were relieved by a Worcester Battery. We were thankful to leave this horrible sector and get back to Albert, and the next day to Béhencourt again.

The war situation at the New Year was that a total of 1,800,000 casualties for both sides had been sustained, the result being a complete stalemate. We sensed something of this sort at the time, together with a disgruntled feeling that now had come the moment, with the 1917 New Year, when the war both could and should be brought to an end.

I lost the diary I kept for the first 2½ months of 1917, or possibly I never kept one, so the following is an account written from memory.

Soon after we came out, I obtained leave for the day to visit Amiens. I was accompanied by Bombardier Roberts, an extremely nice and intelligent man. It was a red letter day. I had been in no town, walked on no pavements, looked in no shop windows and sat in no restaurants since my leave eight months ago.

The first problem was to get there, the distance being twelve miles, and needless to say we were not being supplied with transport. The only hope was to cadge a lift. We walked to the main road. The traffic in both ways was continuous, and lorries, cars, jeeps and motor bicycles were tearing past at speed, as it was a straight road. No one had any intention of stopping to pick up two waving gunners. However, a military policeman, an hereditary enemy, who was on point duty, took pity on us and, stepping forward, peremptorily ordered various cars to stop to see if they had room for us. Eventually he got us into a car. He was the first nice M.P. I had ever met.

It was quite an extraordinary sensation to walk all the time on a hard surface with no mud, mingle with civilians and shop for mementos. We sat in a cafe and ate omelettes, chicken and peas with a bottle of Bordeaux. We felt different beings and marched about as if the place belonged to us. The lovely Cathedral was much sandbagged inside and out and was so far undamaged. I was impressed with the tremendous height of the interior and especially with the lovely blue glass.

A very cold spell came on with the New Year. I had never experienced greater cold in my life. I believe we had at times 30 degrees [°F] of frost. Our barns at Béhencourt were completely draughty and, if there had been any strong wind, which fortunately there was not, it being a long anti-cyclone, I don't quite know how we should have survived. We were never warm day or night, and I came to dread the night. Going to bed consisted of putting on all the clothes one had, including spare underclothes and all woollies, and wrapping blankets round one and in addition any old sacks or newspapers that could be found. Even so, I would soon start shivering, but I knew enough physiology to know that that was nature's way of creating heat, so I was glad I could shiver and let myself go on doing it until I slept from exhaustion, which was as good a way as any other.

In one village while on our next trek where we had barns, ours was roof-less, so we were sleeping in the open. The water in my water-bottle froze. I had a cold to begin with, a rare event, and felt miserable, but later found that being permanently and terribly cold did me no harm at all. I had the sense therefore not to worry about it, as I realized that all our germs were long since dead, and that, as I wrote, 'there was no possibility of being ill', however frozen or soaked we might be (perhaps a slight exaggeration). One effect the cold did have, however, was annoying. We had throughout the war really only one pleasure in life, namely food. It was therefore rather tragic that the one and only effect the great cold had upon us was to take away our appetite to the extent that, though we continued to eat, and nothing could stop us from doing that – we ate like horses, that is, kept on as long as there was anything there – we had no appetite and had to force the food down and then found it difficult to digest it. Looked at another way, this was lucky, because as usual there was not enough to eat anyway; but we did not look at it this other way.

I had suffered in this way only once before; the symptoms were the same, but the cause different. On my expedition in Formosa to climb the 13,000-feet Mount Morrison, at the end of the third day of tremendous scramble, I was surprised to find I could eat no supper; after twelve hours' rest on the summit I was all right again. Obviously then great cold has the same effect on one's digestive organs as has great fatigue.

But there was still joy in life left. Huge dixies of steaming hot strong, sweet tea were prepared by good Jennings for our three daily meals, and I never forgot the breakfasts during that cold spell, when we stood round the cook's fire with our round billy tins full and literally thawed out our frozen insides. We had to drink it quickly because experiment showed that it froze in five minutes in the open air. Bread, butter, jam and bully beef were all frozen solid, and the former had to be sawed or chopped.

This cold spell was, I believe, universal, and thousands of people, under-nourished because of the war, died of cold in Germany and Russia.

6

PÉRONNE

Towards the end of January we moved off over frozen roads, free for once from mud, and, billeting in frozen villages in barns, passed south and crossed the Somme to Corbie, a nice old town, where we spent a few days.

We then did a long day's trek to Cappy to the east.

The next day another long march east on the Péronne road took us through Herbécourt and Flaucourt to where, on the further side of the latter place, a French position had recently been evacuated.

We were now taking over the whole Péronne sector from the French, who were moving further south, their infantry having already gone, but only part of their artillery had as yet departed. There were still many of their Seventy-Five Batteries about, with their jolly, friendly gunners.

The position was in the open in a sea of mud, but the casemates were good. The Germans had put over a number of 8-inch onto the position and approach routes, and were doing so every day. In fact their attentions were more than we appreciated.

We were here for over a month and a miserable place it was.

The signallers' dugout was partly hit in, also 'B' and 'D' casemates. Fortunately, there was a very deep tunnel to take cover in. While the frost lasted all was well. The cold and frost that had plagued us so much on trek was here most welcome. But with the thaw, which soon came, there developed the worst mud conditions we ever did experience. The mud was of the sticky kind, it held you and you might have to yell for somebody to come and dig you out.

One day all twelve of our ammunition wagons came up laden. The position was some distance from the road, and they rashly plunged off it and made a valiant attempt with whips flying to rush themselves through to us. The front team got within a hundred yards of us and then stuck, and then all of them. I heard sounds and saw them there, drivers and horses all motionless, tired out and hopeless, just waiting for something to happen. No one had seen them, so I took a shovel and yelled to three gunners to come and help, no N.C.O. being visible, and the four of us went out and stood on our pathway and looked at them. The drivers could not get off their horses or they too would have become stuck. I felt a surge of pity for the poor drivers as it seemed to me that on the whole they had a worse time than we gunners did.

So I jumped down into it and sank and stuck, but I had my shovel and proceeded to dig myself clear and then to make a pathway to the nearest wagon, and told the gunners to form a chain behind me. I then started unloading and passed the rounds back to them to pile on the path. So we unloaded the twelve wagons so that, empty and light, they could manage with a supreme effort to surge ahead, wheel round and plough back to the road.

There was some headquarters near the neighbouring village of Flaucourt behind us, which had to be communicated with daily. There were two routes to it, and the Germans plugged one or the other with 8-inch all day, but generally not both at the same time. Our main occupation became that of speculating and advising upon which route our daily party should take. The trip was no joke and we all dreaded our turn. The Germans always seemed to start shelling the route we had taken as soon as we were on it, just as if they had direct observation.

On my first trip all went well, but I was nevertheless somewhat shattered. Passing near the ruined village of Flaucourt, I was puzzled as to the nature of a quantity of dark coloured round heaps on the open field next to the village, and went to investigate. There were quite fifty of them. I thought they were heaps of old rags that had been dumped there. However, looking closely, I saw shrivelled white faces and skeleton hands. They were French infantrymen who had obviously been mown down by machine gun fire from a trench parapet which fronted the village. The French had charged the parapet in their assault on the village last autumn, we were told, had taken the village and these were the casualties which had lain there ever since and were now frozen hard like rocks, preserved by the frost from further decay.

To make this winter of our discontent more so, our food rations, which were now always short, diminished still more, and we began to wonder whether in time no food at all would reach us. We argued with undoubted truth that the longer the distance between ourselves and Divisional A.S.C. H.Q., the shorter the rations would be, owing to the greater opportunities for pilfering en route. Our bread ration on which all depended was now half what it should have been. Nobody did anything about it, so we, taking the Colonel's advice about self-help, took the only course open to us, which was a course of carefully planned thieving expeditions made upon the remaining French batteries. After all we had to live. Tins of lovely small biscuits and bags of dried carrots and onions, the like of which our Quartermaster General could never have produced and of course could never be expected to know existed, materialized silently and unaccountably. The amazing thing was that the kind French gunners appeared to bear us no resentment, merely remarking, as our marauding parties went by, '*Ah, les Anglais, toujours la faim*'.

The winter seemed endless. Would warmth ever return or, as the Chinese say, would the dragon never stop eating up the sun? Was spring so very far away still? Never had I longed for it more.

7

THE ADVANCE

About the middle of March developments commenced which quite transformed our lives, at any rate for a couple of months, which brought us out of our hopelessness and stagnation, and set before our imagination prospects of activities more according to our ideas of war as she should be fought.

The first change, a very welcome one, was the discontinuance of the shelling of the tracks. We were greatly relieved, but thought no more about it. The thought occurred to me that the sound of distant firing seemed much less than heretofore, but I was not in a position to have any opinions about it.

Apparently we were now to start a preparation for an assault on Péronne. In the first week of March right section went forward to a position in the open above Biaches on the edge of the slope leading down to the river and town, to do wire-cutting.

We fired all day and gradually it dawned upon us that there was no enemy response at all; all in front was quiet except for the bursting of our shells. Something odd had happened, but what? We stopped firing and sat about completely at a loss. One of us might have been bright enough to ask, 'Is the enemy there at all?' but I do not think anyone did so.

After several idle days, the news broke. The enemy had retired, that is they had decided to withdraw quietly by night and before the thaw came; moreover they had done so days ago, and in the meantime we had been firing our guns industriously each day at nothing at all. We felt angry at having been made to look ridiculous. It was the duty of our Pioneers and Intelligence to know something of the enemy's whereabouts at all times, so we thought, and our feelings found difficulty in expressing themselves, as we asked each other what, if anything, these people had been doing lately. How the Germans must have laughed. However, we were sure that the particulars of this lapse would not find their way into the papers at home, nor did they.

The German retreat from Péronne was not a mere act of convenience, as I thought at the time, when there passed through my mind the comical French saying '*Reculer: pour mieux sauter*', and I wondered where we should be when the 'jump' came.

We quite understood that he did it in order to straighten out his line and so strengthen it, that is, to retire just here onto the immensely strong second line or Hindenburg Line. But we did not understand at the time that this retreat was necessitated because ever since January our 4th Army of General Rawlinson had been ceaselessly attacking at selected spots and making continual small advances. It had extended itself to the right as far as Roye, where it now linked up with the French; on 29 January the Australians had taken Le Transloy; on 28 February Gommecourt and Puisieux fell and a general advance took place all the way from Arras in the north to Soissons in the south, an advance of ten miles by us and thirty miles by the French. On 17 March the Australians took Bapaume, and just before this the 1/6th Warwick battalion of our 48th Division had crossed over the Somme in front of us and passed through the empty, shattered town of Péronne and out into the country beyond.

It was grand to feel that open action would now be the order of the day, as after all that was what we had trained for. Perhaps, we thought, this was the beginning of the great advance which was to stop only when we reached Berlin. But I never really believed that.

When the news was confirmed, and having one last free, lazy day left, Gunner Wiggin and I slipped away with the object of getting into Péronne. All was completely quiet, the enemy being clear away from the town and the Warwicks following up, but no immediate advance was possible until the Engineers had put bridges across the Somme. Wiggin and I went down the slope to the river, to where we saw a wooden causeway forming a single-file path across the marshes and river leading straight into Péronne.

Fortunately, we knew we must be circumspect as the Germans had left booby-traps everywhere, but it was obvious that the Pioneers had been along before us and had cleared most of these up. We watched the causeway path intently as we crossed, and sure enough we came to a place where an end of a quartering had been carefully sawn through so that a man's weight upon it would cause it to fall a few inches, which thereby would by a wire pull the pin out of a hand grenade fixed below; it was beautifully thought out.

Péronne was a weird and terrible sight, the more so as, standing in the *Grand Place*, we saw not a living soul. Moreover a deathly stillness reigned except for some snipers' shots in the distance. I had never seen an empty town before and it was a most uncanny sight. Nearly all the houses were in ruins, and this was the more tragic as some of them had been beautiful Renaissance-style buildings, the streets were a shambles and impassable as all the trees had been felled across them. On a large board high up on a balcony in the *Place* were written the words, '*Nicht aergern, nur wundern*' – Don't be annoyed, just wonder.

We went out at the far side of the town and looked at the gun positions there, and still there was no sound either of war or of humanity. It got on our nerves.

On 22 March the order came to advance.

We remained in General Rawlinson's 4th Army, having the 1st Australian Corps of Gough's 5th Army on our left, but a special ad hoc force had now been created on the spur of the moment, called General Ward's Flying Column, which consisted mainly of our 48th Division. This was splendid news and added to the excitement. Would it mean open action and living in the open at last, we wondered, and the end of dugout life, would we be firing in the open, moving on and firing again? Moreover, it was lovely weather, dry, cold and sunny and still frosty at night.

The battery reunited at Biaches and started forward on the first advance we had experienced. Down the slope to the Somme we went, across the river over a pontoon bridge, through Péronne and out beyond to the little village of Doingt. Here there was not an unwrecked house anywhere, but 'A' sub did find a tiny cottage with part of its roof intact, where we spent the night.

The next day we moved on to Cartigny and made our lines in front of the village, where the Uhlans were said to have been the previous night, and slept in ruined cottages.

It was here that we saw the results of the order given by the German command for the systematic destruction of the countryside. They had really done it most carefully. Any house or barn not destroyed by gunfire was blown up, furniture was stacked and burnt, and all fodder, wells were polluted, shafts of carts sawn off and the many orchards of fine young trees destroyed by the simple method of peeling off a narrow band of bark on each tree.

That evening a pleasant little ceremony took place. We fell in and Colonel Lord Wynford, our new Brigade C.O., appeared. We were called to attention. The Major called, 'Sergeant Bennett'. The latter stood forward and the Colonel pinned the M.M. medal on his tunic. I do not remember what it was given for, and in our minds this did not matter much; what we knew was that Sergeant Bennett was one of the finest people that ever was and that he was the one person in the battery whom we most wished should receive a medal, and we all cheered like mad. This was the only medal-giving parade that I remember. The British Army did not go in for that sort of thing much, thank goodness.

The next day we had billets in some good well-built barns of a farm in the village; they had evidently been used for this purpose and had not been destroyed by some oversight. We were told to look out for Uhlans, though what we did if we came face to face with them, our six rifles being with the guard on the gun-park, we were not told. This complete defencelessness on our part appeared to us to be so ridiculous as to be almost, but not quite, funny. Sure enough, at dead of night I woke suddenly, as we did in that war if anything sudden happened, to the loud sounds of horses galloping at speed through the village. It was a relief to feel that, from the sound becoming fainter in the distance, they seemed to be in a hurry to get away. They could have been our horses stampeding, but there seemed no reason why they should do so in such a quiet spot. We listened for frantic orders, but hearing none, went to sleep again, humming, 'We are Fred Karno's Army'.

There was a village nearby called Tincourt, into which the Germans had moved all the civilians who had remained in the district; all the other villages were then destroyed and somehow an agreement was come to by both sides not to shell the place. It was crammed with wretched peasants and their families, most of whom had lost everything. We passed through with our guns several times and were received with pathetic cheers. We were running in food to them as they were starving. The Germans had fed them fairly well, but they had suffered much. I would have liked to have talked to them, but had no opportunity.

Sir Philip Gibbs apparently came here five days later and talked to them. They told him they had suffered much from looting, and had had all their stock taken, including poultry, and that all their pretty young girls had been taken away by drunken soldiers and had not so far returned; they were a tragic community. But, incredibly, they also stated that most of the German rank and file were decent men, who said they regretted the misery that was inflicted and were sorry for the people, and who tried to explain that they disliked carrying out such destruction but were compelled to do it by orders. One woman asked a German soldier, 'Why do you go?' He answered, 'Because we hope to escape the new British attacks. The English gun-fire smashed us to death on the Somme. The officers know we cannot stand that horror a second time.' Of course this was not the reason.

On the 26th March we went into action in the open for the first time above a quarry opposite the village.

Next day we moved to Buire-Courcelles and the next day left section went into action between Longavesnes and Villers-Faucon, and on the 30th the whole battery was in action in [the] open between Longavesnes and Saulcourt. It was great fun, but we saw nothing and there was no reply, but on the 31st we were shelled.

On 1 April we were alerted early for an attack. Our infantry was to take Épehy and we put up a sort of barrage for them, but had to stop as they went out of range. They were the 4th Glosters, and the next day they took Sainte-Émilie.

On 3 April America came into the war, but I don't know if we were aware of the fact.

On the 4th we moved off at 05.00 hours to Sainte-Émilie. This position was a weird one outside a completely wrecked *sucrerie*.

It snowed and became like winter again, but we discovered a wonderful flue, an underground tunnel, which had been opened up by a shell most conveniently, and made this quite a comfortable, dry and also clean billet.

On the 5th there was a sudden attack by us at 05.00 hours and we took the two little villages in front of us, Lempire and Ronssoy, with three machine guns and thirty prisoners, this by the 5th Glosters.

The *sucrerie* was a most dreadful sight of collapsed and twisted girders and it was unsafe to go near it in case the whole thing collapsed on you. However, I noticed some little booklets and managed to get one. It was a German 'Outline History of the World'. I glanced through it, and noticed that in their view the American 'War between the States' was waged entirely so that the Northerners should dominate the Continent, and slavery was given [not] as a reason only as an excuse.

While we were here things again became delightfully slack. I never remember seeing an officer at all and there was after the first barrage very little firing to be done. 'A' gun alone seemed to have anything to do and that was all night and every night. It had to fire one round a minute on an exact point, which was some meeting place of several trenches, and we had to be very careful with the laying. The guard did it and it was fun to saunter up, slam the lever, out case, in round, slam breech, check line and range and saunter off. I always liked having the gun to myself.

After a time I became aware of our men continually wandering off to a small wrecked house nearby, and wondered what the attraction was. I asked, and was told to go and look. When I asked why, they said, 'We're looking inside the Uhlans head.' I didn't know what on earth they were talking about, so went along. Inside on the floor on its back lay the body of a young good-looking Uhlan in his smart uniform. He looked very peaceful and as if he was merely asleep, but as usual he was frozen stiff. The point of interest to our fellows, however, was that the top of his skull was blown off showing the top of the brain with all its wonderful convolutions. The sight depressed me.

On the 11th 'F' sub went forward with gun to a position in front of Lempire opposite Petit Priel Farm, the gun having to command the road through the village and shoot at tanks or armoured cars, actually at anything that came along.

On the 16th 'A' and 'D' guns moved off at 04.00 hours to a position in a cut wood behind Lempire. The rest of the battery came in later. At first weather was awful with snow, rain, hail and wind. There was a lot of night firing, as there were several unsuccessful attacks on Petit Priel, Tombois, Sart and Gillemont Farms, which were taken after severe fighting. The Hindenburg Line, to which the Germans had retired, ran along a crest just behind these farms and consisted of three rows of very thick wire. Unfortunately, it was just out of range of our guns and there was absolutely no cover between it and the village of Lempire.

The Hindenburg Line, which had been prepared by Ludendorff many months previously as a strong second line of defence, ran roughly between Arras and Soissons, and this was the line we were now up against. In spite of our knowledge of the three rows of wire, I think we did not at all comprehend what its strength really was. Two tremendous events happened during this April, events determined geographically by the location and strength of this Line.

The plan was set by the French who in their wisdom appointed General Nivelle their Commander in Chief and, what was worse, proceeded to agree to his plan to stage a tremendous attack in Champagne which was to finish the War. Instead of that it nearly finished France and might have lost us the war. To draw off some of the pressure that was building up against him, thanks to the news of the attack having become public property, our 3rd Army put up the Arras Offensive on 9 April, when by a most gallant and successful attack they took Vimy Ridge, this being beyond the north end of the Hindenburg Line. The enthusiasm of the troops over this victory was unfortunately somewhat damped by the failure two days later of Gough's 5th Army just south of Arras in its attack on Bullecourt.

On the 16th, Nivelle, in supreme and arrogant confidence made his attack south of the Line in Champagne, and by the second day had advanced two miles with the loss of 120,000 casualties. The effect of this slaughter upon the French soldiers had appalling results, news of which was concealed as long as possible, with the result that for a few weeks we were in ignorance that anything was wrong.

Our 48th Division, in spite of some sharp fighting in the capture of the many little villages during the advance and not inconsiderable casualties, was now brought to a halt, and we found ourselves from now onwards in a fairly quiet sector, but uncomfortably aware that terrific fighting was going on at either end of it.

On 28 April, when the above mentioned offensives had petered out, and things were again quiet, we had our first warm weather, which soon turned into a perfect blazing hot summer.

This was our third lovely outburst of spring and my mind went back to the other two at Neuve-Église and Coigneux. How many more would there be? On this date there was no fresh green, only wood anemones. A week later hawthorn and mountain ash were out, willows, sorrel, violets and the true oxlip, so rare in England, taking the place of the primrose, as it does in Essex. Desolate gardens in empty Lempire were bright with polyanthus.

Suddenly our wood was full of migrants, willow warblers and chiff-chaffs singing in every bush and a nightingale by our shack. The winter of our discontent was over.

There was now little firing to do and we were not shelled at all. The heat, to which we were so unaccustomed, now became quite oppressive and made us feel very slack. Whether it was caused by the warm weather or not I do not know, but an epidemic of impetigo broke out on our faces, and I had it so badly that I could not shave for several weeks and grew a beard. To my embarrassment it proved to be a yellow one and I was told I looked exactly like a German, and was subjected to a lot of rude remarks.

A note in my diary here states, 'We didn't know, but this was our best time in France, and our last good time'.

I thought of this lovely Lempire wood many times thereafter and wished myself back in it.

On 11 May we came out of action with the whole 48th Division, the 42nd Division, whom we compared with ourselves to their disadvantage, taking over. Our lines were at Marquaix, where the men had made nice shacks, but there being no shade the heat was bad.

On the 16th we moved off and went via Templeux-la-Fosse, Moislains, Manancourt, Sailly-Saillisel, Le Transloy to Beaulencourt, where we went into lines about a mile from Bapaume. Our whole brigade was under canvas in an empty Canadian camp. I managed to get an evening in Bapaume, where there was a very good Australian cinema.

On the 18th we moved to Vélu in nice open, undulating chalk country, where all the villages had been destroyed.

8

HERMIES

About now incredible rumours began to pour in about the French. The result of Nivelle's offensive appeared to have been that on the 3rd of this month entire regiments of infantry decided they had had enough of it and just marched off on their own to Paris, where they demonstrated and then dispersed to their homes. History gives the opinion that the French Army from this moment ceased to be a fighting force; it was fortunate that we did not then know this.

During one of our encampments in this area, exactly where it was it is perhaps as well that I have forgotten, but it must have been in a district formerly occupied by the Australians, something happened, which was highly improper and extraordinarily funny.

I remember a wide open grassland area without habitation or cultivation, and it was full of horses running wild, literally hundreds of them. I understood that they belonged to the Australians, and that they were a reserve supply and that this was the extremely sensible way they were kept. No horse lines with hundreds of soldiers feeding, watering and grooming them all day long as we always had to do, but simply one slouch-hatted and slouchy-looking man on a horse would ride round their area once a day at a fixed time. The horses fed themselves and watered themselves at troughs and never strolled away very far from the latter. The point was, some of them were extremely nice horses, which point was apparently not lost to certain of our sergeants. I became aware that much mystification and subdued laughter was going on, which puzzled me.

At last I knew. A deep plot had been hatched, any discussion of which in too loud a voice earned the rebuke to 'shut up'.

A fine evening was chosen at a time when the guard was not on his rounds and when it was getting dusk. Farrier-Sergeant had his fire going and branding irons heated. A number of N.C.O.s who were good riders assembled, some with lasso ropes, and they sallied forth amid loud guffaws. Terrific gallopings were then heard in the dusk, and one by one beautiful, sweating, frightened horses were led in, up to the forge, where any marks on their hoofs were burnt off and our own R.F.A. number branded on in place. After two or three days of this we had a marvellous collection of beautiful horses that any officer and N.C.O. would be proud to ride, fine 16-hand chestnuts and roans and several hunter types; our horse-lines had never before boasted such beauties. The battery was beside itself with excitement and delight.

But something else had now to be done. We obviously had to get rid of an equivalent number of horses. This was easier still, as anyone with a horse he was dissatisfied with, and there were plenty such horses, merely had to tell his sergeant, and in due course the old crock was collected quietly and in the dark, taken to the forge to have his number burnt off, and then galloped away as a led horse at great speed and on a twisty course, beaten finally with a whip and suddenly abandoned. I fear I thought this inordinately funny, until I discovered that my dear old pal 'Buttertub' had been so treated. However, he was a rotten ride and I got over his loss. He was replaced by 'Marcus', who was a good, smart horse and an excellent walker. As far as I can remember, the Sergeant-Major absented himself, in spite of which he received a magnificent charger, and all our officers were similarly fitted out. The result was that from now onwards on the march we were a magnificent sight, the admiration of all beholders, especially passing cavalry and other R.F.A.; you could hear their surprised gasps of, 'Cor, what 'osses'. How our officers were able to explain our magnificent horse flesh to other battery officers, I cannot imagine.

The best of all was that we did not break the eleventh commandment: we were never found out. It was enormous fun; it was terrific; it was abominable.

On 19 May we went into action, taking over from where an Australian battery had been. We were a little west of Hermies on a westward open slope near the top of a ridge. It was on fine chalk grassland and the ground being solid chalk it was difficult to dig dugouts in, so the emplacements were merely camouflaged and dugouts were scooped out places with low sandbag walls. Weather was perfect and I write that I was 'thankful to be back in action again'.

We were here for some time and at first everything was quiet. However, we became aware that the front line was a bare mile away over the ridge and ran through Hermies Wood.

Right section soon had work to do, which was to go forward every night and dig a forward position. It appeared to be a nasty place where two

Australian batteries had recently been shelled out. There were shell holes all round and we took a poor view of it. One morning on returning from the forward position, we had heard much shelling behind and were rather anxious. On arrival we found shell holes everywhere but no damage done, and the odd thing was the effect the hard ground had on the bursts, the shell holes being merely saucer shaped and shallow. However, reaching our shack, we had a shock; a shell had pitched just behind our low sandbagged wall, blowing it in onto our kit and also blowing much of our belongings right out and some distance away. The extraordinary thing was that none of our kit was damaged at all. This was nearly, but not quite, my No. 3 'near one'.

One evening I was really frightened. My turn on gas-guard was at 23.00 hours. Gas-guard's job was to smell for gas and watch for lights. There were various combinations of lights, such as green-red-green, meaning 'danger', but the only ones we ever took serious note of were three reds in quick succession, S.O.S. I proceeded at the exact time to contact the guard and take over from him, he saying that there were some red lights about, but not seeming to be worried about them. S.O.S. lights mean only one thing for a battery, gun-fire on night line, and the guard has to yell it out pretty loud. As he spoke to me, I saw what I took to be a mixture of lights, both green and red. I went to our officer, Mr Carter, and told him what I had seen, and that was all. Soon a furious telephone call came from the Colonel, to the effect that S.O.S. signals had been sent up by infantry for us to open fire, and we had not done so; why the hell had we not done so? Mr Carter sent for me. I explained what I knew, namely that there had been green and red lights going up, both before I took on and after, but I saw no three reds. I was frightened, but not half as frightened, it seems to me now, as I ought to have been. Nothing happened. I awaited the morning in trepidation, but nothing happened then either.

But it was a shock to me, and I felt that familiarity with our work was making us take too much for granted.

On the 6th June we were strafed properly. Apparently we had a wireless receiving set at this time, as the Major was able to pick up messages from a German plane directing the fire of the battery. The Major ordered a 'nip' and we cleared off, racing with the shells, several bursting parallel to us, to the bank behind. My diary says, 'Strafed sometimes with gun-fire, shells seemed to be 5.9 percussion; position plastered with shallow holes; shelled later close to bank and we cleared off down to light railway; even there bits were too thick in the air, so we went across the fields; no one hurt and no damage done, though quite a hundred shells were fired. Our usual luck.'

On the 7th news came of the taking of Messines, a great advance and many prisoners up there. 'Tomorrow we (No. 1 gun) go forward "close up" somewhere and lead the way for the rest of the battery afterwards. Some game. We can do it.'

June 8: 'Went up in dark. Put gun in position in open by side of a road on right of Hermies beyond cemetery. Very close to line according to sound of Boche guns and machine guns. While unloading ammunition, a machine gun opened fire. Didn't pay any attention. Driver Dudridge called out 'I've got it', with a bullet in his foot as he sat on his horse. Two gunners and I got the camouflage net in such a muddle that, as it was getting light, we threw it all tangled up over the gun and went back to the sunken road, where we dossed down. The next day we were back on the gun and did some firing at 2,600 yards. After every round a tremendous cloud of dust rose off the road and blew back over us; very dangerous for observation.'

9

REST CAMP

Then, while in this forward, active, excited state, what should happen, but something entirely unexpected. A signaller came up and told me the order had come on the phone for me to report to the wagon-lines to go to Rest Camp (5th Army) for a fortnight at Saint-Valéry-sur-Somme with Corporal Rice, Bombardier Dennis and Gunner Willie. I was stunned and others were envious, also I didn't stop to think, but said good-bye and walked off, noting in my diary, 'Don't like our position here with machine gun bullets sweeping it at night. Have a feeling something will happen. However I'm going, but feel anxious for the chaps'.

Our horse-lines now were at Haplincourt, a pretty spot though village destroyed; horse-lines were under trees and shacks had gardens.

Next day, as no arrangements had been made for our transport, I borrowed a bicycle and went to Bapaume. The train was packed with infantry, including Anzacs, and artillery. We travelled in vans. It was a warm night and it was interesting to see the ravaged countryside literally the whole way between Bapaume and Albert, especially as we passed Achiet-le-Grand, Miraumont, Beaumont-Hamel, which we had done our first barrage upon, Authuille and Aveluy. All was desolate, churned up waste and summer had hardly yet been able to overgrow it all with its greenness. We travelled all night through Amiens and Abbeville and from there along the little branch line to Saint-Valéry, a really attractive small seaside town at the mouth of the river. We arrived early next morning and marched some distance out onto open heath to the west of the town, where was an enormous tented camp with literally hundreds of tents. I really enjoyed myself here.

Whether it was purposeful, or else due to inefficiency, there seemed to be no organization or discipline whatever, and what was more incredibly delightful was the abundance of food, you could have as much bread and butter as you could eat, when, as I note, 'There were times when I would have given five francs for one biscuit.' We were thirteen in a tent, which did not appeal to me in the hot weather, so I slept under some trees outside. We were supposed to parade every day at 09.00 hours, and so we all did except the Anzacs, who to a man disappeared on arrival and were said to have practically taken possession of the town of Le Tréport, their overwhelming need being a social one. The mild-mannered British did a few camp chores and indulged in games on the shore, well organized by a jolly gym instructor. He introduced us to the game 'Fox and Geese'. I, being the tallest, was always the gander, having about two dozen geese clinging on behind me in a row, and a small trumpeter was the fox. The smallest man of all at the end of the row whom the fox had to catch was often thrown up in the air during our violent convolutions. It was enormous fun. There were advantages in being a ranker.

I always remembered Lena Ashwell's Concert Party, who gave two concerts in a big tent. They gave us good music and songs, and for once there was an absence of the everlasting comic and lewd. I thought at first, with dismay, that they would not be appreciated, but I am glad to say I was completely wrong. Everyone appreciated the change.

Every evening our little party, and we were a happy little party liking each other, would walk into the town and go to a small hotel called Hôtel la Colonne de Bronze, which fortunately had not been discovered by too many, and where we could have a nice table with cloth in a quiet room and actually eat with a knife and fork. We had many lovely meals of fresh fish, veal or omelette. I wrote, 'We soon forgot that we had ever eaten our meals in any other way,' which shows how old habits have a preference over new. We also found a teashop, where proper English teas of bread, butter and strawberries were provided. We could not have been in a nicer place, in spite of whatever the Anzacs thought.

There was a monument in the main street commemorating the fact that William I, the Conqueror, sailed from here to conquer England. I think some of the men on reading this became partly unbelieving or partly angry.

One day we got a pass to go to Ault, which was a twenty-mile walk there and back. It was a sad place and practically uninhabited. We sat about and bathed and walked back. It became dark and feeling tired we lay down in the grass and had a sleep. It was such pretty country of small meadows and orchards, little villages and poplar-lined roads, and it was wonderful to see unspoiled countryside. It was peaceful, the only sound being the barking of dogs we had disturbed.

One day I got a pass for Abbeville on the strength of visiting a cousin, who was a V.A.D. at the dressing station at the station there. She had gone home and I wandered off disappointed into the town and visited the Church of St Wulfram, and St Gilles, shopped, ate and sat in the lovely garden of the Museum. Inside the latter was a British officer with a very pretty French girl. My diary notes, 'Why can't I have one?'

With the end of our fortnight the Anzacs all turned up from nowhere, and we marched back to the station and entrained. I felt a different person and very grateful to the High Command. I do not remember anyone, including myself, ever expressing gratitude at any time. I suppose we had all lost the habit, that is those who ever had it.

We reached Bapaume late and were told that our division had come out and gone to Albert. Somehow we must have got transport and we arrived there at 02.00 hours, and found quarters in a Church Army hut.

The next day we heard that our wagon-lines were at Montauban [-de-Picardie] and we had to walk the distance. The lines had huts and that was all that could be said for the place. The battery had been there several days and did not know when they would be moving.

I wrote nothing at the time about our stay here, but the following is an account I made later from memory.

It was a desolate country with the stink of dead things. This area was just behind Delville Wood, where the most appalling fighting had taken place, so the whole of the ground was a ghastly sight. Though midsummer, I can't remember anything green; stark, shattered trunks everywhere and the yellowish pocked earth was covered entirely with trenches and wire. Graves were everywhere with rough wooden crosses having names, sometimes lists of names, pencilled on them, sometimes pathetic lines about 'comrades'. There were no signs that man had ever occupied the place in all this desolate valley, no sign of his belongings, houses, fields, roads, crops, the vegetation being a riot of weeds. One weed I had never seen before, a dark blue round spidery flower head. I thought I knew all the weed names, but this plant I had never seen before. I sent a specimen to a botanist friend at home; it passed the Censor, and the reply was, it was *Muscari comosum*.

One day friend Wiggin and I, as we never had much to do, wandered off to explore. Everything was completely quiet, which made it all the more difficult to imagine what it had been like here. We came to a place which had been made into a small cemetery, and there we found our Padre vainly trying to unwind rusty barbed wire in order to make some sort of a wire fence round it. He was a delightful man, and did his job well, moreover he knew every man by name, which is probably more than could have been said of most Padres. He called out, 'Here, Price, Wiggin, give me a hand will you?' We helped him and talked. Wiggin felt that the subject of religion was the natural one, and expressed scepticism as to whether anything in the Bible gave excuse for 'things like this'. They argued together in a most friendly way, and, as I liked the Padre so much, I forbore to join in.

I did not do so out of any feeling of false superiority, but entirely because their argument was to me meaningless.

The difficulty in discussing religion lies in the manner of its presentation. For what were presumably considered good reasons, a special language has been created in which special meanings have been given to words and phrases, which are entirely different from the meanings understood in ordinary conversation, and which are divorced from rationality. Religion is really an attempt to solve Man's dream-wishes and subconscious fears, but progress in this direction is not made nowadays through the language of personal salvation, rewards and punishments. Man's outlook on life and the Universe requires rational reorientation and concentration on a moral code of co-operation, toleration, sympathy and co-existence between all classes, colours and nationalities.

The Stoics in the third century B.C., with their assertion of the equality and brotherhood of man, made a valiant effort in this direction, but with their decline the emphasis to the present day seems to have been all in the opposite direction, towards defensive alliances, armaments and tariffs. If the Stoics had not been so soon submerged, humanity might by now have learnt how to live peacefully together like rational beings.

The only comment possible over Wiggin's argument would have been the question: why are we surprised that society is completely acquisitive, and, in the matter of terminating war, apathetic? It is running away from life not to consider these things.

We continued eastwards and came to the 'Devil's Wood'. It was a stinking, awful place of dead, shattered trees, with deep, narrow trenches everywhere. We scrambled along some of these, and all the time we passed wooden crosses with long lists of names, messages and pathetic poems of farewell pencilled upon them. We could not stand it and came back.

Our time on the Somme had now come to an end. We had arrived in the area on 21 July, 1915, and we were leaving tomorrow, 5 July, 1917, having spent nearly two years there. We felt we had done our bit in that part of the line. The question was, would any move have any relation to the frying pan.

10

THIRD YPRES

July 1917. Since late 1914 the Allied plan had been to stage an attack in Flanders. However, the offensives in 1915 took place further south, 1916 was taken up by the 'Somme' and most of 1917 was squandered by Nivelle. Field Marshal Haig desired an attack in Flanders as early as January 1916, and in May 1917 he made his definite plan for it, and, after much trouble to get over the strong opposition of Lloyd George, started preparations for it for a date in July. It was to be a great final attack, with the Navy co-operating, the infantry to break the German lines at Ypres, to be followed by the Cavalry Corps which would sweep on to Ostend and Bruges. It was to be the Third Battle of Ypres. We heard rumours of it, and, in view of what the First and Second Battles of Ypres had been like, we concluded, first, that the largest concentration of troops that had ever been would be necessary, and, second, that it would be HELL.

On 5 July we moved off, we were told, for a long trek. Again, and for the last time, we said, 'We're for it now'.

Our route was Albert, Aveluy, Mesnil-Martinsart, Englebelmer to Mailly-Maillet, parking near this village. The whole division and many others were all moving north at the same time, causing some congestion, but it was impressive.

Next day we went via Acheux, Louvencourt to Sarton. It was very hot, but fortunately the whole movement had been arranged to start in such good time, that the journey could be made slowly and in easy stages.

Next day we went through the pleasant little town of Doullens, and parked in an avenue in front of the Château de Rebreuve. There were no billets and we all slept out, I being on guard. In the night a terrific thunderstorm burst with torrential rain and the poor chaps were soaked through. Moved off for Saint-Pol-sur-Ternoise, parking at Ramecourt, a short way out. Here we had lovely straw in a barn. Incredibly I received a cake from my kind factotum.

The next day, the 9th, we were given a rest. In the evening we were allowed into the town, but took a poor view, as everywhere were notices 'Officers only', and the town was full of Portuguese troops. Portugal had kindly come into the war recently. We wished they had not bothered. On their first time in the trenches at Béthune, at the first German attack, they simply came out; they were probably used as Pioneers thereafter.

On this free day, our last 'pay parade' was held. These parades were held if and when possible, and there had been none for some time. I had never bothered myself unduly about them, in fact I had got into the habit of ignoring them. Money was no use to us, as we only wanted it to buy food and we were never, literally never, near canteens. However, on this day our efficient battery clerk, Bombardier Willis, came to me and said that I had the equivalent of £30 owing me, and wouldn't I like to draw it before somebody else did, or words to that effect. So I rather grudgingly agreed. When my turn came to go up to the table before a new young officer, saluting I replied to his question, 'How much?', 'Thirty pounds, Sir', with the result that he nearly sprang into the air and accused me of impertinence, almost threatening to put me under arrest. I remained impassive, so he appealed to the bombardier, 'He's not entitled to that sum, is he?' 'Yes, sir', was the reply. A huge bundle of francs was counted out by the officer, gasping with indignation.

The next day we moved off again and made a long march, watering at Pernes. We passed through Ferfay, noting that the *château* wood, where we had been two years before, was now a large infantry camp, and made our lines at Amettes, a pretty little place.

It was dull work. At every slight incline the order came, 'Gunners dismount', and sometimes I found it less trouble to continue walking. I remember an occasion when, the dismounting pause being rather prolonged, I instinctively lay down on the grass verge and went to sleep. I could always sleep at a moment's notice and get up again. On this occasion after half a minute the sound 'walk-march' penetrated my sleep and I got up; it seemed quite natural, just as one sprang up instantly when asleep if a shell burst near.

An occasional pleasant interlude during a wayside halt, or even while en route, was Levy's violin. He had smuggled his little fiddle out with him and had somehow preserved it intact, and was always happy during quiet intervals to strike up a tune, often singing a quiet accompaniment. He played softly and in tune and we all enjoyed listening to him.

Again, looking back, I am struck with the fact that probably the most characteristic part of the British armies of this war was its system of transport.

It is worth now, at this distance in time, to remind what may possibly be an incredulous public what our transport consisted of – legs. Until I stood one day on the Amiens road at Pont-Noyelles in December 1916 and watched a stream of light motor vehicles, cars, vans and bicycles speeding in both directions, I had not been aware that we had any mechanized transport. The complete absence of these in early days produced the brain-wave of bringing out London buses for use as troop transport. By 1917 R.G.A. heavy ammunition went up to their guns in motor lorries, though I do not remember seeing them. Also emergency movements of troops came to be made by motor lorries.

The R.F.A. moved on their own feet always and throughout the war, and the feet of men, horses and mules can cover a certain distance without rest and no more.

In these days we think of armies 'breaking through' and continuing in victorious advance without pause for days and weeks, as happened in the second war. The extraordinary thing is that military leaders in 1914 apparently thought along the same lines; they apparently thought that men and horses could go on and on and on, as motor lorries go on and on. It was because living things are not machines that the Germans were held up at the Marne. If we had ever broken through on the Western Front, we could have only made limited slow advances for the same reason. On the Eastern Front no rapid advances were possible for the same reason. In the First World War armies were not mechanized; we walked and walked, literally, and the slowest of trots were almost unknown.

This trek to Belgium which we were now making measured up to exactly one hundred miles and, allowing for a day's rest at St Pol, it took us nine days. That meant we did eleven miles a day. True we were in no hurry and our time schedule had been a generous one. We could have moved along faster, but anything like a fifty percent speed increase would have seen us arriving in Belgium in a fair state of exhaustion. We could have done the distance in half the time no doubt, but we certainly could not have done another hundred miles at that speed, or at any speed.

It was a curious war, a mixture of hell and sleepy boredom.

I often thought, as I walked throughout these dull hours, about how fit I felt and I definitely appreciated the fact; I appreciated that under normal circumstances, to be young meant to be fit and with a surplus of energy. What started these thoughts was my realization of foot comfort. It is almost difficult to appreciate comfort or good fortune in little things; it does not occur to be grateful. My Manfield & Co's field boots were the cause of this joy. The leather was soft and kept my feet dry except under the worst conditions, and I often thought, as I walked along the French roads, how comfortable I felt, not a pain anywhere.

Now after the years it is easy to be envious and nostalgic about it, to envy the young and accuse them of being unaware of their good fortune, but this reasoning is of course fatuous. The young pay for it in worry, work and war, just as the old pay for their probable luxury and ease and more developed understanding, by the inability to walk miles. If Life is a FLOW, this fact of compensation is surely the factor that makes of it an even flow.

About now we lost our good Sergeant-Major Parker. He had done his bit if anyone had and was not getting younger, and was transferred to some home job, much to all our regrets. In his place came Sergeant-Major Clarke, a surprisingly young man for the job, but a man, it seemed to me, extremely suitable for our unit. He knew his job, kept normal discipline and did it quietly and without noise; we did not require shouting at. We were lucky to have him.

The next day, 11 July, we came down off the chalk plateau of the Somme, down a long gradual slope into the plains of Flanders again. We followed the St-Omer road to Aire-sur-la-Lys, where we branched right to Pecqueur, a pretty little place among trees by a canal. I was interested to see that our Command had had some imagination, as they had made use of the canal for barge transport, many barges laden with material passing along it eastwards all day, manned by Engineers.

The next day was a short march to Staple, where, arriving early, we could make ourselves comfortable in deep straw and buy fresh milk.

The next day we passed along pretty by-lanes towards Cassel Hill, that extraordinary mountain visible for miles.

During a pause, as I lay on the grass, I looked up and saw a little old brick or stone shrine by the roadway, a little thing with a small image in its cavity. On it were written in old lettering the following words:

Indienst Gott.
In Sturm, Waeter, Donder und Fyr
Fur Drei Hunderd Jaeren
Bin Ich Noch Hier.

The lines rang in my head and still do even now. It had survived.

We passed the foot of Cassel Hill, went through Steenvoorde, to Godewaersvelde, a tiny village among meadows and woods. Horse-lines were on a pretty common. After tea we wandered about and came upon a little *estaminet* on the common, quite by itself and not even on a road. Its name was delightful, 'À la Tranquilité'. Some of us went in and started to have drinks. Suddenly I had an impulse. My pockets bulged with franc notes that I did not want; what an opportunity. I called to the young girls of the house for '*cinq franc vin rouge*' and started pouring out. 'Come on chaps, what about it, let's have fun, who knows when the next time will be.' Then *encore* and *encore* and *encore*, others joined in with a 'What's all this?' We laughed and sang and I continued to call for *encore* and to pay for it, and it was really rather lovely, though to me it was obvious that this would be the last chance for how long? Eventually we were all there, that is, all the gunners and drivers, all my friends. Then came, '*Finis, Messieurs, partir*', and out we poured with *au revoirs* onto the common and sang our way back to the lines over the grass in the dim light of that perfect summer evening, my last recollection being of Gunner Wiggin trying to run races with himself.

We knew that the next day would see us into it.

Next day we started early and crossed the frontier into Belgium and went on to Poperinge, passing through it and on along a byroad to Peselhoek, where we were to have our lines for some time to come. I noted that I had never seen so many troops in any area.

The next day, though we did not know it, the preparatory bombardment for 'The Third Battle' began. Ever since crossing into Belgium we had been conscious of distant guns, but what made us contemplative was their note and tone; we knew at once that it was all heavy stuff and very heavy, from the lowness of the tone and a certain vibration in the air. Long-range high-velocity shells were bursting sporadically in all the wagon-lines zone.

We went into action in the evening following along military tracks through Brielen to near a *château* at Reigersburg about a mile due north of Ypres, and half a mile behind the Ypres Canal. We took over quite a nice position, which consisted of a shallow trench from which access was made to emplacements and quite good dugouts with bunks. This was the only proper position here, all the other batteries being in the open. We could see the shattered walls of Ypres not far off, but we never, thank goodness, had to go any nearer than this to that hell-spot.

The following is my diary account of our life here preliminary to the actual commencement of the bombardment:

Germans shelled pretty heavily every day on and off with 5.9s and 8-inch, but always on our flanks and behind. One day some of us were drawing water from a well by a brick tower near a crossroads. Enormous shells were bursting, and did so most of the time, on the point where the main road entered Ypres. We thought we were far enough off to be safe, but suddenly we heard an increasing singing sound, and a huge piece of shell, it was obvious, was coming straight at us; it passed within feet and hit the tower with a 'wump'. I knew now what the word momentum meant. The Brielen road behind us was the main target, fortunately for us. We were gassed heavily on the second and third nights. Otherwise stood easy. Heavy work ammunition running. On most nights we had some 2,000 rounds in boxes to unload from a Decauville train a hundred yards away. Used to do it in 1½ hours. D.A.C. parties came to help us. One day 11-inch shells fell on the road and canal in front. Another day 'D' Battery had all its guns bar one knocked out and went out. Many casualties in Brigade. Bombardment became continuous and entirely by heavies, and continued day and night with occasional lulls. Very few shells came near the position so far. One day I went forward with a message to the O.C. of one of our batteries on the canal. A Big Bertha had dropped a shell at the end of the position, making the largest crater I had ever seen, into which two buses could have been put. Their gun stood undamaged on the actual precipitous edge.

The Colonel and another officer in a tent offered me a whisky, my first for a year, and we chatted. They were wonderfully calm. I could not make out if they were there when the shell fell, and did not like to speak about it. Then one of them said there was a rumour of a German gas that respirators would not keep out; the Colonel replied, 'Why will they tell us these things?'

One dark night we heard an extraordinary rumbling noise and then a roar of some kind of traffic along the track at the end of the position, called Queen's Road by us. Dashed out and saw a sight we had never seen before. A long procession of tanks was rumbling along, quantities of them all 'going up'. An infantryman walked in front of each. We were fascinated. They looked like evil monsters of the night, which in fact they were.

One quiet day I explored a short distance on this flank, and came to a minute pond, which actually had not been disturbed by any shell. It was a peaceful little place, full of water beetles, and water-boatmen, and water buttercups. I made a sketch of it. A few days later, after much shelling, I went there again. A shell had fallen right into it and it had just become a shell hole of mud and water: destruction *ueber alles*.

Every night teams went up with ammunition to the position beyond the Canal which we were preparing. They stopped to pick up one gunner per wagon, generally four of us. I suddenly realized that my periodic 'turn on the ammo', the corporal's brief order 'Price on ammo tonight', was something to be feared and dreaded, for the simple reason that every night at least one of the party was wounded. In other words, we were 'windy'.

On 17 July we heard that Zero Hour would be on the 29th. The following is my diary account for the next fortnight up to Zero hour:

22nd. Right Section up forward to dig emplacements at forward position a mile beyond the canal and opposite St Julien; by poplar trees about a mile from the line, our nearest yet by a long way. Our bombardment now becoming heavy, each field gun having a front to fire on of only six yards.
23rd. Ammunition up by pack horses by night. Centre section working party got so shelled they had to run for it.
24th. U DAY. Went up with another lot of ammunition by pack horses. Much shelling. Couldn't get through trenches owing to dead horses filling them up, so went along the top all the way. German planes flew low firing machine guns, however, fortunately too dark for them to see us.
25th. V DAY. Another ammunition party went up. Lieutenant Isaac in charge with Sergeant Gore as guide. Party was shelled all the time and I felt anxious about them. They had awful time, getting jammed in a long line of traffic on the cobbled road in the open and shelled like hell. Somewhere a shell caught them and Sergeant Gore and Gunners Havens, Bevan and a D.A.C. gunner all wounded. They got to a dressing station somehow and were sent back, but the Sergeant developed shell-shock and went to the rear.

This matter of shell-shock had interested me for a long time. It is curious to know that till now, it was invariably looked upon as a 'swinging it' device, a condition that anyone smart enough could act up to. Consequently, any suspicion that anyone thought he was suffering from it was discounted by us all with obloquy; no one dared to suffer from it, so great was our ignorance.

But now we had begun to learn a little about what the medical profession had to say, and what steps they were taking about this terrible affliction. We understood that the doctors could now easily distinguish true from feigned shell-shock. Consequently, when my good friend Sergeant Gore was shocked, and witnesses left no doubt about it, there was nothing but sympathy expressed, which was very pleasing. I missed him a great deal and never saw him again during the war, as, although he recovered, he was not back in action till after I had gone.

26th. W Day. Ammunition train at 04.00 hours. Miss our Sergeant very much. Don't feel windy myself (lie!), though I know that we are up against something this time. When your pals begin to go the feeling is 'that forward position is a death trap'. Think to myself it will be all right when the attack is on. The road by the canal this morning is, they say, an awful sight, dozens of wagons, lorries, horses, some drivers and a train all hit out and lying about. It's hard to realize that the chances of getting out of this aren't good.

27th. X Day. Germans reported retiring. Very heavy barrage on road behind us. Later 8-inch fell round battery. Did a nip into shell hole in field on left. Immediately after, shell pitched a few yards behind centre section while whole battery was in trench. Thought they were all done for, but they had all nipped to flank. Lieutenant Isaac badly wounded, also Sergeant-Major Clarke and several gunners and D.A.C. men were hit by shrapnel. A marvellous escape. Position shelled for some time. Our only hit was a direct one on left front of 'A' gun emplacement, putting gun out of action, piercing buffer and shield and breaking a wheel spoke. Did night firing on 'C' gun.

28th. Y Day. Last ammunition party forward. The drivers always reserved their horses' strength for crossing the canal. The Boezinge bridge had of course gone, and it was the task of the R.E.s to keep communication across the canal open by putting pontoon bridges across. This they did in the most wonderful manner, keeping at least three open on this front. But as fast as they put them up, the Germans spotted them next day and blew them to hell. No words can be too good for these men who never gave up and never failed to keep our crossings open. Their casualties must have been enormous.

All this meant that the canal was an unhealthy place to be near, so when our teams were close to it their drivers whipped up, and the horses obviously well knowing, they took their bridge at a mad gallop. On this day I was on our wagon; it was exciting and exhilarating as we tore with rattling hooves and shouts across and thankfully reached the other side without being hit by anything, when we went back to the stipulated walk, which was necessary for avoiding shell holes. On this night shelling was pretty intense on the other side, but appeared to be indiscriminate. The thought occurred to us gunners that it was a fool's game to sit perched up on the top of the wagons, and we soon put ourselves at a lower level sitting on the footboards.

I noticed on this occasion extraordinary sounds all round us, thumping noises which seemed to shake the earth. This, I found, was caused by a large number of the shells, which were now falling all round, simply going into the soft, deep, wet, peaty earth, with so small an impact that they did not all explode.

The cause of this softness of the earth was the fact that all this area had been at one time the sea bed, which became dry land in the course of time, either by the rising of the land level, or because of intensive drainage undertaken by the Belgians, or for both reasons. It was consequently a deep peat with no hard soil or rock within reach and, which Haig had been told but did not heed, with a water level of eighteen inches. Consequently, the country which Haig had chosen for his greatest of all offensives was an area where trenches of whatever depth would fill with water in wet weather and soil which, in spite of duds, would be churned up into mountains of loose, slimy, waterlogged earth by the terrific bombardment that was now going on, a bombardment which was to entail on our part the firing into this bog of an estimated 4¼ million shells. Another important piece of information which the Army's meteorological department supplied was that, with the regularity of a tropical monsoon, in this bog district of Ypres the weather always broke on the first day of every August, and had never been known to fail to do so.

It would be reasonable to think that these two facts relative to one, the soil, and two, the weather, might have received some serious consideration by Haig before he definitely committed us all to this useless, futile hell. Apparently they received no consideration at all.

29th. Z Day. This day was originally Zero Day, but when it dawned, the meteorologists were proved right, or practically so, for it was a pouring wet day, and Zero Day was postponed.

30th. ZZ Day. We learnt that Zero Hour was 03.40 hours tomorrow.

31st. ZZZ Day. This was IT. At stated time we fired 200 rounds at battery fire 30 seconds for two hours, making continual lifts to keep ahead of advancing infantry. A terrific bombardment. The sky was lit up with German red S.O.S. lights.

We were now in Gough's 5th Army and in Maxse's XVIII Corps, having the 11th and our 48th Divisions in front, their objectives being the village of St Julien in front and Pilckem Ridge to the left. Our infantry took St Julien, but were held back by the II Corps on the right getting stuck at Zonnebeke, and both advances were partly lost later in the day. Our division took 600 prisoners.

In the afternoon our teams came up and we went forward to the prepared position, the position we came to dread, the St Julien position.

As we expected, and as always happened in a big attack, we had no shelling whatever on the way up, neither at the Canal nor elsewhere, the German guns being far too busy attending to our infantry. Crowds of wounded and prisoners passed us on their way back. 'B' Battery, who were already in position to our right, had a few shells and three drivers wounded.

Our position was completely open behind a deep trench and in front of a large clump of very tall black poplar trees. A track reached us on the left from a minor road, which had been named Buffs Road, on a slight crest, which was the beginning of Pilckem Ridge. Our cook-house was in a ditch under the poplars. There were fairly good dugouts, except for 'A' sub. However, we had a tent scrounged from somewhere, or rather a large sheet, and seeing a thick tall hedge to our right we carried it with a view to putting it up there. However, in the very place where we needed to put it to be convenient for reaching the gun, we found the dead body of a very large and stout infantry machine gunner. He must have been there some time, as his gun had been collected. We were disconcerted and no one even suggested that we lug the poor body to one side. So we temporarily found another place. We fixed an upright post, then a slanting ridge pole and threw the sheet over it, laid our blankets in a flat pile and had plenty of room for all six of us to sleep.

Then at 16.00 hours it rained and kept on heavily all night and we got fairly wet.

The meteorologists continued to be correct.

All the shell holes and old trenches quickly filled up with water and wherever you went you slipped and slid.

I often wondered just how we would do it if the teams came up to take us further forward in an advance over the slimy waterlogged, water-holed ground, where a gun could suddenly disappear under water, and a man, heavily equipped, could do the same and drown, as happened to many of the infantry.

I often wondered also how Haig's pets, the Cavalry, a division of whom was now being held in reserve on either flank of our Corps, were going to dash forward at the prescribed time and pursue the retreating enemy over such a surface, one that a man could hardly stand upright on, one over which you did not walk anyway, but over which one climbed, in and out of holes and trenches and over wire entanglements. Over such a surface, and in pouring rain, the Cavalry were, in Haig's imagination, to gallop – to Ostend.

At about this time came terrible news from the east, that is, the farther east. We knew there had been a Revolution in Russia, but Kerensky seemed a good sort of person, and we were not interested anyway. But now we heard that Russian resistance was collapsing, in fact had collapsed, their armies just disintegrating and going home, as the French had been doing on a small scale. This, it was said, would enable the Germans to transfer forty divisions from that front to this. We had every sympathy with the Russian people, but we wished they had not decided to do this just at this particular time.

We knew that American troops were on the way and that certain units had already arrived, but we had no confidence that much help would be forthcoming from that source during the rest of the year 1917.

Consequently, the dull apprehension, which I had systematically fought against for the past year, returned with this news with panic intensity. How can we possibly survive now, I thought.

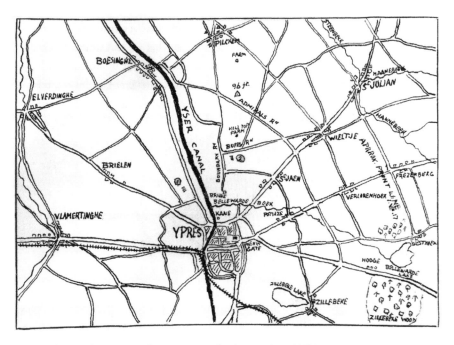

First and Second Positions of C Battery at Third Ypres, Aug. 1917.
Scale 1 mile = 1 inch

Fortunately, the matter was not discussed, and Russia was the very last subject of interest to the men, and it was well that it was so. If this is what 'Third Ypres' is like without these forty extra divisions, what sort of a place would this be with them? I felt a deadweight of depression, but fortunately there was no time to brood and if ever there was nothing to do, I went to sleep.

The next day, 1 August, it was obvious that the weather had broken, as it rained all day. Teams came up all day with ammunition and, as things were now quiet, we worked hard carrying the fairly long distance, especially for 'A' gun, as the nearest point the team could reach was a little wide of the left section. We carried, carried, carried, and stacked. We had to have a thousand rounds per gun and keep this supply up. We stacked on both sides of the gun and partly behind it, the piles of rounds gradually creeping up and up.

2nd. Rained most of the day and mud awful. Some small time-shells came over the position, the first we had had since Neuve-Église times. We again treated them with hilarity; we weren't used to anything so insignificant. It was unwise. Suddenly an S.O.S. came through and we put up a burst of gunfire, which, not being repeated, indicated to our minds at any rate, that we had stopped them. The rumour was, 'Boche, attacking all along the line', but it came to nothing. While unloading from pack horses in afternoon, several 4.2s burst a few yards from us in front of 'C' gun. It was so sudden that we didn't realize at first what had happened. Driver Tansell wounded. Shells then fell to our rear, but then one fell straight into 'D' sub's shack, blowing it and men's kits in the air; marvellous luck that no one was inside. In evening was another S.O.S. Well, that was what we are here for.

3rd. Rained all day and night. Mud appalling. Conditions of drivers who had to walk up leading horses pitiful. Short S.O.S. in early morning. Shack nearly swamped.

4th. Sun came out. Thank goodness. Dried ourselves a little.

I had wandered off to the left for a little relaxation and was sitting on the ground watching one of our old reconnaissance planes come over me very low on a very leisurely flight. Suddenly a German Fokker tore down out of the clouds firing machine gun bursts on it. The old plane replied leisurely and continued its slow course towards the rear. The German attacked again and again and I was just lamenting that the poor old slow-coach's days were over when slow-coach fired a longer burst at its tormentor, who suddenly tipped forward and shot down to earth behind some trees at an angle of

75 degrees. I heard no sound, except the delighted cheers of hundreds of surrounding gunners.

On another clear day I saw a sight that has haunted me always. Far away high up to the north a dog-fight was going on. I had not been watching it especially as it was too far away. But I suddenly became aware that one of our planes was hit, as there was a gas cloud and the plane was turning over. Then I saw two tiny black spots below the plane. I watched, and saw them coming down lower and lower, and there were no parachutes. I looked away, and perhaps half a minute later looked again. They were still there, lower down, and still falling. What a long time to take to fall to your death.

There was one aspect to our life on the St Julien position which we regarded with unbounded appreciation.

For the first time we had reached, by force of circumstances, the point where the guns, and only the guns, mattered, and where all our work and attention was given to them and their ammunition supply, and where nothing else but the guns counted. For the first time we were free altogether from parades, horses, grooming, harness cleaning and spit and polish.

But it had taken exactly three years for us to arrive at what was to me 'gunners' life', life with the guns, concentrating on firing guns, or rather firing 'A' gun, our gun – the life that I joined up for on August 4th 1914.

I developed a feeling, and surely all of us did so without speaking about it, that we had served our apprenticeship, learnt our job and had 'got there', and a certain feeling of satisfaction pervaded us. And so, when we were not firing nor 'ammo thumping', and when things were quiet, we could lie down in the sun, and I could get out my pipe and appreciate it as never before, smoke, finish it and have a nap. At such times we felt and were free, provided always that we did not wander off the position further than a hundred yards.

I never, or rarely, wanted to leave the position and 'go down' to the horse-lines. The gunners were my pals and our interests were the same, the guns. The drivers were good fellows, but their interests were different, being naturally with their horses. I liked riding and hunting, but not to the extent that I was in any way 'horsey'; any tendency there might have been in that direction had long ago been cured by life in the horse-lines.

We seldom saw an officer. They rarely came round to inspect because, I always supposed, they knew that we were doing our job, and they had other things to think about than to see that we shaved.

Mr Leslie, whom everyone liked, would come round at quiet times, and sit and chat to the detachments.

I do not remember any other officers on the position, other than those in charge of wagon parties, except Mr Leslie and Mr Carter. After all, only two were necessary, one to be in charge at the position, and the other at F.O.P; these two seemed to take it in turns. F.O.P. was definitely a nasty place right in the open later; another officer and a signaller were killed there. We were fortunately spared many F.O.P. fatigues, but I remember vaguely going on one at night and crawling the last few yards on hands and knees to reach a kind of hole. Mr Carter seemed usually to be there, and rumour said that he was quite used to 'getting it' from both front and rear, the latter not now being due to our guns' prematures, but to epidemics of their firing short, due in some way to the buffer trouble.

Our other officers all had comfortable billets at Peselhoek, which I never saw. Mr Leslie and Mr Carter had an officers' shack to the left of the position, one just the same as ours; when it became sodden with rain, it fell in just as ours did. I don't think they had even one gunner as officers' servant, and they were most considerate about ever asking us to do anything for their comfort, in fact they never did. They appeared to have no cook or mess, our Cookie taking them their meals, which were the same as ours, from 'cook-house hedge'.

We did not realize our good fortune in having such nice officers.

The time came when I wondered vaguely why it appeared that Mr Leslie was always at the position. I had never talked to him alone, nor had I talked alone with any officer since my political argument with Todd on observation at Hébuterne in the early hours of a summer morning two years previously.

But when twelve days later, on what I came to know as 'that day', he came and talked to me as I sat on a log, it occurred to me afterwards, from one of his remarks – 'I thought you would want to go down' – that our two minds might unconsciously have been working in parallel. I thought he might have developed a feeling for life at the guns in preference to that at the horse-lines, an unaccountable and illogical preference, and that somehow he sensed that I had the same feeling.

It seemed, then, that that was the explanation very probably of his continual presence on the position, and that was no doubt part of the reason that I liked him.

So, on this St Julien position we lived a free, un-army type of life after our own hearts.

But there was very obviously a price for this freedom, which had to be paid, and which more and more cancelled out our sense of satisfaction.

The price of course was the indiscriminate shelling, which went on almost unendingly with unpredictable degrees of intensity and interludes of time. Shells would fall just anywhere at any time and in any numbers: at one time bits would be flying all over the place and you could not hear yourself speak, and at another time there would be complete quiet for a short interval, and I could enjoy my pipe, but always in the knowledge that the quiet was a mere interlude. Our only remarks to each other about the War were on one subject of When are we coming out? This subject monopolized our thoughts at quiet times, this subject of 'the time factor': 'It's just a question of how long they keep us here.'

5th. A lovely day. How we appreciated it. Dried ourselves still further. Could sleep very little at night owing to continuous indiscriminate shelling.
6th. Easy day. Shelled near shack in evening. Germans 'tanked' road with 8 inch.
7th. While preparing to put up barrage at 21.00 hours, Germans counter-attacked. Fired gunfire on S.O.S. Report said the Glosters, who were preparing to go over, met the Germans halfway, that the latter caught a cold, and that the Glosters took the remaining half of St Julien.

Our gun had had a lot of firing to do, and now the trouble developed again – buffer trouble. We had been fairly free from it since the Somme, as firing had not been very continuous at any one time. But now the confounded springs were reacting to it; I suppose it is a physical property of all metal to react to strain if continued in the same direction for too long a time. It was dreadful, in the middle of gunfire, to find the barrel hanging back and barely being pushed up again by the springs. We had to push it, then push it more, then the springs gave out altogether, and two of us had to put our shoulders to the breech and push up slowly and laboriously. When speed was essential, it made us frantic, the two pushers soon becoming exhausted and two others taking over. Instead of the exhilaration of gunfire, it became a prolonged agony, especially with the knowledge that we were not giving the infantry a quarter of the support they were calling for. Cooling the gun did no good. Ceasefire and a rest for the con-founded springs appeared to be the only thing. However, later an extraordinary cure, though a very temporary one, was discovered and ordered. It was found that if we took out the springs, took them to a road or any hard surface, and threw them violently and continually on the hard surface, they would recover their recoil power. I do not understand the physics of the matter, but apparently steel is composed of a crystalline structure, and in the case of springs their nature is due to the crystals of the metal all facing in the same direction, that is, longitudinally. The wear and tear had forced the crystals out of their longitudinal position and into indiscriminate positions, but if the free, unpressed springs were violently jarred, the crystals automatically resumed their proper positions, and springiness returned. Fortunately, we had a road near, a very dangerous one to be on, but it enabled us to get going again with the gun. But the cure did not last long. We were continually dismantling and carrying springs and setting up again.

Friend Wiggin was, and always had been, our very good limber gunner. All No. 2s were automatically limber gunners, that is, they were responsible for the condition and working of the gun, they had to know how to dismantle it and clean and oil it. I once said to Wiggin I thought I would like the job, to which he reacted violently with a 'Don't you do it, Gunner. You don't know what they put you through down at Ordnance.' He knew. It transpired that our Divisional Ordnance was presided over by a terrifying Warrant Officer who was convinced that all limber gunners should know their job and their whole job. Apparently No. 2s were originally chosen at random and, for the purposes of action, it was the easiest job, practically just opening and shutting the breech. They were never given any instruction on the gun, neither were they warned that, when repairs were required, they had to accompany the gun to Ordnance, where they would have to jump to it. Wiggin was a handy man and became a good limber gunner, a self-taught one, and he survived several visits to Ordnance, though he always returned somewhat shattered with hard work.

We had several lots of new springs fitted and towards the end the trouble abated somewhat. (About this time the spring buffer mechanism was replaced by an air pressure mechanism.)

While I was on guard from 23.00 to 03.00 hours that night, the enemy gassed the batteries behind like hell, including the 4.5 Howitzer Battery of our brigade, who were in the hedge immediately behind us. Fortunately, there was no wind and the gas did not come across to us.

8th. No entry.

9th. Lovely day. All quiet, except much shelling on the road. But catastrophe came to 'A' Battery. Two of their officers were killed and two wounded. The battery went out.

Our 'D' gun was taken out to go to Ordnance for new springs and repairs. Rain at night again and the usual S.O.S.

10th. 'D' gun had got stuck in a water-hole on the side of the road and had been there all night. Apparently the teams had left it, but had now come back early and required our help to pull it out. Just as we reached it, tremendous shelling commenced on the road and all round it. I saw here a very fine action by a bombardier. A team of some other battery came dashing past, led by a smart young bombardier on a nice horse, and as they were passing us, a shell exploded within a few yards of all of us, wounding the bombardier and his horse, both of whom were covered with splinters, bleeding wounds in front and the poor horse's nose slashed and pouring blood. The bombardier carried on without turning a hair and exactly as if he had been unaware that he had been wounded, shouting orders back and pointing their direction forward, and speeding forward at almost a gallop. He deserved a medal.

It was perhaps not surprising that after that, we extracted 'D' gun from its hole with drag-ropes at very quick speed, hooked it up, and team and we departed with speed in our opposite directions.

11th. Lovely day. Germans very quiet, except for their heavies, which quietened later. Our heavies played hell with them.

12th. Field batteries very active. Firing contests between us and 'B' Battery. Earth fairly shook. Dangerous game.

13th. German planes dropped two bombs between us and 'D' Battery.

14th. Germans 'crumped' right flank of battery like hell. Our shack was so near to the bursts that we considered ourselves comparatively safe as all the pieces flew over us, so we just lay in it.

We had given up the idea of dugouts. We had never had them on this position, only sandbagged surface shacks with single-layer sandbagged roofs, and we certainly were not going to start digging down now into the sodden waterlogged earth. We had given up the 'nipping' habit completely, provided of course that there was no question of the position receiving one of the German's systematic pastings. Shelling on this position was always indiscriminate, except for the ridiculous little shrapnel, and on the whole we would have preferred, from our own point of view, to have been without the indiscriminate, but subject to the occasional pasting, the latter was always in our imagination at such times as we were not in action.

So interest in bursts had now become academic, a matter of comment solely on the question of nearness, with no action taken. The casemate-camouflage controversy had long since died; the time factor was literally all we thought about all day at all, all that counted in our lives. That and (to me) the forty Russian Front Divisions.

So, as my diary notes on this day, 'we just lay in it and let the bits fly over us.' Could it be contempt resulting from familiarity? Well, to a degree. What sort of degree?

15th. Prepared all day for a stunt next morning. I never knew what the barrage was for or anything about the attack or whatever it was. Afterwards I did not care.

16th. It was a warm, still, dry morning and barely daylight, when 'A' detachment rolled themselves out of their blankets under the large tarpaulin. As far as I remember, I slept the farthest man in, so if others were there I could only get to my sleeping place by crawling over them. Consequently, when at 04.30 hours our Corporal called 'show a leg, come on out of it' and we all crawled out yawning, I came last, not from laziness, but so as not to have to crawl over the others. Next to me was Gunner Havens, so when I stood up and stretched outside, I found only Havens, the other four being already on the gun some twenty yards away, and in their positions. Corporal was standing by the trail, Wiggin No. 2, little 'Cocker', who had recently come to us from being a driver and was keen to do gun-laying, was in my seat as layer, and Gunner Prosser was preparing the ammunition as No. 4. Four men were all that were necessary on a position like this one, as long as a rush of fuse-setting or rounds carrying was not required. So Gunner Havens and I stood behind Corporal and yawned and waited.

Barrage began at 04.45 hours, we only firing at slow rate battery fire. The bombardment broke out almost instantaneously and was simply tremendous. The sky in front was lit up with German signal lights. After we had been firing a little time, Corporal remarked casually to Havens and myself that we could turn in again if we liked and he would call us as soon as he wanted us, but at the moment there was nothing for us to do.

We said, 'Right Corp', but for some reason we continued to stand there. I always remember that moment, how my mind thought sleepily, 'Shall I turn in, or stay here and watch and see if anything happens – how warm and still the air is.' I decided to stay there and we both continued to stand and watched.

Then, whether it was due to a feeling of sleepiness or boredom I do not know, but I simply thought, 'I'll turn in', and said so to Havens, and we both sauntered back to the shack, crawled onto our blankets and were soon asleep.

There had been no shells over. However, after a little I was aware in my sleep of a few shells bursting somewhere near. Then an incendiary shell burst quite close behind the shack and woke us. I said to Havens, 'Where was that?' He, being near the entrance, looked out and said, 'Pretty near, nasty'.

We were nearly asleep again when there was a loud burst quite near, and simultaneously there was a noise like chhht and our upright post supporting the ridge pole collapsed, cut through like butter by a piece of shell, which must have passed within a few inches of Haven's head. We were in the dark under the large tarpaulin and proceeded to scramble our way out. I had farther to scramble and got all mixed up with tarpaulin and blankets, and as I bored my way along, called to Havens, 'Where was it?' He was out by now, and his reply froze my blood, 'My God, it's on them'. I was still tied up with the blankets and fighting furiously with them, tore myself free and rushed out, dashed onto the position. It had taken me so long to free myself from the wrecked tent, that by the time I reached the position, that is 'A' gun, only a few yards away, Havens had disappeared, and there was nobody there, nobody on the whole position.

I was standing there alone. 'A' gun and emplacement was all a sheet of flame, the cordite in the cartridge cases of the rounds had ignited, and all the rounds were blazing and the cases popping off from heat. There was no one there. I was absolutely rooted with horror. Suddenly I saw Corporal behind me staggering and falling, and as I rushed towards him, two others were there first and were carrying him back to the cook-house hedge. I went mad and don't know what I did but run frantically round the gun, into the water of the trench in front, and round again yelling for them, calling their names, 'Cocker, Wiggin, Prosser'. I stood again behind 'A' gun and thought where are they, they must all be hit up, the whole lot, all 'A' gun detachment gone except Havens and me.

Then a shout came from cook-house hedge, 'All off the position'. I ran there, and there they were, all four of them, with the rest of the detachments. The chaps were trying to make them comfortable, if such a word at such a time is not an insult, two [of them] on our only two stretchers. They were all burnt, their hair black, in fact they had been on fire; they were bleeding everywhere from quantities of small wounds made by the fragments of the incendiary shell.

The shell had fallen on the ammunition pile at the Corporal's very feet, and the whole pit must have been a blazing inferno.

The gun was uninjured except for the elevating handle which was broken, and little Cocker's hand had been on that handle.

Wiggin, a fellow of quick reactions, had thrown himself, a sheet of flame, from under the net forward and head foremost into the water of the trench, an action which may have saved his life. Fortunately, Corporal Rice saw him do it, ran out and fetched him in. Corporal, Wiggin and Prosser lay as dead, but little 'Cocker' lay looking up at us, his face all blood and sweat, and he smiled and, as they started to lift the stretcher, he said, 'Good-bye chaps' and held out his right arm to shake good-bye, but his hand was swinging on a piece of skin.

Some things I can never forget.

With three others I carried Corporal to the dressing station. It was about 500 yards off at a crossroads, and was in a mere trench. It took some time to get there with a stretcher, as there was no path and there were many old trenches to get the stretcher across. We were as careful as possible, but I thought the Corporal was dead, as he never moved or spoke.

At the station was one R.A.M.C. man in charge. Of course the time had been chosen to shell the crossroads like mad. I saw an antiquated horse ambulance standing by itself there, the driver evidently sheltering, and marvelled at the two old horses standing quietly with lowered heads. We got the stretcher carefully into the trench and lifted Corporal out onto a sort of platform.

He still appeared to be dead. I watched the Orderly and marvelled; he was completely calm and did his work mechanically, preparing for and giving a morphia injection. All the time the shells crashed outside. Then suddenly Corporal spoke, 'Put me out', he said. The Orderly spoke quietly, 'Keep quiet, old chap'. I couldn't bear it, but now worse happened, just as we were filing out. There were screams of 'make way there' and four R.G.A. artillerymen literally ran in with a stretcher with one of their number lying screaming with one thigh a pulp. We just ran to get away from the hell-place. When we got back, we found that 'Cocker', Wiggin and Prosser had all been carried off, and that when they left they were at any rate alive.

News came that evening that Corporal, Cocker and Prosser were all dead.

Dear old Wiggin got back home, but he suffered tremendously as he was a mass of wounds and they never really healed. I met him fifteen years later and he seemed well, but he died soon after, I always thought on account of his wounds.

Havens and I were too upset to do anything but stand about. I felt stunned and numb and wanted to be alone, and the chaps left me alone.

The battery was not in action any more and all was quiet again.

The stunt was supposed to have gone well, but history records it as 'a disappointing action'. The 48th carried all before them, but the division on their right was held up, so that they were left in a dangerous position. Report said that there were not many casualties and no prisoners, but hundreds of dead.

I heard that Gunner Birch had been killed at O.P. and that Mr Edwards of H.Q. had been wounded and died later.

Gunner Havens went down to the wagon-lines, and I was then the only one of 'A' sub detachment left on the position.

I sat on a log a little away and pondered. This, I decided, is 'near one' number three, and there will not be another; three is quite a good number, after which one can no longer expect any more of these misses … and I was right.

I thought, what determined that I said to myself that morning that, after all, I would turn in? The answer of course was that nothing, that is, no <u>single</u> event, object or motion, determines things; every event is determined or caused by an <u>infinity</u> of causes, from the macroscopic to the microscopic, to the infinitely small causes inside the molecule and atom and electron. Events flow in life, as life flows, and their nature is determined by the flow of life, call it chance or not, as you like, and of course Man's mind is part of and affects the flow. But to talk about one determining fact, thing, creator or whatnot in the Universe, is meaningless.

Yes, it was chance, and I could not go on depending on it.

I decided another thing, irrespective of the machinations of chance. I wanted to stay on the position. This desire was only partly due to my hatred of the wagon-lines, the bloody grooming. It was chiefly because I wanted to stay with the gunners; I felt I belonged with them, I always liked 'B' sub and their nice Sergeant 'Frizzle' Bennett; they were always a nice lot and 'A' and 'B' subs were never rivals and always friends. I knew they would be sorry, and I wondered if they would have room for me.

I saw them glancing in my direction. Then Mr Leslie appeared. He walked along behind the battery, and suddenly turned towards and came up to me with a 'Don't get up, Price, you all right?' 'Yes, thank you, sir.' Then, after a silence, he said, 'I didn't send orders for you to go down', and paused again, and then, giving me a quick glance, 'I thought you wouldn't want to'. He was a completely understanding person; what nice officers we had.

I said, 'Can I go into "B" sub, sir?' He said, 'Of course. They are one short, as Gunner Webber has had one in the arm and gone down'.

We stood now in silence again. Then he said, 'The Major wants me to ask you whether you will take a stripe. You have been so long with us and with "A" sub; three years isn't it? He says you can hand it back any time if you want to. There have been so many casualties that he is short of N.C.O.s.' He knew my difficulty that I was uncertain about getting out words of command. I didn't want it and I feared I would lose my name 'Gunner'. But I felt I ought to help and have a shy at it, so said yes. He walked away.

Again I saw 'B' sub looking my way and then someone waved and called 'Hi, Gunner, cha up'. I walked over to them and said, 'What about it, Sarge?' Kind Sergeant said, 'We were just coming over to fetch you, Gunner'.

17th. I was completely out that night and slept like a log. Fortunately, all was quiet and also in the day.

We had 'lashings' of food. I never fed like it and could eat till I could eat no more. Then I realized why. We had all 'A' sub's ration; it was dead men's food, and I felt like choking.

Our infantry were, they said, all back in their trenches, and the 5th Glosters lost hundreds. 'A' gun went out to Ordnance.

On 19th at 04.00 hours there was an attack, and we took a 'fort' and some farms. Gunner Dearlove was wounded in the hand.

I had kept quiet about my stripe, but one day now Bombardier Willis came along with Brigade Orders, which he nailed up every week on a board on a poplar tree. Seeing me, he called out, 'Congratulations, Bombardier'. I was furious. All that day I was miserable, everyone I met saying, 'Cheerio, Bombardier', or words to that effect. I hated it. But I need not have worried, because next day I was 'Gunner' again, so all was well.

After a few days 'A' gun came back repaired and with it five men for the detachment, Bombardier Cove and Gunners Havens, Smith, Driver Jones and a reinforcement who was practically a boy. We built three little huts on the right front of the gun, roofed them with elephant irons and made them very cosy. There was no work and no action and we had an easy time.

On the 26th we fired all day. It was an attack on Inverness Copse. Infantry got into shell holes early and at 14.00 hours we started barraging and continued without a break till 21.00 hours. As usual when anything was on, it rained all day. We fired shrapnel, smoke shells and no end of different barrages. Infantry were said to have done well, but there were neither casualties nor prisoners. Actually the attack failed and from now on till the end of the month Inverness Copse was taken by us and lost again eighteen times! Wolff says: 'The senselessness of it all grew like a cancer into the minds of the Allied troops. One historian writes that "these strokes, aimed at the morale of the German army, were wearing down the morale of the British."'

On the 31st I went down for a rest. The wagon-lines now were by a *château* at Vlamertinghe. Walked down and it was a relief to be away.

Had no work to do and could lie about. Things fairly quiet except for a high-velocity 'India-rubber' gun.

One evening I saw Sergeant-Major and a smart looking young Captain on a smart horse walking over to me. The young Captain introduced himself to me as the brother of a family friend. He was Captain L of our A.S.C. and had his billet and mess at Peselhoek. He said he had heard about 'C' Battery and about me, and he and his mess had decided to invite me over for dinner one evening if I could come. He added that tomorrow night their Major was dining out in 'Pop' [Poperinge], so it would be convenient then. He was so friendly and Sergeant-Major said O.K.

So on Sept. 2nd after feeding, and after Marcus had had his feed, I saddled him and rode off along the route given. It was a lovely evening and Marcus was a splendid hack and I felt once more on top of the world, or would have felt so if it had not been for memories. Arriving at a very nice house quite isolated in the country, I was met by an Irish orderly, who saluted and took Marcus. Captain L came out, took me in and introduced me to another Captain and a Lieutenant. I felt extremely awkward. This was the first time I had associated with officers all the time I had been in France, now 2 years. I had made a rule always to keep off any social contact, and now, in a moment of weakness I had broken it. I felt an urge to experience once more a good dinner and good talk and drink after it. The three of them could not have been nicer. We sat down to a wonderful meal, I forget what we ate; two orderlies waited, and I was as happy as could be as long as the latter were out of the room. They made me tell them the story of 'C' Battery, all about the Somme, and I was just beginning to speak of the events of the last few days when I heard a car draw up outside. Captain L looked out of the window and exclaimed, 'Good Lord he's back.' I jumped up and said, 'I'll clear out by the back.' Captain L pushed me back in my chair and said, 'You'll do nothing of the sort. I'll fix him.' In came the Major, a stout, elderly man, in what appeared to me a bad temper. I was introduced as 'My friend, Gunner Price, sir'. He nodded at me without a word, said his dinner had fallen through and that he wanted food. Orderlies ran and brought him his meal, which he proceeded to tuck into in silence. An appalling silence reigned. When he had finished his plateful and had some cheese, he called for some port and started to sip it. He then, and not till then, gave me a quick sideways glance and said, 'You been on the Somme?' To my 'Yes Sir,' he said, 'Tell me about it'. I sketched out our last year's movements there briefly. He then said, 'Where else?' Later he asked, 'What sort of life?' Finally, 'What's happened to you at St Julien?' I gave him a description ending up with the story of 'A' gun.

A long silence followed, during which we all sipped port and continued to do so through several bottles, which the orderlies kept bringing in. I kept very quiet and he kept making quick sideways glances again and again at me. He could not quite make me out, I think. Suddenly he got up and said, 'I'm turning in, good night all', with a final glance at me.

When he had gone the other three proceeded to make explosive ejaculations. I said in agony, 'Did I do the right thing? He didn't seem to like me much.' Captain L burst out laughing and when he could speak said, 'I've never seen him be so polite to anyone.'

We went on with the port and with stories and reminiscences and it was the evening of my wartime life.

At a late hour I said good-bye to my very kind hosts, went out into the back yard, where the Irish orderly already stood to attention at Marcus' head with a 'Good evening, sir. He's had a good feed.' 'Oh, thanks so much, thanks a lot', I said, and 'Good night, thanks again'. 'Good night, sir'.

I rode out into the autumn night, and I am certain Marcus felt as I did, on top of the world. He must have done so, because he at once broke into a gallop and we tore along the grass track over meadowland and past vistas of bushes and trees in the dim light when distant vegetation turns a velvety green-black, the prelude to night. I thought, this won't do, we shall be back too soon, I must spin this heavenliness out a little; I shall never enjoy anything like this again in France, or perhaps ever. I slowed him down into his beautiful walk, which was better than any gallop. There was no sound and even the guns were silent. If I had listened, I am sure I should have heard the nightjar. I thought of the past war and what the future war would bring and of my three 'near ones', of which there would never be another, but something else, and what? 'HALT WHO ARE YOU?' All I could think to say was 'Night Boozer'. 'Halt who are you? And if you don't answer properly, I'll shoot you, bloody Gunner. Where you been anyway, you old b–?' I didn't tell him, but led Marcus to his place, tied him up and unharnessed him and went off to my tent. This I found had thirteen people asleep in it, so I pinched a saddle and feeding bag for a pillow, found a grassy spot and lay down under a blanket and slept.

3rd. Went for a bicycle ride with Bombardier Willis to Dickebusch in the evening, a glorious evening.

4th. Borrowed bikes off Quarter and went off all day with Gunner Havens. Went through Poperinge and on to Watou. Here we had our hair cut by a Belgian soldier on leave at his home. He suggested that the war would last another two years. I suggested that the League of Nations might be the only way, to which he said 'Ah oui Monsieur, by fighting the war will last another two years.'

Spent the evening at Talbot House, where we lay in hammocks in the garden and smoked Egyptian cigarettes, ending up with a cinema. I am not sure, and it sounds ridiculous, but I think that cinema was the first I ever went to.[5]

On 11 September I went back to the guns, starting at 02.00 hours, as I had to replace Gunner Strange, who was a casualty. There had been fearful doings there the previous day, though these did not concern our battery, one might say by a hairsbreadth, but 'D' Battery, our 4.5 Howitzer Battery, who were in the hedge behind us on the other side of the poplar grove. They must have been making a nuisance of themselves for the Germans, who proceeded to retaliate in their usual thorough way by putting a good and proper barrage down on them, which was both concentrated, accurate and continuous, and what could be more efficient artillery procedure than that. The result was that by the end of it Don Battery had been literally and completely blown away and had ceased to exist in any form other than scattered fragments.

My diary runs as follows:

The piece and axle of one gun was blown up spinning in the air and landed near the signallers' dugout in a trench about 200 yards away. Four guns hit out and dumps of gas shells blew up later. Shell cases and debris rained down on the position, several shells fell short on the position and others all round, also shrapnel. Men, ours and theirs, scattered and eventually got over to the deep dugout at Hill Top Farm. Several slight casualties, but meanwhile a 5.9 burst just by our cook-house, severely wounding poor old Dick Woodward and Gunner Strange. Came up on ammunition wagons with shells bursting all about and a good deal of gas about. Turned in in 'B' sub. Poor chaps so tired they did not wake. Had several S.O.S. firing in the night and so many shells over that we began to get light-headed. A reinforcement, a mere boy who had only just arrived, and whose army life till now must have been in entirely quiet, uneventful training camps in England, was afterwards called to mind by a note in my diary: 'Fool of a reinforcement lost his head, couldn't understand anything said, couldn't do anything, was just a bloody nuisance. We told him, "get out of the bloody way"'.

---

5   Apparently not: see above, p. 116.

I often thought afterwards how brutal we must have been to that poor lad. I remembered his bewildered, scared face, unable to understand anything yelled at him in the din of the bombardment and being pushed away and told to get out of the way. I wish I could remember ever having said a kind word to him afterwards.

Went over next day to Don Battery position to look at it. It was an awful sight, ground all churned up and several great craters where dumps had been, no vestige of casemates left, no guns, no sign that a battery had ever been there.

'A' gun and detachment came up late that evening. Germans gassed hard that night. We managed to keep it out of our shack with blankets, but Corporal Cove got some of it in him and chlorine gas too. Fortunately, no more firing to do.

12th. Tested 'A' gun. Found it fired short and nearly got Mr Carter at O.P. So 'A' gun had to go out again. Heard that Don Battery horse-lines had been bombed in the morning and many horses killed and some men. Everyone with wind up. Things get worse and worse in this damnable place. If we don't get out soon, we'll all be done in. Casualties in Brigade have been awful.

13th. On this date began the preparatory bombardment of the Battle of the Menin Road which was launched on the 20th. On the position we noticed nothing unusual and only heard rumours that there was going to be an attack on St Julien.

What had happened was that it was discovered that the Germans had concentrated the greater part of their strength now on the Menin Road just outside Ypres, and it was considered that everything must be held up until that concentration could be broken. An adjustment of the two Armies of this sector was made whereby their meeting point came slightly further north, that is on a line with Zonnebeke. General Plumer, who had command of the operation, had his 2nd Army to the south of this line, and General Gough's 5th Army was to the north, the latter comprising our XVIII Corps of Maxse on the left and Fanshawe's V Corps on the right, their dividing line being the Wieltje–Gravenstafel road.

Our 48th Division in front of us had been replaced by the 58th, a second line London Territorial Division which had done good work, but had not yet been in a major action. Our brigade therefore was on Maxse's extreme right and next to Fanshawe. The only thing that happened to us this day was a 5.9 in the hedge close to our shacks.

15th. Much shelling every evening and small shrapnel by day, which later we unwisely continued to ignore. Battery shelled at medium rate in the evening and we all cleared. No damage.

On the 16th I was sent to the wagon-lines with a note; these had now moved to a place beyond Peselhoek. I had to walk and the distance was 8 miles. However, it was a lovely day and I started out happily. I had not gone far when I saw approaching a marvellous looking officer followed by a cavalryman with a lance, which indicated a General. I recognized him at once as General Fanshawe, and panicked on the ridiculous supposition that he might ask me what I was doing there all by myself. I could not avoid passing him close to. I carefully saluted, but he appeared not to see me, rather naturally. He made a marvellous picture, a handsome, tall, spare man, mounted on a splendid horse, followed by an equally well-mounted cavalryman. His face had a sad expression and he was looking straight ahead of him in deep thought.

After a time I became aware of large shell bursts ahead. The country was desolate waste with many large poplars; there were many tracks, but I saw not a soul. Then I saw the bursts and they were big fellows and they seemed to be on my course. As usual it was impossible to tell whether any definite track was the target or not and I decided to carry on. The bursts came nearer and I seemed to be walking into them. I decided that if I ran a distance, I should get out of their area. I did so, and of course as always, the bursts seemed to keep up with me. I began to panic, because it occurred to me that the complete absence of anyone might mean that the area was a banned one for lines of communication and that possibly I should not have come that way, although I had been given no instructions about it. I ran and ran, glancing back as each terrific roar occurred. I properly had the wind up. It seemed ages before the bursts sounded further off and I stopped running. It was a relief to reach the canal and cross it by an engineers' bridge and find things perfectly quiet there.

After that I enjoyed my walk. Arriving at Peselhoek, I had no idea where the lines were, when suddenly I met an officer I knew, who was in charge of our supply depot. He was most friendly and made me come into his billet and have a whisky, my second for this year. He then sent me on in a sidecar to the lines, which proved to be the best we have had yet, there being proper huts, which even had flower beds round them. Stayed for tea with the chaps and then got a lift part of the way back. The walk from the canal again by myself was rather a nervy one, but all went well:

18th. Much ammunition up. Shelled nastily by [the] dumps in evening.

We had been working all morning either at the guns or on fatigues when there was the usual call of 'Ammo up', the prelude to the endless 'Ammo thumping', which invariably for 'A' Sub necessitated carrying all our rounds in the 4-spaced canvas carriers the whole width of the position, because teams always seemed to arrive on the left flank.

I was beginning to develop at this time a feeling of tired apathy, which seemed to me to be a reaction to the now non-existing satisfaction of grumbling, that old habit which we had long ago forgotten to indulge in. We were all of us experiencing this.

On my 'umpteenth' walk back to collect four more rounds, I suddenly stood still at the sound of something I heard, something not of this world of the St Julien Position. I saw no vision of 'Angels' or a cross in the sky, but the something I heard was more unexpected, and beautiful. It was a violin being played, and with the plaintive little tune came the words of a song softly sung: 'For I love every mouse in that old-fashioned house …'. Of course we all knew who was playing and, looking up, there we saw him, our popular Levy, playing his violin lying on his back on a lot of bags on the G.S. wagon, with his legs up in the air. He always played quietly and in tune, and when he sang it was the same; he never played jazz, but always quiet little ditties reminding us of home.

Such a nostalgic surge came over me that I had to sit down. But I was up again almost at once in a revulsion of anger. What had this window into past happy days got to do with us here in this St Julien Position life? It was as when our Mother first visited us at preparatory school, and I was acutely miserable all the time, because I was experiencing two worlds which could not mix.

Old-fashioned houses, music, poetry, love: what had they to do with life at Third Ypres?

How did we know that we should ever experience these again? They were things of the past, and the real past does not return. Forty German divisions with their guns were on their way here from the Russian front.

Levy's reminder of old days might well be the last, in which case let apathy and four more rounds in the carrier carry on.

'For I love every–' Crash.

19th. All the previous night the most concentrated heavy firing I ever remember went on. Our heavies appeared to be firing at their maximum. We now learned that the big battle (which was later to be called the Battle of the Menin Road) was to commence at 05.00 hours next morning.

20th. The big stunt began. Firing was continuous all day practically without intermission. Thank goodness the buffer springs functioned. Also we had the help of D.A.C. men for carrying rounds from where the drivers dumped them, otherwise we could not have kept the dumps supplied. Rumour says we took a ridge, probably Pilckem Ridge (how often had it been taken and lost?), with prisoners and guns. Not a shell back all day. We had come to expect this, so that stunts, though hard work, became welcome periods free from strain.

21st. Barrage again early, but firing slower. A lovely bright, fresh autumn day. Rubber-nosed devil in trench by 'B' shack; enormous hole. By the end of the second day we were tired and dirty. To fire at even a slow rate is wearisome, if it continues all day, and we had now been at it for two days. Thank goodness there was no night firing.

September 22 opened with a lovely sunny morning. I woke early, some time before firing was to re-commence. I stretched and yawned and looked at the other five asleep and nearly went to sleep again. But I suddenly thought how dirty, unwashed and unshaven I was. Our officers never worried us on the position about our appearance when stunts were on. I decided that I had not washed at all for nearly three days and, though dirt in those days did not worry me as long as we were living in the open air, there were limits. So I got up, went outside and fetched a bucket and filled it at a large shell hole nearby. There was no one else about. I had a good wash and then a shave and then I thought how nice it was to be clean again and how well I felt, in spite of the many times when I thought I felt like death; also how abominable it was here and what a death trap it was and how none of us could survive unless we came out soon. While I pondered, I was sleepily aware of poppings over-head. I looked in their direction and noted the absurd little shrapnel bursts some thirty feet up in the air, which were obviously meant for our battery as their range was so good. The day before one of them had burst in the soft earth on percussion in the field just across the hedge from our shack while I was standing outside. It sent up a shower of earthy sods and one came flying over towards me, and I caught it. I thought of these stupid little shrapnel as ridiculous now, as we thought them 2½ years ago at Neuve-Église, when they were the first shell bursts we saw.

I stopped thinking about them and started to polish my field boots and had nearly finished them, lost in reverie, when I heard a shell coming and dodged down instinctively by the empty shack by which I was standing, a shack in which we merely kept our kits. BANG. It was as if some tremendous force hit me between the shoulders, and I did not seem to fall but simply was down with my face in the earth partly inside the shack, a shrapnel bullet between the shoulders. I couldn't breathe nor move and thought, this is it. I decided that all depended upon whether I could move a toe. It appeared that I couldn't, but fortunately I did not give up but had another try and succeeded. So that was that; nothing to worry about, as I thought there might have been.

I was on the top of the stretcher this time instead of under it.

I couldn't talk to the four sub gunners who carried me to the dressing station as breathing was painful, but I kept on thinking.

I thought: I'm out of 'this bloody lot'; I've got a Blighty One; and the words of our song came back to me, 'Shan't I be glad when my time's up, we'll groom no bloody more'; I'm out of it; the time factor is taking me out; back to England; away from C/240; away from these fellows, with whom I have spent the whole of the last three years, less a week.

Suddenly I realized that this endlessly longed-for event, this happy ending which had come, was bitter.

There would never be comradeship like this again.

There can assuredly never be contentment without discontent, happiness without unhappiness, good without evil, nor absolute good, nor absolute bad, nor absolute Truth.

I looked down on Gunner Havens' head and wondered why the four gunners carrying me swore so little as they struggled getting the stretcher over the old, disintegrating communication trenches.

I kept on saying to myself, 'I'm leaving these fellows', and I couldn't bear it. 'Good-bye, Gunner'.

Some weeks later at Wimereux Base Hospital near Boulogne I received a letter from Sergeant Gore: 'we came out four days after you went. They have put us on road repair work. There is a rumour we are going to Italy. I do miss you so much, old fellow.'

It was hell being away from them; it was hell being in such an atmosphere of disillusionment, disgruntlement and later of lead-swinging, shirking and near insubordination. But why should anyone have been surprised.

The outstanding feature of military leadership at this time, it has been said, was that the only defence known was indiscriminate slaughter. Earl Haig apparently relied entirely upon what he was told by Charteris, his information officer.

On the first day of Third Ypres the latter was somewhere behind the lines watching our wounded coming back. He saw one man on a stretcher make the thumbs up sign. He probably meant it when, describing the incident to Haig, he intimated that the man's words, which he obviously didn't hear, were to the effect that it was a great victory, that the enemy was on the run; in fact, it was a case of '*on les aura*'. Poor man. What that man was saying was, 'I've got a Blighty one. I'm out of this bloody lot.' It was a good thing that the troops did not know Haig's interpretations of Third Ypres thumbs up. It would, on the other hand, have been an immense relief to the troops if they could have known that Lloyd George, in the words of Lord Derby, 'was to spend the rest of the war attempting to prevent Haig from launching offensives' for the simple reason that no more reinforcements were available.

The senselessness of it all became apparent when it was learned that the Germans had decided months previously, with their invariable common sense and thoroughness, to fortify their support lines on this front, and probably elsewhere, by the construction of numbers of underground concrete forts and hundreds of machine gun pill-boxes. In this way they were able to contain all our attacks with a relatively small number of men under cover, suffer comparatively small casualties, and inflict enormous casualties upon us. If they could think out such common-sense strategy, we could have done the same, avoiding the whole battle and economizing our strength till American help was at hand.

The Allied casualties of Third Ypres (including Cambrai) for the period July to December 1917 have been estimated as nearly double those of the Germans, but it seems impossible to find reliable figures.

At the end of November the 48th Division with our 240 R.F.A. Brigade went to Italy, where they had quite a good and amusing time.

The cadre of the Brigade returned to England, after the Armistice, in April 1919.

Of 'C' Battery, the only man in the party who was received at the station by the Mayor, who had come right through with the Battery from the beginning, was little Corporal Benny Cove.

If I could have avoided that bullet, I would have been the other one.

11

POSTSCRIPT

At midnight on 12 September, 1958, I drove my car onto 'Twickenham Rail Ferry' at Dover. The young passport official thought that his father had been at Ypres, at which remark his companion laughed, but at whom I was not sure.

My sleep was interrupted by trains being rolled along above me and by a feeling of excitement, but then there was dead silence with only a faint hum of engines.

At 04.00 hours I made the deck and found a perfect, still night and a brilliance of stars, even the Pleiades were bright and clear.

After no undue delay, I was off alone through Dunkerque's lifeless docks and past notices all saying '*Toutes Directions*'. I wanted the Lille road and it was hard to find, but eventually saw a sign marked Bergues, which was, I knew, on the route.

Then I was away south on a lovely surface and in the pitch dark. Small billows of white mist across the road caused some anxious moments, but they did not last. Everywhere was so dark that I could not read the signs, but stopped when I saw what seemed to be an old town on my left, which turned out to be Bergues.

I got out to go across the road to read a signpost, and literally bumped into two *gendarmes*. I was apprehensive, as an Englishman by himself with no luggage at all at 05.00 hours might invite questions. It did, from the elder one, a kindly looking old man, who addressed me in perfect English, 'Where do you wish to go, sir?' My heart warmed towards the kindly Frenchman. His instructions were to turn left and look out for the *Douane*.

I did so, but too soon, and found myself going over a drawbridge and through a most perfect medieval *porte* and into a completely medieval town over cobbles and under timbered overhanging upper floors on both sides.

It seemed as dead as Péronne had been and lightless, except for a solitary lamp in the little *Place*. It was enchanting, but of course I had to turn back.

Then a solitary black figure approached and a young, rosy-faced priest came along, and to my question for 'la route à Ypres', replied, '*Après la porte la première à gauche*'.

I found the road and sped south.

Dawn was breaking and, the sky being almost cloudless, a lovely sunrise was certain. The first pink streaks gradually expanded till the whole eastern sky was a rosy glow, the climax being reached, as always, just before sunrise. At one point on a long flat horizon some distant round-topped trees and several church towers and spires stood out wonderfully against the brilliance.

I seemed to have the whole country to myself. Luxuriant crops of sugar beet, maize and tall, lush red clover, all soaked in dew, were everywhere.

I stopped for some minutes. Here surely is the time and place to appreciate the world we live in.

Unexpectedly I came to the *Douane* at Oost-Cappel, first the French one which occupied a bare minute, and then the Belgian one which, being devoid of a bar, I nearly passed by.

Having waited in vain for developments, I resorted to an *estaminet*. To my enquiries, the owner replied in perfect English that I must await the arrival of the *gendarmes*, but that they would appear shortly. Soon one arrived, a polite young man on a bicycle, also speaking excellent English. After a quite friendly argument as to why I had omitted to obtain an import authorization for the car, my incipient panic was eased by handing over thousands of French francs, and I drove on after compliments and salutations.

The countryside was now waking up. Young men and girls on bicycles, and small country buses, appeared.

Poperinge now appeared.

I stopped in the *Place* to consult my map, when a voice in my ear said, again in perfect English, 'Can I direct you anywhere, sir; if so, please ask me'. What charming people. I had wondered with what degree of amused non-comprehension a lone Englishman of advanced years seeking First War recollections might be regarded. This kind remark at once set me at ease.

My mention of '*artillerie anglaise dans le secteur St Julien en dix-sept*' caused a polite 'Ah' from the little crowd, and the query, '*Votre première visite?*' As I drove on, someone called, 'Cheerio, have a good trip'. It seemed that my right to be there was recognized, and that I was welcome, and I felt happy and grateful.

Poperinge has been beautifully rebuilt without an ugly spot anywhere.

Soon I was entering Ypres, and for the first time.

The *Grand Place* and wonderful new Cloth Hall are unbelievably impressive, and all the colours of brick and stone are mellow and blended.

I breakfasted in a cafe in the early morning sun and watched the *Place*.

I walked to Menin Gate, which I had never seen, and stood on the ramparts. It was a shock to see some damage on the walls, obviously done by shell bursts of the Second War. The words of our first Major came back to me tragically about not having to fight 'all over again'.

I had two objectives for my eight hours of exploration, first, our first position at Neuve-Église, and, second, our last position in front of St Julien.

I decided on the first first.

I sped along the Armentières road, for time was precious, passing Voormezele on the right and Hollebeke on the left; then came Wijtschate and rising ground, and then I was on 'the ridge', the one we had looked and fired at for so long in 1915, speculating always as to what lay on the farther side. Nothing particular did lie beyond it except the Germans, but what we did not realize then, but I did now, was the magnitude of this great Messines Ridge and its height. You do not expect such elevations on this part of the Continent. No wonder the Germans held on to it. The view west extended for miles and the spires and towers of Bailleul were very clear.

Speeding through Messines (Mesen) village, an unattractive place, I dropped down and took at a venture a very small road to the right. After a time I came to a place where the little road plunged down a short, really steep hill, where the view below showed me all the former haunts. I parked and sat on a wall. An old farmer came hesitantly along and I welcomed the opportunity for a talk, as surely he would know my reason for being there. Alas, his French, and it was French and not Flemish, was almost incomprehensible to me; it must have been some dialect. I had brought my photo album with me and showed it to him. He was interested, but made no comment. He understood me sufficiently to point out all the places I was not sure of: Neuve-Église looked quite a town now, then came Wulvergem, and down the slope and to the left was, of course I could see it, Ploegsteert Wood. It was all quite clear and it was the first time I saw laid out before me this former no-man's-land by the side of which we had lived so quietly that warm summer. I opened a tin of Worthington, or rather two tins. There was nothing else to drink to except '*À bas la guerre*', so I tried it with slight apprehension. His reaction was nil, and rather worse than nil, as he began

a long dissertation from which by frantic effort I thought I understood the
following bits and pieces: he was a Reservist, his H.Q. was Bruges; he was
even now in touch with his Colonel; Indo-China was a trouble; he might
have to report to Bruges at any time because he thought there might be war
within three weeks. I prefer to think I misunderstood him. I then had the
appalling realization that he had never been in the First War as he must have
been a child at the time. That went some way to spoiling my trip. However,
we parted friends.

I went down the hill and there was Ploegsteert Wood, a beautiful dense
wood of full-grown oak. I wanted to go and wander in it, but it looked well
fenced and private and I had not the time. I followed the small road into
Neuve-Église.

It was a smart, big town with quite a large town hall.

I went along the Nieppe road to find Desiré's farm, passing a bare spot
where our Brigade H.Q. house must have stood, and must have been blown
up and not rebuilt. As for the farm, there was no farm at all, but a huge factory
of some kind. I went back into the town and bought postcards and choco-
late. Returning to my car, I found it surrounded by school boys. They were
interested in it. I tried their reactions to my statement that their town was our
first arrival place 'en quinze', that our artillery were in that field 'la bas'. They
stood very quiet, were very polite, and they knew about the battles at Mesen
and they knew about the war. Then one was pushed forward and spoke quite
easily and naturally in good English. I was impressed at their good manners.

My objective was that first position under the elms. With the natural
features of the ridge and wood, I could orientate myself easily, but the
position was some distance from any road. I went out of the town on the
Wulvergem road, at the point where anyone on it was completely open
to enemy observation, and took the first turn on the right, went a short
way and left the car at a place where there were many potato gatherers,
who characteristically worked so hard that they never even looked up, and
walked along a track to a farm. But it was not the farm where we had been.
I studied the lie of the land rather despairingly and my sense of direction,
which is good, told me that I was in front of the position. I then noticed
that the farm road turned here and went back in the direction of the town.
I followed it; it was new and made up with large concrete blocks; a rise
obstructed the view. I came round the rise and a small farm came in view
and our old position was there right in front of me looking exactly the
same as my memory picture of it 43 years ago.

I ran, holding in my hands my photo album, passing a postman, who did not seem to exhibit any surprise.

I came to the little field and there it was exactly as I remembered it. But there were many changes, the old barn was replaced by an iron one, the farmhouse by a small concrete bungalow, and the track I was on, not yet finished, ran up the field just behind where the guns had stood. The elms had gone and a row of fresh ones had been planted in their place, forming low, bushy trees. I looked for the stumps of the old ones and sure enough I found them, nine of them, as in the photograph. They had evidently grown into big trees, as the stumps, which had been neatly sawn off, were two feet in diameter.

It seemed to me that interest in the battles of history waxes and wanes, and then may return with increased intensity. Like most boys, I liked to read in history books how battles were fought, especially victorious ones. Then came a reaction, reason-based and perhaps political. School history, it was said, was taught exclusively in terms of kings and their battles to the exclusion of things that mattered, that is, social and economic development. And they were right, or nearly so. But the time came when I read wonderful Trevelyan's accounts of Marlborough's battles, and his vivid descriptions of the actual battlefields, their fields, hedges, roads and villages, which he had himself visited and walked over and identified; his description of how the 'field of Blenheim' had altered since those days, and how it looked to him standing on it and trying to visualize its outlines in the past; also his descriptions of the 'fields' of Ramillies and Oudenarde.

And so there grew in me a desire to do just this, to visit the 'fields' of all the European battles of history, and make them come alive to me in terms of eyesight rather than in those of military maps in history books. To go to those places is of course the only way to learn history or be taught it.

It was not possible for me. However, I had succeeded in bringing back before my eyes a war landscape picture, albeit merely of the location of a quiet period after Second Ypres.

I stood among nettles on the spot where 'A' gun had been.

I compared the outline of Messines Ridge with the outline in my photographs; the skyline was of course the same, but naturally the trees and fields looked different. Nature is dynamic.

There used to be fields on the flat ground with tall untidy hedges, where 'A' and 'B' Batteries used to play cricket. Now all the hedges had gone and it was one very large field. Obviously agriculture had been stepped up in efficiency since those days.

I walked up to the bungalow. A girl came along on a very smart motor bicycle and went in. I did not like to go there and knock.

I returned to Ypres through Kemmel and with Dickebusch away on my left, past cemeteries innumerable and beautifully kept.

The country round Ypres was a different proposition for me in my search for my second objective, the St Julien position, it being dead flat with no natural features to look for and with many new and smart looking farms.

I followed the road out of Ypres along the canal to Boezinge, where I crossed the canal by a new bridge. I took a photo from the bridge looking up the canal, and realized for the first time what a really marvellous job those R.E.s did in keeping it bridged under that intense and continual bombardment.

I drove south-east along little byroads. French maps appear to be exclusively Michelin and for the use naturally of motorists only, who are not expected to be interested in byroads which do not lead anywhere; also they show no natural features except the larger woods. So my map was no help and I developed a feeling that my search was a hopeless one. There were large black poplars, but always by beautiful, new farm buildings. All the people were scattered out in the fields getting in their harvest in the lovely sunny weather. There was no one to talk to and I met no one on these roads either on foot or in cars.

One of the first of these farms which I saw, standing amidst its poplars, seemed to me to be in the right situation for our position, the towers of Ypres being in the remembered compass position and distance. It might well have been built on the very ground of the position.

I did a round through Wieltje, St Julien, Langemarck and Pilckem twice. Once I left the car and walked through a deserted farm, where furious dogs barked, and found myself on the canal and saw I was perhaps a mile too far south.

I returned to the car and drove on a little and then stopped and consulted the map for the hundredth time. I was on Pilckem Ridge. It is not for me to speak about what happened here, as I was never here in the war, only some 1,000 yards away down the slight slope to the south-west.

I looked south to the towers of Ypres over the endless flats on which Third Ypres was fought, over and over again, interminably and hopelessly, on and on, while I was there and afterwards, throughout that autumn of 1917. The battle never let up, it just died of exhaustion as the Somme had died of exhaustion. No one gave in. And thereby lay a thought.

Of all the armies which fought in the First World War from its start in August 1914 until 1917 and 1918, omitting the remnant of the Belgian Army, which carried on bravely to the end, the French Army was reduced in potential perhaps by a half by loss of morale due to desertions following upon Nivelle's fiasco of April 1917; the Russian Army, demoralized by incompetence, starvation and politics, just walked home at the end of July 1917; and the Italian Army could practically be written off as from Caporetto in October 1917.

The British Army made practically its whole effort upon the Western Front, where it, with the French Army, endured two years of the greatest continual bombardment which the World had ever known, or is ever likely to know; where it suffered probably more than any other army from prehistoric leadership in the doctrine of frontal assaults upon entrenched positions, and in Haig's ridiculous cavalry complex; and where it never squealed for help, but always had to give it.

One conclusion arises from the above retrospect, one which it will not be fashionable to pronounce, and which I therefore propose to give.

Excluding the Belgian Army and the late-arriving Americans, and including enemy armies as from October 1918: ALL THESE ARMIES at different times and indifferent degrees RAN AWAY, but THE BRITISH ARMY NEVER RAN AWAY.

I had now been motoring for fourteen hours, years were beginning to tell, and a weariness was coming over me.

What was I trying to do? I was searching for the past, for something which in terms of space was not there. The grandchildren, who live enthusiastically in the present, scarcely know what the past is; they are wiser than I.

We are surely part of a stream of life in which past and future are inseparable from the present; time is only an hypothesis.

If only this flow of knowledge and understanding could have been free and natural over the last two thousand years, concentrating upon humanity and its need for co-existence and understanding between classes and peoples, instead of upon personal salvation and the supernatural, we might by now have grown out of wars.

If there is hope, it does not come from traditional teachings, but, oddly enough, from the scientists, who have given us a terror which can destroy all. In future the choice will not be, had better not be, between one armed group and another, but between peace or annihilation.

You do not find conscious suicide among animals, and Man in the mass is an animal.

I turned north and drove slowly through Langemarck and Veldhoek, and then I was in Houthulst Forest, where men fought each other without ceasing for three years, and there was a sunset as beautiful as had been the sunrise.

Two lines of a poem entitled 'The Night Express' came to mind:

White roads leading faint and far
Into the land where the good dreams are.

If good dreams can be of the future, and if their realization comes by way of terror, and one would have preferred a different way, that is better than no realization.

I followed the route towards Ostend.

I was at Dixmude …

APPENDIX

ARTILLERYMEN MENTIONED

Below are such biographical details, including service numbers, as we have been able to discover for those artillerymen mentioned in the text: if a surname is not in this list then no identification, even tentative, has been attempted. The notes are included to assist any reader inclined to further research, and the editor is heavily indebted to the efforts of Evelyn and Christopher Wilcock in compiling this list, although any omissions, errors, etc. remain his own.

Bannister, E.: 1219/825215.

Bennett, Fred ('Frizzle'): 966/825093; M.M. *London Gazette* 24 April 1917.

Bevan, Cecil B.: gunner 1803/825599; b. c. 1893, son of a grain broker from Churcham, Glos.

Browne, Geoffrey Dennis: b. 10 May 1888, son of a clergyman; joined territorial unit 1906, promoted Major 7 January 1915, killed 19 September 1916.

Carter, Ernest: b. 26 April 1887, clerk to directors, City of London brewery; enrolled as a gunner 5 October 1914; commissioned RHA September 1916; killed fighting with 240th in Italy.

Cove, Benjamin ('Benny'): 1513/82537; b. c. 1889, son of a carpenter (Frank Cove) in Gloucester; engine cleaner on Great Western Railway; survived the war.

Gore, Charles Reginald Newbury: 589/825047; a railway clerk from Bristol; joined territorials 1909; promoted sergeant December 1915.

Havens, Edwin Arthur: 2674/826009; from Bristol; attested 27 May 1915; suffered gunshot wound to left hand, August 1917, but later rejoined 240th and served in Italy.

Hawling, George Fisher: corporal, later sergeant.

Isaac, W.R.M., lieutenant.

Leach, Daniel: 1752/825562; b. 1892; a gardener from Bollow, Westbury on Severn; embodied 3 September 1914; became a saddler to 240th 5 February 1915; went to Italy with brigade, serving as a driver on the ammunition column; disembodied 2 May 1919.

Levison, Arthur J.: 1754/825564; b. 1893, Gloucester; the son of a sculptor; a woodcarver; discharged wounded 27 November 1917.

Murray, Ernest Reginald: 998/825102; a clerk, joined TA 1911; hospitalised after being gassed 20 July 1917.

Parker, William Joseph: 29/825001; Regimental Sergeant-Major, MC (1918).

Phipps, Charles E.: 1210/825210.

Price, William V.: sergeant; died 23 August 1916.

Prosser, Hebert William: 825670

Roddick, George: 1211/825211; b. 1896; grocer in Mssrs Southern's Stores, Gloucester; enrolled in territorial brigade 1912; served with brigade in Italy; disembodied 24 February 1919.

Ryan, William Owen: lieutenant, later captain, and MC (1916); transferred to Royal Air Force.

Shurmer, Frank: 1226/825219; b. c. 1892; postman from Churchdown, Glos; enlisted in territorial artillery 1912; survived the war.

Smith, Daniel Charles: 1786/825588; b. 1889; a miller from Stroud, embodied 3 September 1914; served in France and Italy; married Louisa Alder summer 1918; survived the war.

Stanley, Albert P.: 1278/825242; wounded on Somme 1916, discharged 3 July 1918.

Strange, Albert Edward: 1785/825587.

Todd, Matthew Edgar, 2nd Lieutenant.

Wiggin, James Henry: 1850/825631; b. 1894; a fruit porter; severely wounded in abdomen during Third Ypres, and discharged unfit for service 14 January 1918.

Williams, Edward J.: 43/825003; sergeant, later quartermaster.

Willie, Leonard T.: 2730/826047; killed in action 9 April 1917.

Wright, Herbert E.: 1783/825585.

Wynford, Philip George Best (1871–1940): succeeded father as 6th Baron Wynford 1904; Captain, RHA; served European War 1914–18 (DSO).

GLOSSARY

Aiming posts/rods	a type of gun-aiming point, sited close to the gun, and used to compensate for the movement of the dial sight when the gun recoiled on firing, or was traversed
Ammo/ammunition thumping	carrying shells, i.e. from an ammunition wagon to a gun emplacement
Angle of sight	the calculation that was used to compensate for the difference in altitude between the gun and its target
'arps	unidentified slang, but in context a reference either to army pay or to French money
AP/AAP.	aiming point/alternative aiming point
A.S.C.	Army Service Corps
Big Bertha	British Army slang for a super-heavy German howitzer
Billy	cylindrical container used for cooking and carrying food or liquid
BL	breech loading (as opposed to muzzle loading)
Blighty one	First World War military slang for a wound that was serious enough to merit being sent back to England, possibly permanently, to recuperate
Bombardier	in the British Army, an artilleryman, equivalent to a corporal
Buffer	part of the mechanism that dampened the recoil of the gun after firing

Casemate	an earth and timber fortification, built to protect a gun emplacement
Cha	British Army slang for tea; derives from the Mandarin *ch'a* ('tea')
Clinometer	an instrument used for measuring the angle of elevation of a gun
CO	Commanding Officer
cordite	a low explosive, nitro-cellulose-based propellant, used during the First World War
Crumped	shelled by any German HE shell, but especially the 5.9; the onomatopoeic name derives from the distinctive sound made on impact
DAC	Divisional Ammunition Column
Dixie(s)	large (e.g. 12-gallon) iron pots, with lids and carrying handles, used in the British Army for cooking or brewing tea; the lids were used for cooking and eating, and saw service as frying pans; the etymology of the word shows its Hindi, that is Indian, origins
Estaminet	small café selling, *inter alia*, alcohol
Fokker	German aeroplane manufacturer, founded by the Dutch aviation pioneer Anthony Fokker (1890–1939)
FOO	forward observation officer
FOP	forward observation post/point
Fray Bentos	city-port in western Uruguay famous for meat processing; it gave its name to a brand of corned beef popular in the United Kingdom
Funk holes	small dugout or shelter, just big enough to accommodate one or two men, usually scraped into the front wall of a trench
Fuse key	a tool, similar to a spanner, that was used to set the length (i.e. the time to elapse before initiation) of a time fuse
Goerz	German manufacturer of cameras and lenses; founded in 1886 by Carl Paul Goerz (1854–1923)
GS wagons	general service wagon
HE	high-explosive; of a shell that exploded on, or soon after, contact; there were many operational uses of HE, which was particularly effective against any kind of fortification, and it was designed to achieve different results to shrapnel (see below)

HQ	headquarters
Layer/laying	the gunner responsible for aiming the gun, using its sights
Limber	the horse-drawn, wheeled and detachable front part of a gun-carriage, used to carry ammunition chests and gun crews; it fixed to the trail of the gun-carriage proper by means of a hook
liquid fire	flame shot from a flame-thrower
Maconochie	a tinned beef and vegetable stew, served as an army ration; tolerable when eaten hot
Menin Gate	gateway on the eastern edge of Ypres leading to Menin, 11 miles ESE; hundreds of thousands of British and Empire troops passed through the gate on their way to the front, and in 1927 Field Marshal Lord Plumer unveiled the memorial arch that stands there today, upon the walls of which are the names of nearly 55,000 British and Empire missing
Naval guns	Royal Navy guns, adapted for use on the Western Front to compensate for the British deficiency there in heavy artillery
NCO	Non Commissioned Officer
NCT	nitro-cellulose tubular propellant; caused less erosion than cordite because its temperature at explosion was lower; this, however, necessitated a heavier charge to achieve the required velocity
OC	Officer in Charge
OED	Oxford English Dictionary
ODNB	Oxford Dictionary of National Biography
OO	Orderly Officer
OP	Observation Post
pavé	a French or Belgian cobblestone road; painful under-foot during long journeys, and consequently loathed by British infantry
Pop	Poperinge, Belgian town *c.* 8 miles west of Ypres
porte	(Fr.) in this context, a hall or gate
QF	Quick Firing; of an artillery field gun that could fire pro-jectiles at a rate in excess of six rounds per minute, the gun barrel recoil and recuperator mechanism absorbing the

	energy of the blast, stabilising the gun when firing, and ensuring that it did not have to be reset for the next firing
range	the maximum distance that a shell could be propelled, this distance varying according to the type of projectile, e.g. gas, HE, shrapnel, etc.
RAMC	Royal Army Medical Corps
RE	Royal Engineer(s)
RFA	Royal Field Artillery
RFC	Royal Flying Corps
RGA	Royal Garrison Artillery
RHA	Royal Horse Artillery
rounds	shells, when fired in sequence, i.e. '25 rounds to the minute'
Sub	short for 'sub-section', the most basic unit of a British artillery field battery
sucrerie	sugar refinery
'Seventy-Five'	or *soixante-quinze*; renowned French 75mm quick-firing gun, highly effective and extensively used by the French Army during the First World War; it had an advanced recoil system, which meant that it did not have to be re-aimed during firing, and could deliver fifteen rounds per minute on target
Shrapnel	shorthand for 'shrapnel shell', essentially an anti-personnel weapon, designed to explode above the ground, showering lethal projectiles (sometimes called 'bullets') over the forces below; to be contrasted with HE, the shells having different tactical uses; ideally artillery had plentiful access to both, but in the early stages of the war the British had plentiful access to neither; shrapnel is often misleadingly used to refer to the fragments and splinters thrown out by a HE shell
Star lights	'star shells', artillery projectiles used to illuminate the battlefield
Stokes bombs	British trench mortar named after its inventor, Sir Wilfred Stokes
Territorial	a member, or a unit, of the Territorial Force, which was created during the army reforms of 1907 as the main reserve of the regular army; over 300,000 strong, it had

	the same structure as the regular force, its regiments organised into fourteen divisions, commanded by serving major-generals, with small staffs drawn from the regular army
trail handle	the part of the gun carriage resting on the ground when the gun is placed, used to fix its position and alter the direction of fire
traversing wheel	part of the gun mechanism, used to rotate it in a horizontal plane
Uhlan(s)	generic British term for German cavalry, much in evidence at the beginning of the war
VAD	Voluntary Aid Detachment, its members, men and women, provided field nursing to the British Army
Waverley Mixture	one of a number of types of tobacco purchased by the Army Service Corps for sale to the troops
willies	'whistling willies', slang for German shells
Windy	scared, fearful
Worthington	beer brewed by the Worthington Brewery, founded in Burton upon Trent in 1761

British and German artillery mentioned in the text

NB. WRP gives the calibre of German guns in inches, rather than millimetres/centimetres

4.2 (inch)	German 105mm light field howitzer; 'The 4.2 was, in the main, strangely lacking in character. Close acquaintance was nasty – very – but it somehow kept to the open spaces more than the others. It was very popular with the Germans as a "woolly bear" – a high burst with thick yellowish or pinkish smoke, and a lateral burst of Time HE, instead of the nasty whipping forward cone of shrapnel. It was, of course, a swine – everything they hurled at us was that – but a lesser swine' (F.S. Gedye, *An Outline of the War History of the 240th (1st South Midland: Gloucestershire) Brigade R.F.A. (T) (nd)*, 23 (hereafter *240th Brigade*)
4.5 (inch)	British Army field howitzer (QF); had a range of 7,300 yards, and fired gas, HE, incendiary, shrapnel, smoke and star-shell projectiles

4.7 (inch)   British Army field gun (QF); had a range of 10,000 yards, and fired gas, HE and shrapnel projectiles

5.9 (inch)   German 150 mm heavy field howitzer. 'The 5.9 was different [from the 4.2]; very, very different. To every field-gunner the 5.9 must have been a dominating life influence. It was a howitzer, and the quality of the shells – from a purely German standpoint – was superb. Duds were practically unknown, but such was the "five-nine" character that even a dud was effective. There was no feeling of rejoicing when one didn't burst. It was sinister; it rocked the ground and shook your dug-out, and you felt that the next would be doubly appalling' (*240th Brigade*, 23)

6-inch   British Army howitzer (BL); a 26cwt howitzer used in both the First and Second World War; it entered service late in 1915, its range, firepower and mobility making it one of the most important British artillery pieces of the war

8-inch   British Army howitzer (BL), Mk VI, VII, VIII; siege howitzer, fired from mobile carriages and capable of firing a 200lb shell up to 12,300 yards; *or* a German 210mm heavy howitzer

12-inch   British Army howitzer (BL); siege howitzer, the Mk II was introduced to the Western Front in August 1916

15-inch   British Army howitzer (BL); developed late in 1914, and originally operated by Royal Marine Artillery detachments of the Naval Brigade, but later transferred to the British Army, who used it against strong enemy fortifications on the Western Front

18-pounder   British Army field gun (QF); the Mk I was superseded 1915 by the Mk II; it was a 3.3-inch calibre gun with a range of 6,535 yards, and fired gas, HE, incendiary, shrapnel and smoke projectiles

15-pounder   British Army field gun (QF); a 3-inch calibre gun with a range of 6,400 yards, which fired shrapnel projectiles

60-pounder   British Army field gun (BL); a 5-inch calibre gun with a range of between 10,300 and 12,300 yards, firing gas, HE, shrapnel and smoke projectiles

CHRONOLOGY

~ 1914 ~

June	28	Assassination of the Archduke Franz Ferdinand, heir apparent to the Austro-Hungarian throne, in Sarajevo; Austria–Hungary holds Serbia responsible
July	6	Germany communicates support for Austria–Hungary
	23	Austria delivers an ultimatum to Serbia; Serbia appeals to Russia for support
	25	Serbian army mobilises against Austria–Hungary
	28	Austria–Hungary declares war on Serbia and bombs Belgrade; the Tsar orders partial Russian mobilisation
	30	Russia proceeds to general mobilisation
August	1	Germany declares war on Russia; France begins mobilisation
	3	Germany declares war on France; the British Cabinet authorises mobilisation
	4	German army invades Belgium; Britain (and Empire) declare war on Germany
	5	Austria–Hungary declares war on Russia
	6	Kitchener appointed Secretary of State for War
	7	Kitchener appeals for 'the first 100,000' volunteers for the new armies
	15	Russia invades East Prussia
	23	British Expeditionary Force (BEF) engages German army at Mons, Belgium (until 24 August)
	24	Beginnings of the 'retreat from Mons' (which ends at the Marne in early September)
	26	Battle of Le Cateau: BEF II. Corps, led by Smith-Dorrien, delivers a 'stopping blow' to von Kluck's advancing First

Army; Battle of Tannenberg, East Prussia (to 30 August): German victory over Russians

	29	Kitchener's First New Army ('K1') created from first six volunteer divisions
September	2	French government leaves Paris
	6	1st Battle of the Marne (to 10 September): Germans retreat and entrench
	12	1st Battle of the Aisne (to 15 September); beginnings of trench warfare on the Western Front
October	1	1st Battle of Arras (to 4 October)
	4	Beginning of defence of Antwerp by units of the BEF
	10	Fall of Antwerp; BEF moves from the Aisne to Flanders, and engages with the Germans in a series of outflanking manoeuvres commonly known as the 'Race to the Sea'
	19	1st Battle of Ypres, Flanders (to c. 22 November)
	29	Turkey joins the war on the side of the Central Powers
November	29	German offensive at Ypres (to 13 December)
December	10	French offensive in Champagne (to 17 March 1915)
	16	German navy bombards Scarborough and other east coast towns
	25	British and German troops share unofficial Christmas truce on Western Front

~ 1915 ~

January	19–20	First Zeppelin raid on Britain, over East Anglia: four killed and sixteen injured
	28	War Council approves naval attack on Dardanelles
February	4	Germany announces submarine campaign in British waters (begins 18 February)
	19	Anglo-French naval bombardment of Turkish defences at Dardanelles
March	10	BEF attacks at Neuve-Chapelle (to 13 March)
	11	Britain bans all 'neutral' parties from trade with Germany
	18	Naval attempt to force Dardanelles Straits fails, leading to plans for invasion

April	22	2nd Battle of Ypres (to 24 May); first use of gas by Germans, near Ypres
	25	First Gallipoli landings, at Cape Helles and Anzac Cove
	26	Treaty of London, by which Italy joins the Entente
May	7	Sinking of the *Lusitania* off Ireland
	9	Aubers Ridge offensive: British attack impeded by shortage of shells
	14	*The Times'* military correspondent alleges shortage of shells on Western Front
	15	Fisher resigns as First Sea Lord
	17	Asquith visited by Bonar Law: he agrees to form a coalition
	18	Turkish offensive at Anzac Cove (to 24 May)
	23	Italy declares war on Austria–Hungary
	31	First Zeppelin raid on London
June	4	Allies attack on all fronts in Gallipoli
August	6	Allied landings at Suvla Bay in Gallipoli (to 10 August)
September	25	Beginning of the Battle of Loos (until c. 14 October)
October	12	Execution of nurse Edith Cavell by the Germans
	14	Decision taken to replace Hamilton by Monro as Commander-in-Chief, Gallipoli
December	7	Anglo-Indian forces besieged in Kut, Mesopotamia
	18–20	Evacuation of Suvla Bay and Anzac Cove, Gallipoli
	19	Haig replaces French as commander-in-chief on the Western Front

~ 1916 ~

January	8–9	Evacuation of Cape Helles, Gallipoli
	27	Military Service Act introduces conscription of single men age 18 to 41
February	21	Start of German offensive at Verdun (to 18 December)
	25	Germans take Fort Douaumont, Verdun
March	9	Germany declares war on Portugal
April	16	Second Battle of Aisne (to 9 May)
	24	Easter Rising in Dublin (to 1 May)
	30	Fall of Kut
May	3–12	Execution of the leaders of the Easter Rising in Dublin

	25	Second Military Service Act extends conscription to married men
	31	Battle of Jutland, North Sea (to 2 June)
June	5	Lord Kitchener drowns in sinking of HMS *Hampshire*
	24	Beginning of bombardment of German positions on the Somme
July	1	Start of Allied Somme offensive along a 25-mile front (continues to 18 November)
	4	Lloyd George becomes Secretary of State for War
	14	Battle of Bazentin Ridge on Somme (to 17 July)
August	29	Hindenburg appointed Chief of German General Staff in place of Falkenhayn
September	15	Allies take Flers, Martinpuich, Courcelette and High Wood on Somme; tanks used for first time, at Flers-Courcelette
	23	Germans begin construction of the Hindenburg Line
	26	British capture Thiepval
October	1	Beginning of the Battle of Ancre Heights and Transloy Ridge
	24	French retake Fort Douaumont, Verdun
November	13	Battle of the Ancre: British take Beaumont-Hamel
	18	Winter ends Somme offensive: casualties in region of 419,000 for the British, and 204,000 for the French; estimates of German losses vary greatly
December	5	Asquith resigns
	6	Lloyd George becomes premier; forms a coalition government
	18	President Wilson's 'peace note' issued

~ 1917 ~

January	22	Wilson's 'peace without victory' speech to Congress
February	1	Renewed German campaign of unrestricted submarine warfare
	3	USA breaks off diplomatic relations with Germany
	24	British retake Kut
March	8	Beginning of the 'February Revolution' in Russia

	15	Tsar Nicholas II abdicates; beginning of 'Operation Alberich' – the German tactical withdrawal to Hindenburg Line
April	6	America declares war on Germany
	9	Battle of Arras, in support of the Nivelle Offensive (to 17 May)
	29	Mutinies in the French army (to early June) following the failure of the Nivelle Offensive
May	15	Pétain replaces Nivelle as the French commander-in-chief
	26	First American troops arrive in France
July	31	Beginning of the 3rd Battle of Ypres (Passchendaele) (to 6 November)
November	7–8	The 'October Revolution' in Russia
	15	Clemenceau becomes premier in France
	20	British tanks attack in force at Cambrai (to 7 December)
December	9	British take Jerusalem, Palestine
	16	Armistice on the Eastern Front

~ 1918 ~

January	8	Wilson's programme for peace, or '14 Points', announced
March	3	Treaty of Brest-Litovsk between Germany and Bolshevik Russia
April	9	Beginning of the German Lys Offensive
	12	Haig's 'backs to the wall' order of the day
	14	Foch appointed Allied commander-in-chief on Western Front
May	27	3rd Battle of the Aisne: Germans reach the Marne (to 5 July)
June	3	German offensive on the Aisne halted at Château-Thierry and Belleau Wood
July	20	Beginning of the German retreat on the Marne
August	8	Allied counter-offensive in Amiens (to 15 August) triggers German collapse: Ludendorff's 'black day of the German army'

September	29	Allies cross the St Quentin canal on the Hindenburg Line
October	4	Germany and Austria–Hungary seek an armistice with American government
	5	Main Hindenburg Line positions taken by Allied armies
	30	Turkish government signs armistice of surrender with Allies; German High Seas Fleet mutinies
November	2	Allied Sambre offensive on Western Front (to 11 November)
	3	Austria–Hungary signs armistice with Allies
	5	Allied Supreme War Council accepts the terms of German armistice
	8	Foch receives German armistice delegates
	9	Kaiser flees to Holland, and abdicates; republic proclaimed in Berlin
	11	German delegation signs armistice of surrender; armistice on all fronts
December	14	Wilson arrives in Paris; Lloyd George coalition wins general election

~ 1919 ~

January	18	Peace Conference opens in Paris
June	21	German High Seas Fleet scuttled at Scapa Flow
	28	Treaty of Versailles signed by Germany and the Allies

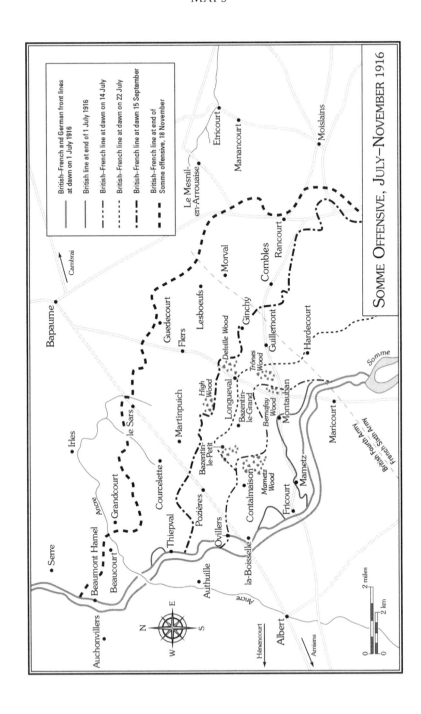

SOMME OFFENSIVE, JULY–NOVEMBER 1916

British–French and German front lines at dawn on 1 July 1916

British line at end of 1 July 1916

British–French line at dawn on 14 July

British–French line at dawn on 22 July

British–French line at dawn 15 September

British–French line at end of Somme offensive, 18 November

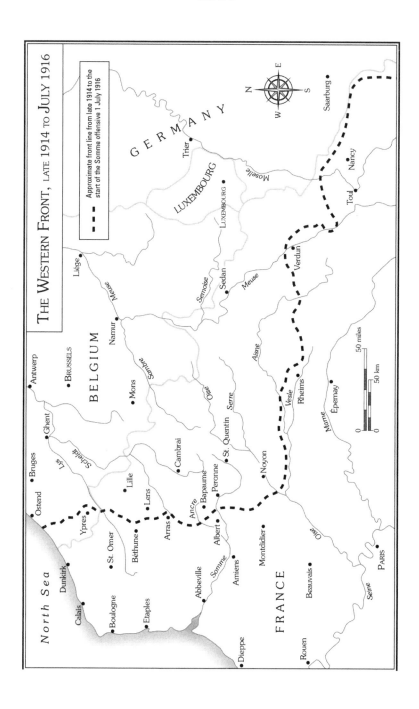

THE WESTERN FRONT, LATE 1914 TO JULY 1916

- - - Approximate front line from late 1914 to the
start of the Somme offensive 1 July 1916

179

NOTES

[17]   *I remembered while at school being told that the Boer War would be over by Christmas.*

The Boer War, or Second South African War (1899–1902), was fought between the Boers, descendants of the Dutch who first settled in the Cape colony in the seventeenth century, and British imperial forces whose presence was increasingly felt in the region during the nineteenth century. Hostilities began with the Boer declaration of war on 11 October 1899, following several years of tension; the Boers proved much tougher opponents than the British had expected, and although the war was eventually won by the British, the tide was slow to turn, and the methods used to end it controversial.

[17]   *I wandered off on that day of August 4, 1914 into the county town [Gloucester] with a vague idea of joining the Artillery of which one Battery, the Third or 'C' Battery of the County Territorial Royal Field Artillery Brigade, had its headquarters at the Barracks there.*

The Gloucester-based 3rd (C) Battery of the 1st South Midland Brigade, a Territorial Brigade of the Royal Field Artillery (RFA).

[18]   *later moving to Crown Hill under canvas.*

Crownhill Fort was one of a number of forts and batteries built in the 1860s to protect the naval base at Plymouth: situated on the summit of a ridge overlooking the town, it dominated the approach to the Royal Navy dockyard there. During the First World War it was used, among other things, as a staging post for troops bound overseas: 'When we later moved to Crownhill the men of the Brigade began to throw off the spirit of a long camp and to realise that it was to be more than a 14-day job' (*240th Brigade*, 4).

[19]   *It did occur to me, however, on the way back to camp, that the Kaiser had said most definitely that God was, indeed had always been, on the side of the German Nation, but I noted that neither he nor our preacher had produced any definite evidence.*

Wilhelm II (1859–1941) of Prussia, *né* Prince Friedrich Wilhelm Albert Viktor, German Emperor and King of Prussia 1888–1918; abdicated 9 November 1918 and fled into exile in the Netherlands, where he died. Referring to German atrocities in Belgium in August 1914 a *Times* editorial averred: '[The Kaiser] could stop these things with a word. Instead, he pronounces impious benedictions upon them. Daily he appeals for the blessing of God upon the dreadful deeds which are staining the face of Western Europe' ('The March of the Huns', *The Times*, 29 August 1914, 9). Douglas Haig's information officer, Brigadier-General John Charteris, later recalled: 'Our French friends are fond of telling a story attributed to a highly placed Roman Catholic cleric in Paris who said, "I am telling my people that undoubtedly God is on their side; my revered brother of Cologne is telling his people the same thing at the same time, only *le bon Dieu* knows which of us is lying!"' (Brigadier-General John Charteris (1877–1946), *At G.H.Q.* (London, 1931), 262).

[19]   *I had not then discovered that any organized rationalist thought existed.*

Perhaps an allusion to the work of the Rationalist Association in Britain, which was founded by the radical publisher Charles Watts in 1885 as the Rationalist Press Association; it published works of science and free thought, as well as critiques of organised religion, all aspects of human inquiry in which WRP had a natural interest.

[20]   *I bought a pocket edition of Major Straubenzee's 'Manual of Artillery Drill and Procedure'.*

No book of this exact title can be found on library catalogues: perhaps a reference to Major-General Sir Casimir Cartwright van Straubenzee and Norman Goldsmith's *Notes on gunnery for the assistance of the officers and permanent staff of the territorial artillery* (Woolwich, 1913). Straubenzee (1867–1956) was a Canadian officer who served in the British Army, and was an instructor at the School of Gunnery, 1909–12, and Chief Instructor RH and RFA, 1914–15.

[20]   *Our guns were 15-pounders. We were pleased with them, knowing no better, though somewhat daunted when we heard that they had been through the Boer War.*

'[…] the Brigade was still [i.e. April 1915] equipped with 15-pounder guns which had outlived their effectiveness. Modern conditions necessitated an accuracy of fire [of] which the 15 pounder was incapable' (*240th Brigade*, 7).

[22]   *Taking up position practice was, however, our chief exercise on our bi-weekly days on Roborough Common.*

Roborough Down in Devon, now within the Dartmoor National Park.

[22]   *From what we could learn, however, it seemed that open action days had finished after Mons, and that henceforth static action would be the order of the day, and indeed it was so.*

For the British, 'open action days' of mobile warfare began with Mons, 23 August, and continued during the retreat to the Marne, which was reached at the beginning of September; there followed Joffre's famous counter-offensive, beginning 6 September, which led to the First Battle of the Aisne, *c.* 12–15 September, following which both sides began entrenching, eventually bringing about stasis on the Western Front.

[24]   *The First Battle of Ypres had not altered the general course of the front lines*

In a series of battles collectively known as First Ypres, 19 October–22 November 1914, the British, French and Belgians resisted German efforts to reach the Channel ports and take the strategically important town of Ypres. British losses were heavy, and the BEF action there has been described as its 'chief glory', but also the reason why it 'practically ceased to exist' (C.R.M.F. Cruttwell, *History of the Great War* (Oxford, 1934), 106 (hereafter Cruttwell)).

[25]   *We hardly knew the word camouflage in those days and our efforts in that direction were limited to sticking a few branches in the ground in front of the guns.*

The word *camouflage* is borrowed from the French. In its military sense it came into use during the First World War, and began to appear in *The Times* early in May 1917, although it was certainly in use before that date: a war diary of the 7th Battalion of the Bedfordshire Regiment refers to 'methods of French confluage [i.e. camouflage]' in August 1915 (OED).

[25]   *We had now given up our Territorial nomenclature. Our Brigade had become the 240th and we belonged to the 48th Division and were in the 2nd Army, replacing the 4th Division.*

Originally there were three artillery units in the South Midland Division, which was redesignated the 48th (South Midland) Division in 1915; these units were the 1st (Gloucestershire) Brigade, the 2nd (Worcestershire) Brigade, and the 3rd (Warwickshire) Brigade. When reorganised they lost their Territorial designation 'South Midland' and were renumbered, the 1st Brigade becoming 240th Brigade (Gloucestershire).

[25]   *Unfortunately, we could do very little firing owing to shortage of ammunition, our battery ration being 8 rounds per day.*

The chronic shortage of shells in the British Army, especially of high explosive, in the opening months of 1915 was judged a fatal bar to success at Neuve-Chapelle (10–13 March) and Aubers Ridge (9 May). After the latter attack the Commander-in-Chief, Sir John French, personally briefed *The Times*' military correspondent Charles à Court Repington, whose published report had serious political ramifications. The 'shell shortages scandal' was one of the factors that brought an end to the Liberal government of H.H. Asquith, resulting in a coalition government, and, crucially, the appointment of David Lloyd George to the newly created post of Minister of Munitions.

[26] *It was our first premature, a time shell having burst on firing.*

The implication here is that the time fuse of a shell malfunctioned, causing it to explode prematurely over friendly troops.

[26] *They were heavy and unwieldy guns in spite of their small size, and we daily longed and enquired for the new 18-pounders which were promised and plied our officers with questions about them.*

Such was the feeling in the brigade about the unsuitability of the 15-pounder guns to the task at hand that one of its officers, Lieutenant E.L. Gedye, wrote home and engaged the support of a local MP, Sir William Howell Davies. Davies subsequently gained an interview with Lloyd George, now installed as Minister of Munitions. The effect of this is unclear, but nevertheless the problem was quickly solved: 'Within a very few weeks, all of the 15-pounders in action in France and Flanders were withdrawn and 18-pounders issued' (*240th Brigade*, 8). The 240th Brigade got their new guns – the Mk II model – at Thièvres in the third week of July 1915.

[28] *On April 22 we aroused to find our eyes smarting and stinging. Of course we knew what it was, in view of the Germans' first use of gas recently at Ypres.*

WRP's chronology is slightly askew here: the first use of gas by the Germans at Ypres was *on* 22 April, during the Battle of Gravenstafel Ridge: around 17.00 hours they released chlorine gas against the front line around Langemarck, which was held by the French 45th (Algerian) Division; the gas attack was followed by an infantry advance.

[28] *Authority could not have been much impressed, or we would not now have been completely without protection.*

The British and French forces in and around Ypres had some foreknowledge of the possibility of a gas attack by the Germans opposite them, but the true nature of the threat was not understood, and the information was consequently disregarded: 'At that date no British officer believed that the enemy's leaders would deliberately depart from the usages of civilized warfare' (James E. Edmonds, *History of the Great War Based on Official Documents … Military Operations France and Belgium, 1915 (vol. 1)* (London, 1927), 163–6, and nn.)

[28] *In due course thick flannel hoods with talc eye spaces, soaked in some solution, were issued.*

Early gas masks were improvised, and the 240th Brigade experienced an ad hoc design that took advantage of the plentiful supply of crepe in haberdashery shops in Belgium and northern France: 'the earliest gas masks [took] the form of respirators of cotton wool covered with crepe, which were placed over the nose and mouth and tied behind the head' (*240th Brigade*, 7). Later on, masks were supplied with mouth pads soaked in a chemical that would absorb the chlorine gas, and later still, full-length head masks, made of a chemical-absorbing fabric, were supplied. In 1916 these were superseded by the canister gas mask.

[30]   *We were, henceforth, to be in the Third Army.*

Formed in France 13 July 1915.

[37]   *The noise of firing inside the confined space of the gun-chamber was pretty bad, but we found it bearable provided we never stood immediately behind the gun. Sometimes a man would go temporarily deaf. I had luckily provided myself with a pair of Mallock-Armstrong ear-defenders, which, screwed into the ears, completely deadened the shock whilst enabling one to hear orders clearly. Eventually rubber ones were issued to all gunners.*

The heavy use of artillery during the First World War necessitated ear protection to prevent temporary or permanent deafness among gun crews, and the Mallock-Armstrong ear defenders were state of the art, their makers claiming that 'ordinary sounds and conversations [are] heard as usual. Gunfire and shell bursts rendered harmless'. The *British Medical Journal* ran tests in January 1915, however, and concluded that cheaper plastic ear defenders were actually more effective (Science Museum, London, 'History of Medicine' website: www.sciencemuseum.org.uk).

[38]   *Somehow the conversation got onto the subject of Free Trade, and I held forth rather ignorantly in its favour.*

One of the dominant debates in Edwardian politics was over the merits of Free Trade versus Tariff Reform, the former policy solidly backed by the Liberal Party, and the latter policy supported by a majority of, but by no means all, Conservatives (or Unionists, as they were then also called). Free Traders opposed the imposition of duties on imports of manufactured goods and foodstuffs, which were demanded by the Tariff Reformers, who were led by the maverick and influential Joseph Chamberlain. Chamberlain hoped by this policy to defend British manufacturing, while also strengthening the ties of Empire, by offering preferential rates to the colonies and dominions. In July 1903 the Tariff Reform League and the Free Food League came into being, each seeking to sway opinion in advance of the next general election: when held, in January–February 1906, Free Trade helped secure a landslide victory for the Liberals.

[39]   *Hébuterne had been taken by the French in June at the cost of several thousand men.*

In October 1914 the German army had taken Gommecourt, on the Somme, but had failed in its efforts to take nearby Foncquevillers and Hébuterne, to the north-west and south-west respectively, and these villages remained in Allied hands. During the Second Battle of Artois, 9 May–18 June 1915, units of the French Second Army, under the command of Général de Castelnau, attempted to drive the Germans back from their positions east of Hébuterne. Although they gained ground in a series of costly engagements, 7–13 June, they failed to secure the hamlet of Serre, one of their principal objectives; around 2,000 French officers and men were killed, and another 9,000 were wounded or missing.

[40]   *I picked up a German letter encrusted with mud, but I could read it. It was a pretty fancy little sheet of notepaper printed at the top with blue doves and the words 'Aus Liebe'. I prepared to have my heart wrung and was not disappointed, 'Your friend Adler has been wounded in the head and Ernst is dead.' 'Am letzten Sontag war Ich in Waltershausen, das war schoen, Viel schoener wurde es gewesen wenn Du auch konnen Urteil nehmen. Wie lange kann der traurige Krieg lange dauern. Deine treue Anna'.*

Aus Liebe means 'with love'. The correct spelling of the main text is: *Am letzten Sonntag war ich in Waltershausen. Das war schön. Viel schöner wäre es gewesen, wenn auch Du hättest Anteil nehmen können. Wie lange kann der traurige Krieg noch dauern? Deine treue Anna.* This translates as: 'Last Sunday I was in Waltershausen, which was nice. But it could have been much nicer, if you had been there as well. How long will this sad war last? Faithfully yours, Anna.'

[40]   *After the first month in France the order had come that all cameras were to be handed in. It was sent home, but in due course my faithful factotum, on my instructions, returned it to me in one of her food tins, and I carried on, but with much circumspection.*

WRP's faithful factotum was Anna Maria Philips, his unmarried maternal aunt. Anna's older sister, Caroline Trevelyan, lived in London, where there lived also another aunt, his father's unmarried sister Edith Price.

[41]   *All the batteries on this front are firing, the Territorial 18-pounders and 4.5-inch howitzers, the Regular 4.5-inch long barrelled gun, replacing the 60-pounder, and the Kitchener's 6-inch howitzers.*

i.e. the 6-inch howitzers were operated by gun crews from one of Kitchener's New Armies.

[42]   *It is a comical fact that it was not until 45 years later that I took the trouble to look up and see what happened on 23 September 1915. It was start of the Battle of Loos.*

The Battle of Loos (25 September to 14 October 1915) took place *c.* 60 miles north-east of the 240th Brigade's position at Colincamps, and WRP must here be describing a supporting Somme bombardment during the Champagne-Loos-Artois offensive.

[45]   *As time went on the condition of the men's feet became chronic, the ordinary issue ankle-boots being quite inadequate under these conditions. I had a good pair of field boots made by Manfield, and when these were worn out, I just ordered another pair.*

The bootmakers Manfield, who had stores in Piccadilly and New Bond Street, and branches through the United Kingdom, advertised their 'officers' war boots' in the early months of the war. Their regulation army field boot, a calf-length boot in brown grain hide, sold for 84/- in March 1915, nearly £400 by 2016 reckoning.

[46]   *I used to fear sometimes that, in this existence rather than life, my mind would atrophy through lack of stimulus, but I contrived to maintain myself on the 'Weekly Times'.*

After the declaration of war in August 1914, *The Times* began producing a separate weekly supplement of war news and analysis, augmenting the reports that appeared in its daily editions. Every thirteen successive instalments of the *Weekly Times* were intended to be bound in covers especially manufactured by *The Times* and available 'at all good booksellers'. In 1921 the *Weekly Times* was republished in twenty-two large volumes as *The Times History of the War* (1914–21), running to a total of 11,000 pages and 6 million words, including thousands of photographs, illustrations and maps.

[46]   *and 'The Nation', the latter, under the editorship of Massingham, proving a depressing influence with which I failed to disagree. The time came when Massingham's office was raided by the Censors, unsuccessfully, for supposed incriminating evidence, the only result being that the paper was ordered not to send itself abroad in future.*

In 1907 the radical paper *The Speaker*, which represented the anti-imperialist wing of the Liberal Party, was renamed *The Nation* and placed under the editorship of Henry William Massingham (1860–1924). The journal was greeted as the authoritative voice of the Liberal Party, but Massingham's 'declared aspiration … was not so much to support the Liberal government as to interrogate it' (H.W. Nevinson, 'Massingham, Henry William (1860–1924)', rev. A.J.A. Morris, ODNB). Massingham had been critical of the government's pre-war foreign policy, but nevertheless supported the declaration of war on 4 August. Thereafter *The Nation* gravitated from unenthusiastic support to open criticism, and in April 1917 the government informed Massingham that no copies of the paper were to be sent abroad, on the alleged grounds that its war reporting was 'of a nature to help the enemy' and had been 'widely used for propagandist purposes' (Chancellor of the Exchequer answering a question in the House of Commons, Tuesday 17 April 1917, in *The Times*, 18 April 1917, 12). The restriction was lifted in October 1917 after protests. The censor undoubtedly watched *The Nation* during the war, but WRP's report that the paper's offices were raided may be apocryphal. In 1921 *The Nation* merged with the *Athenaeum*, and in 1931 that journal merged with *The New Statesman*.

[46]   *No politics were discussed, and of course all knowledge and opinions emanated from the 'Daily Mail'. It has been said that this war was very much 'run by newspapers'.*

The dominant figure in newspapers in this era was Arthur Charles Harmsworth (1865–1922), created Baron Northcliffe 1905, and Viscount 1917. Northcliffe was proprietor of the *Daily Mail* from 1896, and of *The Times* from 1908, and owned other papers besides. He was independent, and was a strong critic of any government, but leaned towards the Unionist Party (Conservatives), and was influential in the process by which the Liberal Prime Minister H.H. Asquith was replaced by Lloyd George (also Liberal) in December 1916. Northcliffe had long warned of the threat posed by Germany to Britain and its Empire, and he sought the most vigorous prosecution of the war once it had started.

[47]   *I would doubtless still feel oppressed by the same hopelessness now, had it not been for a fantastic event which took place thirty years later.*

WRP must mean the birth of the United Nations, which was established 24 October 1945, replacing the defunct and ineffectual League of Nations.

[51]   *He always sang while he worked, and our winter lines were always associated in my mind with his then favourite, which he sang quietly over and over again. It was in its words ruthless and scandalous and was called 'Again, Again and Again'. It included the lines:*

And when I was single my pockets did jingle,
And I wish I was single again.

We would have felt awkward about it, had we not known that he was a devoted husband and father.

There are various versions of this song in circulation, but they have a common theme: a man laments his married status, wishes he were single, and is given his wish: 'My wife she died, / I laughed and I cried, / To think I was single again, again, / To think I was single again'. He then remarries, only to find that his second wife is worse than the first: 'And I wished I was single again, again'. The lyrics could be transposed to switch genders (i.e. 'My husband he died' etc.).

[51]   *Our undoubted favourite throughout – that is during the time when we sang, for the time came when we no longer did so – was 'Fred Karno's Army'.*

Fred Karno (real name Frederick John Westcott, 1866–1941) was a highly successful British music hall comedian, credited with being an originator of slapstick. He employed a troupe of comedians – 'Fred Karno's Army' – who performed his gags during short sets on music hall bills. Among his 'recruits' were Charles ('Charlie') Chaplin, Stan Jefferson (Laurel of Laurel and Hardy), Will Hay and Max Miller. 'Fred Karno's army' became shorthand for any chaotic organisation, and during the First World War it was immortalised in the lyrics of a British Army song sung to the tune of the popular hymn *The Church's One Foundation*.

[51]   *Hoch, hoch, mein Gott*

'Praise, praise the Lord' / 'Praise, praise my God'.

[53]   *The Wandering Gun was a scheme to deceive the Germans as to the positions of our batteries and the numbers of them. Apparently it is possible to fix the direction of approaching shells.*

Both sides developed the science of detecting enemy batteries during the war, the British pioneering sound-ranging techniques, but these relied on identifying the location of a gun, rather than the trajectory of the shell as it travelled through the air.

[57]   *Start thinking about what to think about, 'Henry Esmond', the war, food.*

'Henry Esmond' is W.M. Thackeray's historical novel *The History of Henry Esmond, Esquire*, first published 1852. Regarded by some critics and readers as his best work, better even than *Vanity Fair*, it established his fame as a historical novelist.

[59]   *We lay about. I had carried Vol. I of a small edition of 'Gibbon' in my haversack since leaving England, and now started on it for the first time when I could get away to a quiet place.*

Historian Edward Gibbon (1737–94) was made famous by his monumental and magisterial *The History of the Decline and Fall of the Roman Empire* (6 vols, London, 1776–88); a small format edition had been published in the World's Classics series 1903–06.

59]   *Gore was a young man and good tempered and tactful with everyone, treating us when off duty all alike and as pals; moreover, he was intelligent and could talk; he was a Godsend. He knew his drill and worked quickly. His job in civilian life had been on the Executive of the L.M.S. Railway.*

The London, Midland and Scottish Railway was established 1 January 1923. Gore worked for the Midland Railway (MR), which centred on the East Midlands, but around the time of the First World War extended as far south-west as Cheltenham, Gloucester, Bristol and Bath.

[62]   *The Somme Offensive was not a British idea. The interest of Britain lay further north in Belgium, where Haig from the beginning of his command wished to concentrate his strength.*

Douglas Haig (1861–1928), created 1st Earl Haig in 1919; became Field Marshal at end of December 1916 (noted in *The Times* 1 Jan. 1917); commander, First Army, 1914–15; commander-in-chief, BEF, 1915–19.

[62]   *Falkenhayn, in spite of his stated belief that there could now be no decisive military decision, concluded that his only route to victory lay in the cracking of the morale of his weakest enemy, namely France, who would give in if only one strong point of famous name could be taken. Such was Verdun, in spite of the fact that there was no strategic advantage to be gained, as a German success here would actually result in a shortened French line.*

Erich Georg Anton von Falkenhayn (1861–1922), Prussian Minister of War, June 1913–January 1915; Chief of the German General Staff, September 1914–August 1916; dismissed 29 August, to be replaced by the more aggressive Hindenburg. Falkenhayn believed that there could be no breakthrough on the Western Front, because of trench warfare, but also that the Central Powers would lose a prolonged war of attrition, not least because of the material advantages of the Allies, who could draw on the immense industrial resources of the United States while exerting – through the Royal Navy's blockade – a stranglehold on supplies reaching Germany. This logic impelled him to seek, if not a breakthrough, then a decisive blow in the West in 1916. He chose to attack the fortress of Verdun because of its military and symbolic value: in this localised war of attrition the French army would be bled to death. In fact, each side lost more than 300,000 men, and the French not that many more than the Germans, during the battle of 21 February–18 December 1916.

[62]   *The other side of the picture, however, was, firstly, that the French armies' casualties, though less than the Germans, were sufficient to set up on their side such a deterioration in will to resist, that only one more slaughter, albeit the smaller one of Nivelle's in 1917, was necessary to reduce them to a state in which, in the words of the historians, 'they could thereafter do no more'.*

French casualties during the Nivelle Offensive, or Second Battle of the Aisne, were exceedingly heavy: there were 134,000 casualties 16–29 April, by far the bulk occurring on the first day of fighting, when Nivelle's strategy unravelled due to the weather, the failure properly to coordinate the infantry advance with the artillery barrage and, above all, the strength and organisation of the German defences. A battle plan that was meant to deliver victory in forty-eight hours petered out in early May, when the offensive was finally abandoned. By this time morale in the French army was broken, and there was mutiny in sixty-eight of its 112 infantry divisions. It would be an exaggeration, though, to say that the army itself was broken, and could 'do no more', as WRP implies here. Nivelle's ignominious disaster led to his replacement as commander-in-chief by Pétain, the hero of Verdun, and the latter restored morale in the army, which played a vital role both in defence and attack on the Western Front in 1918.

[62]   *Secondly, Falkenhayn could afford his casualties, which the Allies could not; German man-power was unlimited and continued so right into 1918.*

This was far from being the case: against the combined weight of Britain, its Empire and France (not to mention the United States, who entered the war in April 1917), Germany had an insufficiency of men, a fact that persuaded Ludendorff of the need for a decisive victory in the west in 1918. With the divisions released from the Eastern Front, he had a superiority of around 10 per cent on the Western Front: 'His real danger would lie in the question of reinforcements … Such serious encroachments had been made on the capital of [German] youth that very few new conscripts could be available in the field before the end of the year. Lack of man-power therefore made it imperative that the "gambler's blow" should be as swift and terrible as possible' (Cruttwell, 489).

[62]   *After Verdun the Western Front and the war itself depended upon the British armies …*

An exaggeration that doubtless reflects a veteran's pride in the British Army: during the great Allied offensive on the Western Front, August–November 1918, which brought the war there to its successful conclusion, the largest army was the French.

[62]   *From 1915 onwards it was always to Britain that her Allies appealed for help. The first appeal came from the Russians in that year, that we should attack the enemy's 'under-belly' at the Dardanelles, and by so doing strengthen the morale of their stalemated armies. As always, we responded, but with forces so inadequate as to lead to a costly failure and the jeopardizing of the Western Front; 'Any further dilution of the military effort was absurd and dangerous.'*

The possibility of a campaign to take the Dardanelles, thereby forcing Turkey out of the war, and relieving both the Russian armies in the east and the Allied armies in the west, was first mooted by Churchill at a meeting of the newly formed War Council 25 November 1914 (M.G. & E. Brock (eds.), *H.H. Asquith, Letters to Venetia Stanley* (1982), 327, letter 222, n. 1). Churchill initially recognised the need for a combined naval and military operation, but he and others subsequently vacillated between that and a purely naval operation. On 28 January the War Council approved his plan for a naval attempt to force the Dardanelles, but a general recognition grew that a substantial military force would be needed, if only to consolidate the navy's gains. After the naval operation was suspended, 18 March, following the loss of three battleships to mines, all hopes were pinned on an armed invasion of the Gallipoli Peninsula. This was launched 25 April, allowing the Turks a month in which to treble their strength on the peninsula. Only at great cost were beachheads established at Cape Helles in the extreme south, and at Anzac Cove 15 miles to the north. Ironically, given the original hopes of a breakthrough, both sides now entrenched, and Gallipoli saw a repetition of the deadlock on the Western Front, with its attendant high casualties. By the time of the Allied withdrawal that winter, more than 140,000 men had died. The quotation is from Alan Clark, *The Donkeys* (London, 1961), 100.

[63]   *In 1917 came an appeal from our third Ally, Italy.*

Italy appealed for military assistance from its Allies following its reverse at the Battle of Caporetto, 24 October–19 November 1917 (see below).

[63]   *The largest Army Britain had ever had, comprising 22 divisions and some three million men, all volunteers, no conscripts having yet arrived, was concentrated round the Somme Salient by the end of June 1916, 'pour encourager les autres'.*

For the opening fortnight of the Somme, twenty-five divisions of the Fourth Army were deployed, but during the whole of the offensive, that is, July to November 1916, there were double this number of divisions involved, including eight territorial divisions, among them the 48th. All of these divisions, however, did not make up 3 million men, and even at its greatest extent the British Army on the Western Front fell considerably short of this figure, there being around 1.3 million men in January 1917 and 1.6 million in January 1918 in total (fighting and non-fighting troops). Nor were they all volunteers, there being still the remnants of the regular BEF involved.

[64]   *We were now in Rawlinson's 4th Army, in which we formed General Hunter-Weston's 8th Corps, which extended actually from our position south to the River Ancre. Our guns covered a sector just north of the river at Beaumont-Hamel.*

The Fourth Army was created by Haig in January 1916, under the command of Sir Henry Rawlinson, and mostly comprised volunteers who had been given their training since the outbreak of war; notwithstanding this, it was given the principal role in the Somme offensive, Haig's major campaign for 1916. WRP's 48th (South Midland) Division was one of four belonging to Lieutenant-General Aylmer Hunter-Weston's VIII Corps, which was charged with capturing the heavily fortified hamlets of Beaumont-Hamel, Beaumont-sur-Ancre and Serre; its ground stopped some way short of the Ancre, which lay within the scope of X Corps. On 1 July 1916, VIII Corps suffered heavy casualties without capturing any of its targets, except for some isolated stretches of the German front line which had to be abandoned soon after their capture. Henry Seymour Rawlinson (1864–1925), KCB 1915, created 1st Baron 1919, commanded IV Corps, and Fourth Army; Commander-in-Chief, Army in India, from 1920.

[65]   *The next day, 24 June, the artillery bombardment of our great offensive was to begin, the date of the actual offensive being 1 July. The bombardment was to last a week, and then the infantry was to 'go over'.*

On Saturday 24 June the Fourth Army began its intense bombardment of the German lines: the bombardment was prolonged after bad weather, which meant that the attack had to be postponed for twenty-four hours, zero hour becoming 07.30 a.m. on Saturday 1 July.

[69]   *July 1st was the fatal day and zero hour was 06.30 hours.*

Zero hour here must refer to the artillery bombardment that day: as WRP implies two sentences later, zero hour for the infantry was 07.30 hours.

[69]   *Reports began to come in. They said that the 31st Division had taken Serre and German third line trenches, but were out of touch.*

The strong German defences in front of the fortified hamlet of Serre withstood the British assault on 1 July. The attack was carried out by units of the 31st Division, which was made up of 'Pals battalions' recruited mostly in Yorkshire; this was its first major action, and it suffered very heavy casualties without securing any of its objectives, although, remarkably, isolated parties did reach Beaumont-Hamel and Serre. The battalions attacking Serre were the 12th (Sheffield), York and Lancaster Regiment, and the 11th (Accrington), East Lancashire Regiment: both were decimated by machine gun fire. One company of the Accrington Pals reached Serre, but contact was lost with them. Of the 720 Accrington Pals who went over the top, 584 were killed, wounded or missing at the end of the day, a casualty rate of more than 80 per cent. Reinforcements from the 13th Battalion (1st Barnsley) and 14th Battalion (2nd Barnsley), York and Lancaster Regiment were also stopped: the latter unit sustained heavy casualties from German artillery and machine gun fire while still in their assembly trench.

[69]   *London Scottish on the left had taken Gommecourt with heavy casualties and had taken 300 prisoners, some of whom we saw walking along the road behind us, the first Germans we had seen.*

The German defenders at Gommecourt also withstood the British attack of 1 July. Immediately to the left of the Fourth Army's VIII Corps was the VII Corps of Allenby's Third Army: it was charged with a diversionary attack on Gommecourt. Its 46th (North Midland) and 56th (1/1st London) territorial divisions sustained nearly 7,000 casualties with no permanent gain. The 1/14th Battalion (London Scottish), 168th (2nd London) Brigade, 56th Division, operating on the right of the line, suffered 616 casualties from its complement of 871 men.

[69]   *Papers from home were all enthusiastic with big headings, 'Battle of Somme Valley' and statements that gains were being consolidated.*

Headlines from *The Times* on 3 July (all p. 8): 'Forward in the West. Start of a Great Attack. Fierce Battles on the Somme. A 25 Mile Front. Strong German Posts Taken. 9,500 Prisoners'; 'British Official Reports. Heavy Enemy Losses Near Fricourt'; 'German Admissions. Withdrawal Both Sides of the Somme'. That day's editorial began: 'The Battle of the Somme. The great offensive in the West has made a good beginning and promises exceedingly well …' (p. 9). On p. 10 there was also: '"The Day Goes Well." Details of the Fighting. Semi-Official Reports. British Headquarters, July 1.'

[70]   *We did not know then that our casualties on 1 July were 60,000.*

British casualties from the first day of the Somme were 57,470 in total, 19,240 dead.

[70]   *Having no guns, the gunners travelled by lorry. Our route was south through Bertrancourt, Acheux-en-Amiénois, Forceville, Hédauville and Bouzincourt to Albert. Enormous quantities of troops were everywhere. Albert was a shambles, the figure of the Virgin on the top of the cathedral hanging over at right angles.*

A statue of the Virgin Mary and infant Jesus, which sat on top of the Basilica of Notre-Dame de Brebières in Albert, was hit by a shell in January 1915: miraculously it did not fall, but instead assumed a near-horizontal position, remaining there until the tower was destroyed by shelling in 1918. The 'Leaning Virgin' became a familiar sight to British soldiers passing through Albert during the Somme offensive. Inevitably, myths attached to it, the British supposedly believing that whoever made the statue fall would lose the war, and the Germans believing the opposite.

[71]   *We learnt that a new Army, the Fifth, had now been formed under Sir Hubert Gough for the purpose of holding and attacking on this left flank of our salient.*

The Fifth Army originated in the Reserve Army that was assembled for the Somme Offensive under the command of Lieutenant-General Hubert de la Poer Gough; the reserve was renamed the Fifth Army in October 1916, and WRP here anticipates that event by several months. Hubert (de la Poer) Gough (1870–1963), KCB 1916; European War, in France and Flanders, 1914–18; commanding Fifth Army 1916–18.

[71]   *News came that the 6th Glosters and Anzacs attacked through gas and liquid fire, the former surrounding the Leipzig Redoubt, and the latter taking Pozières and its crest, thus giving a clear view of Courcelette and Martinpuich. The bombardment continued all day and, at a slow rate, all that night.*

The Leipzig Salient/Redoubt (some sources describe the Redoubt as the west face of the Salient) was a strongly fortified German defensive position that pushed into the British lines opposite the village of Authuille, just south-west of Thiepval. It was taken by the 1/17th Highland Light Infantry, of the 32nd Division, early on 1 July, and remained the only permanent gain in the northern sector of the Somme Offensive until the operations of mid-September. It is unclear which operations WRP describes here involving the 1/6th Battalion, Gloucester Regiment, part of the 144th (Gloucester and Worcester) Brigade of the 48th Division, Reserve Army.

WRP adds here a footnote: 'History records this battle as The Battle of Pozières Ridge and that: "[It] must forever stand as a monument to the pluck, determination and skill of Britain's Imperial Army"': here he quotes Haig, as reproduced in John Terraine, *Douglas Haig* (London, 1990), 234. Pozières was captured on 23 July by units of the 1st Australian Division, part of I Anzac Corps in the Reserve Army. The Germans made supreme efforts to recapture the village, and the Australians suffered heavily in the following days from intense artillery fire, with in excess of 5,000 casualties before being relieved on 27 July.

[73]   *On the 13th we marched to our new position where we took over a six-gun battery from the 12th Division. It was a good position on a steep chalk bank at a junction of the Arras and Bapaume roads near Aveluy, and we called it Crucifix Corner because there was, or had been, a crucifix there.*

There are many instances of junctions being named thus on the Somme, a reflection of the French (and, elsewhere, Belgian) practice of erecting roadside crucifixes: there is a better-known Crucifix Corner just south of High Wood, between Bazentin-le-Petit and Bazentin-le-Grand, while just south of the village of Villers-Bretonneux is the Commonwealth War Graves Commission's Crucifix Corner Cemetery.

[73]   *On the 18th the 7th Warwicks went over near Thiepval and took trenches with the Anzacs and 1,800 prisoners.*

It is unclear which engagement WRP describes here. The 1/5th and 1/6th Battalions, Royal Warwickshire Regiment, part of the 143rd (Warwickshire) Brigade of the 48th Division, captured a fortified position during an attack towards Thiepval, 18 August, taking nearly 600 prisoners, but there is no record of the Anzacs accompanying them.

[77]   *September 3rd was the first day of the Battle of Thiepval.*

The Battle of Thiepval Ridge came later, 26–28 September 1916; 3 September saw the opening of the Fourth Army's offensive against Guillemont (to 6 September), which WRP alludes to below. That battle resulted in the capture of Guillemont on 3 September, and the major portion of Leuze Wood on 6 September, after which further advances stalled in the face of intense German fire from the direction of Ginchy. WRP may here be describing the final stages of the Battle of Pozières Ridge, in which the Australian divisions of I Anzac Corps were again involved.

[78]   *Much has been written about courage, and about fear. The appreciation of the courage which prompts incredible acts of bravery done on the spur of the moment seems nowadays to have become secondary to the appreciation of the capacity to endure. But is passive endurance without prospective alternative necessarily the highest form of bravery? There must be an alternative choice, and passive endurance implies no such alternative. One cannot just walk home out of it, although apparently that is exactly what thousands of French soldiers did nine months later, and later still all the Russians.*

An allusion to the mutinies in the French army following the disastrous Second Battle of the Aisne, 16 April–9 May 1917, which constituted the main action in the Nivelle Offensive. On the Eastern Front the Imperial Russian Army effectively disintegrated that year, against a background of social unrest, political revolution and incipient civil war.

[79]   *He had no time for grumbles, and I remember one occasion when we were hard at it, no doubt to the hindrance of our work, when he came up and said quite calmly, 'Be quiet, and remember this: "Wealth lost, something lost, honour lost, much lost, courage lost, all lost"', and walked away. It was not until years later that I discovered that the words were Goethe's:*

Gut verloren, etwas verloren;
Ehre verloren, viel verloren;
Mut verloren, alles verloren.

An abridged quotation from an untitled poem by the German poet, dramatist and scholar Johann Wolfgang von Goethe (1749–1832). The poem reads in full (followed by a translation):

Gut verloren – etwas verloren!
Mußt rasch dich besinnen
Und neues gewinnen.
Ehre verloren – viel verloren!
Mußt Ruhm gewinnen,
Da werden die Leute sich anders besinnen.
Mut verloren – alles verloren!
Da wär es besser: nicht geboren.

Wealth lost, something lost!
You must quickly make up your mind
And gain new wealth.
Honour lost, much lost!
You must gain glory,
And people will see you differently.
Courage lost – everything lost!
In this case it would have been better never being born.

Source: Johann Wolfgang von Goethe, *Werke*, Berliner Ausgabe, herausgegeben von Siegfried Seidel, Berlin: Aufbau Verlag 1960 ff., Band 2 [Gedichte, Nachlese], S. 369.

[80]   *The next day, 15 September, the Battle opened, the second greatest bombardment since 1 July.*

WRP describes the opening of the Battle of Flers–Courcelette, 15–22 September 1916, which is notable for the first British use of tanks in warfare. Even with the advantages this weapon brought, the attack did not yield the intended breakthrough, but it did result in the capture of the villages of Flers, Courcelette and Martinpuich.

[81]   *With the Major leading and all gunners on limbers and wagons, we sped up a steepish slope, and, passing the celebrated mine crater near non-existent La Boisselle, came onto the main road and dashed along up it.*

The site of an immense mine that was exploded under the German lines just south of La Boisselle at 7.28 a.m. on 1 July. The mine was placed at the end of a tunnel driven from a British trench known as Lochnagar Street, and was dubbed the Lochnagar mine. The resulting Lochnagar Crater, almost 91 metres in diameter and 21 metres deep, is now a war memorial.

[81]   *I have listened to accounts of bombardments in the Second War, accounts by Americans of the bombardments of Tarawa and Guadalcanal, and I can never satisfy myself that these can have exceeded in roar this bombardment of the second Somme Offensive.*

The Battle of Tarawa, 20–23 November 1943, was an engagement in the Pacific Theatre of the Second World War. As a preliminary to an advance on the strategically important Mariana Islands, the Americans first targeted Tarawa Atoll, in the Gilbert Islands; the atoll was heavily defended by the Japanese, who inflicted heavy casualties on the Americans as they effected an amphibious invasion 20 November. In the hours preceding the invasion the enormous US fleet, which included seventeen aircraft carriers and twelve battleships, pounded the atoll from sea and by air. The Guadalcanal Campaign, in the same theatre of war, lasted from 7 August 1942 until 9 February 1943, and involved many independent operations, each a major engagement in its own right: naval gunnery again proved crucial to success, as the Americans inflicted a major strategic and psychological defeat on Japan.

[84]   *Martinpuich, High Wood, Flers, Delville, and Leuze Wood, all passed permanently within the British lines, and the trophies of victory amounted to 5,000 prisoners and a dozen guns. At this stage no less than 21,000 prisoners had been taken by the British and 34,000 by the French since the great series of battles was commenced upon July 1.*

Not so: during the German Spring Offensive, beginning 21 March 1918, the British retreated westwards from these positions, although they were later recovered during the Second Battle of the Somme, 21 August–3 September 1918. The quotation is from Arthur Conan Doyle, *The British Campaign in France and Flanders 1916* (London, 1918), 261–2.

[84]   *[…] the losses of 538,000 troops on the part of the Central Powers compared to 794,000 of the Allied attackers. After this blood-bath a plaintive cry went up, 'No more Sommes!'*
Leon Wolff, *In Flanders Fields* (London, 1958), 4. Wolff's figures are not accepted by historians (see next note).

[84]   *I do not comment. The Censor had to do its work, but equally the truth had to come out, and the longer it was in doing so, the greater the reaction when it did.*

WRP added a footnote here: 'Present day estimates of Somme casualties make them equal on both sides. It seems that reliable figures are unobtainable.' He must have been influenced in this judgement by the discussion in John Terraine, *Douglas Haig: The Educated Soldier* (London, 1963) at pp. 235–6, which notes that the destruction of relevant documents in both German and British archives during the Second World War means that reliable figures are now out of reach. Terraine subscribes to Sir Charles Oman's 1927 conclusion that German losses were 560,000 and the British and French combined 'almost exactly the same' (at p. 236). A.H. Farrar-Hockley, in *The Somme* (London, 1983), comes to much the same conclusion, putting the figure at 600,000 on each side (and a ratio of British to French of 3:1) (at p. 251–3).

[86]   *The troops disposition on this 'Breaking of the Third Line' on our sector of the front.*

During 1916 the Germans reinforced their fortifications on the Somme, constructing a third line of defence; this was almost finished by the time the British offensive began on 1 July.

[86]   *On their immediate right was our 4th Army; first came the Third Corps covering Martinpuich and in High Wood, next on their right the Fifteenth Corps in the trenches opposite Flers, and on its right the Fourteenth Corps joining up with the French on the Somme.*

It has not been possible to check these battle dispositions.

[86]   *What was holding things up on this whole front was the Germans terrific bastion on the extreme left at Thiepval. We had not taken it, and there could be no advance until we had done so. However, on the 21st the Canadians fought down the slope and took Courcelette.*

Courcelette fell to the 2nd Canadian Division on the first day of the battle, 15 September. The village was subsequently destroyed by German artillery.

[91]   *Gradually I became conscious of the roar and of the fact that it was resolving itself out into that of (1) our four guns, (2) our guns behind, (3) the barrage overhead, which we couldn't look at, having no time, but supposed it was there, and (4) a new noise, which most of us had never heard before, the chatter of machine-guns – whose, we did not know.*

WRP surely misremembers here: of autumn 1915, the history of the 240th Brigade reports: 'Although the Brigade casualties were amazingly small prior to the Battle of the Somme, the general atmosphere was not always as healthy as this would suggest. There was always a good deal of machine gunning of the cross-roads in Hébuterne, and "Stuttering Sam", the machine gun which operated in enfilade from the Gommecourt salient, used to throw many a tired bullet during the hours of darkness and maintain a healthy spirit of haste in those whose duty took them along the road. Somewhat ominously, it led to the cemetery as well as to the trenches' (*240th Brigade*, 12).

[92]   *The place proved to be on a crest near Blighty Wood, quite a long way back and facing Thiepval on its south-west side.*

Blighty Wood, just south of the village of Authuille (by which name it was also known).

[95]   *Two days later a Warwick Battery took over and we walked to a position between Sailly and Château de la Haye (Fourth Hébuterne Position), and took over from C.243, joining up with our left section and the left section of C.243 to make six guns.*

C.243 was 'C' Battery of the 243rd Brigade, which had been formed during the reorganisation of the artillery units of the 48th Division in May 1916.

[99]   *ammunition came in panniers on battery horses, each driver leading two, and they dumped the rounds in the valley and we had the endless task of carrying them up to the position in fours in canvas carriers; N.C.O.s carried revolvers to shoot any horse that became bogged.*

The history of the 240th Brigade records that the heavily shelled ground 'had become a glutinous world of mud in which boots were sucked off the feet and to walk across to the guns from the shacks a few yards away became an exhausting effort. The plight of the horses, too, was tragic … Mud-splashed from poll to rump, the tail, belly, neck and legs were absolutely covered with "tags" of mud, which completely hid the matted hair, and, as it dried, rattled as the horse moved. Nothing effective could be done to clean the poor devils on their return from ammunition-running. They stood in lines when resting, in a foot or more of liquid mud, the mud on their coats was bound into the hair and could not be scraped off, and the cold made washing too dangerous, and was forbidden by an Army Order. To walk down the lines at Stables was heartbreaking. Here was unrelievable dumb misery that paralysed by its hopelessness. One looked from one old friend to another, remembered the sleek beauty that was theirs last summer, and could do nothing' (*240th Brigade*, 20).

[101]   *At school I learnt some Greek, but the only words I eventually remembered were* Επεα πτεροεντα.

The Homeric ἔπεα πτερόεντα literally means 'words endowed with wings'. Price misses the accents and 'smooth breathing' on the first epsilon.

[103]   *The war situation at the New Year was that a total of casualties for both sides of 1,800,000 had been sustained, the result being a complete stalemate.*

It is impossible at this distance of time to obtain accurate casualty figures for particular engagements, still less for all participants on a single front (i.e. the Western, as seems to be implied here), and due to the destruction of important records both in British and German archives during the Second World War. But this figure must be a considerable underestimate: losses on the Somme by Germany and the Allies in 1916 are thought to exceed 1,200,000.

[104]   *The traffic in both ways was continuous, and lorries, cars, jeeps and motor bicycles were tearing past at speed, as it was a straight road.*

A slip on WRP's part: the American term 'jeep', used to describe a small, general-purpose (i.e. 'GP', hence 'jeep') military vehicle, did not come into usage until the Second World War.

[105]   *I had suffered in this way only once before; the symptoms were the same, but the cause different. On my expedition in Formosa to climb the 13,000-feet Mount Morrison.*

Known today as Yushan (or Mount Yu, literally 'Jade Mountain'), at 3,952 metres (12,966ft) above sea level the highest mountain in Taiwan.

[105]   *This cold spell was, I believe, universal, and thousands of people, undernourished because of the war, died of cold in Germany and Russia.*

Reuters reported that in Leipzig around 8 February 1917 'the thermometer fell to 50 degrees [F] below freezing point', and that the intense cold in Germany was 'greatly aggravated by the shortage of coal'. The cold affected Eastern Europe, the temperature in the high mountains of northern Romania, where troops were entrenched, averaging 30–45 degrees Fahrenheit below freezing in early February (*The Times*, 10 February 1917, 6; 10 March 1917, 5).

[108]   *The winter seemed endless. Would warmth ever return, or, as the Chinese say, would the dragon never stop eating up the sun? Was spring so very far away still?*

According to ancient Chinese mythology, solar (and lunar) eclipses were caused by a celestial dragon devouring the sun (and moon). WRP perhaps learned of this during his travels in the Far East in 1911. See Foreword, p. 4.

[110]   *'Reculer: pour mieux sauter'.*
The paradoxical 'Retreat to jump further.'

[110]   *We quite understood that he did it in order to straighten out his line and so strengthen it, that is, to retire just here onto the immensely strong second line or Hindenburg Line.*

The Hindenburg Line was the name given by the British to the fortifications along the Lens–Noyon–Rheims front; known as the Siegfried Line to the Germans, it was begun in winter 1916, following the losses at Verdun and the Somme. The strategic withdrawal to this line, Operation Alberich, took place between 9 February and 15 March 1917, Ludendorff's orders being that the Allies should find 'a totally barren land, in which their manoeuvrability was to be critically impaired'.

[110]   *on 29 January the Australians had taken Le Transloy; on 28 February Gommecourt and Puisieux fell.*

British operations around Le Transloy, on the right of the Somme front, 27–28 January, gained ground but the village itself did not fall. Gommecourt was occupied by units of the 31st and 46th Divisions on the night of 27–28 February, and Puisieux fell to the 62nd and 19th divisions on 28 February.

[110]   *On 17 March the Australians took Bapaume, and just before this the 1/6th Warwick battalion of our 48th Division had crossed over the Somme in front of us and passed through the empty, shattered town of Péronne and out into the country beyond.*

On 17 March Australian Light Horse and infantry patrols entered Bapaume. The 48th Division occupied Péronne on 18 March: 'Péronne had been laid to waste – every village behind systematically destroyed – roofs battered, furniture piled up and burnt; every tree-lined road had all the trees felled across it, making it impassable for traffic; cross-roads mined and blown up. Trap bombs caused very heavy casualties until the troops realised that nothing could be touched safely – a footbridge would blow up when crossed, a doorway had a loose wire, which when touched detonated a bomb – and so on. One battalion (6th Gloucesters) H.Q. used the cellar of a house in Tincourt, and many days after the Germans had retired, a time fuse caused the complete wrecking of the cellar, killing practically the whole of the H.Q. staff.' (*240th Brigade*, 25).

[110]   *Péronne was a weird and terrible sight … On a large board high up on a balcony in the Place were written the words, 'Nicht aergern, nur wundern' – Don't be annoyed, just wonder.*

The German should be spelled *Nicht ärgern, nur wundern*: Price's translation is accurate, though literal, and the German idiom here is more subtle than he allows. Alternative translations are 'Don't be shocked/disappointed, just wonder'.

[111]   *We remained in General Rawlinson's 4th Army, having the 1st Australian Corps of Gough's 5th Army on our left, but a special ad hoc force had now been created on the spur of the moment, called General Ward's Flying Column, which consisted mainly of our 48th Division.*

This has not been verified.

[112]   *Sir Philip Gibbs apparently came here five days later and talked to them.*

Philip Gibbs (1877–1962), KBE 1920; author and journalist; a war correspondent with the French and Belgian armies in 1914, and with the British armies in the field 1915–18.

[112]   *They told him they had suffered much from looting, and had had all their stock taken, including poultry, and that all their pretty young girls had been taken away by*

200

drunken soldiers and had not so far returned; they were a tragic community. But incredibly, they also stated that most of the German rank and file were decent men, who said they regretted the misery that was inflicted and were sorry for the people, and who tried to explain that they disliked carrying out such destruction but were compelled to do it by orders. One woman asked a German soldier, 'Why do you go?' He answered, 'Because we hope to escape the new British attacks. The English gun-fire smashed us to death on the Somme. The officers know we cannot stand that horror a second time.' Of course this was not the reason.

WRP quotes from Philip Gibbs, *From Bapaume to Passchendaele 1917* (London, 1918), 78–80, quotation at p. 80. WRP appears to mean that the Germans retreated for strategic reasons, that is, to withdraw behind a better defended line, and not because they were broken. He adds a footnote here citing Terraine's *Douglas Haig*: 'See ... Ludendorff's statement on the Somme Battle that, "our troops would not be able to withstand such attacks indefinitely"' (p. 230).

[113]   *On 3 April America came into the war, but I don't know if we were aware of the fact.*

Actually Friday 6 April 1917, after Congress voted for a declaration of war against Germany; war was formally declared against Austria–Hungary the following day.

[113]   *However, I noticed some little booklets and managed to get one. It was a German 'Outline History of the World'. I glanced through it, and noticed that in their view the American 'War between the States' was waged entirely so that the Northerners should dominate the Continent, and slavery was given [not] as a reason only as an excuse.*

WRP refers to the American Civil War, 1861–65, fought between the Northern (Union) forces and the Southern (Confederacy) states of the USA. The abolitionist (i.e. anti-slavery) cause was an important catalyst in the political tensions that led to the outbreak of war in April 1861.

[114]   *On the 11th 'F' sub went forward with gun to a position in front of Lempire opposite Petit Priel Farm, the gun having to command the road through the village and shoot at tanks or armoured cars, actually at anything that came along.*

The German A7V tank, of which around twenty were built, did not make its appearance on the Western Front until March 1918; WRP *perhaps* means British tanks captured and used by the Germans.

[114]   *The Hindenburg Line, which had been prepared by Ludendorff many months previously as a strong second line of defence, ran roughly between Arras and Soissons, and this was the line we were now up against.*

Erich Ludendorff (1865–1937), Prussian general; chiefly responsible, with Hindenburg, for German military strategy in the latter years of the war.

[114]   *To draw off some of the pressure that was building up against him, thanks to the news of the attack having become public property, our 3rd Army put up the Arras Offensive on 9 April, when by a most gallant and successful attack they took Vimy Ridge, this being beyond the north end of the Hindenburg Line.*

In the Battle of Arras, 9 April–16 May 1917, British and Dominion troops attacked the German defences around the city of Arras. The success of the Canadian Corps in the Battle of Vimy Ridge, 9–12 April, was one of the most remarkable victories achieved by the Allies on the Western Front: the meticulous planning and preparations, overseen by Lieutenant-General Julian Byng and Major-General Arthur Currie, resulted in the capture of the ridge on 10 April, an achievement that had twice eluded the French.

[114]   *The enthusiasm of the troops over this victory was unfortunately somewhat damped by the failure two days later of Gough's 5th Army just south of Arras in its attack on Bullecourt.*

In the First Battle of Bullecourt (south of Arras), 10–11 April, poor communication and leadership exposed the 62nd Division and the Australian 4th Division to heavy losses, with no appreciable gain.

[115]   *On the 16th, Nivelle, in supreme and arrogant confidence made his attack south of the Line in Champagne, and by the second day had advanced two miles with the loss of 120,000 casualties.*

For the Nivelle Offensive, see above.

[115]   *A week later hawthorn and mountain ash were out, willows, sorrel, violets and the true oxlip, so rare in England, taking the place of the primrose, as it does in Essex.*

True oxlip (*Primula elatior*), a woodland plant now rarely found in Britain, but widespread in continental Europe; Price here distinguishes it from 'false oxlip', a naturally occurring hybrid between cowslip and primrose.

[117]   *The result of Nivelle's offensive appeared to have been that on the 3rd of this month entire regiments of infantry decided they had had enough of it and just marched off on their own to Paris, where they demonstrated and then dispersed to their homes. History gives the opinion that the French Army from this moment ceased to be a fighting force; it was fortunate that we did not then know this.*
An overstatement: see above.

[120]   *On the 7th news came of the taking of Messines, a great advance and many prisoners up there.*

WRP refers to the opening of the Battle of Messines, 7–14 June 1917, which aimed to capture the Messines Ridge south of Ypres in advance of the main operations there weeks later (Third Ypres). The battle began at 03.10 hours on 7 June with the detonation of 450 tons of explosives in tunnels under the German lines. The massive explosion devastated the ridge line and was clearly audible in London, so was certainly heard by WRP in France. The tunnels had been eighteen months in the making, and were the key to an astonishing success on the part of General Herbert Plumer's Second Army, which secured its objectives in the first day of the battle with relatively few casualties. Further ground was gained in the repulsing of German counter-attacks, and by 14 June the whole of the Messines salient was under British control.

[122]   *The mild-mannered British did a few camp chores and indulged in games on the shore, well organized by a jolly gym instructor. He introduced us to the game 'Fox and Geese'.*

A game of tag; not to be confused with – though perhaps similar in tactics to – the traditional board game for two players, in which one player assumes the role of the fox and tries to eat the geese, while the other tries to trap the fox.

[122]   *I always remembered Lena Ashwell's Concert Party, who gave two concerts in a big tent. They gave us good music and songs, and for once there was an absence of the everlasting comic and lewd.*

Lena Ashwell (real name Lena Margaret Simson née Pocock, 1872–1957) was an actress and theatre manager. A strong believer in the educative and emotional value of theatre, she organised an enormous number of concerts for the troops in France, and as far afield as Egypt, during the First World War. By the Armistice there were as many as twenty of her companies performing in France, and she was appointed OBE in 1917 for this work. Her concerts were deliberately high-brow, including songs, short plays and recitations of Shakespeare.

[122]   *Every evening our little party, and we were a happy little party liking each other, would walk into the town and go to a small hotel called Hôtel la Colonne de Bronze, which fortunately had not been discovered by too many, and where we could have a nice table with cloth in a quiet room and actually eat with a knife and fork.*

A hotel of the same name exists in Saint-Valéry-sur-Somme today.

[122]   *There was a monument in the main street commemorating the fact that William I, the Conqueror, sailed from here to conquer England. I think some of the men on reading this became partly unbelieving or partly angry.*

William I ('William the Conqueror') (1027/28–87) assembled his ships and men for the invasion of England at Saint-Valéry-sur-Somme, crossing the Channel on the night of 27–28 September 1066, reaching Pevensey in East Sussex before dawn.

[123]   *There were no signs that man had ever occupied the place in all this desolate valley, no sign of his belongings, houses, fields, roads, crops, the vegetation being a riot of weeds. One*

weed I had never seen before, a dark blue round spidery flower head. I thought I knew all the weed names, but this plant I had never seen before. I sent a specimen to a botanist friend at home; it passed the Censor, and the reply was, it was Muscari comosum.

Muscari comosum (syn. *Leopoldia comosa*), commonly known as the tassel (or tassel grape) hyacinth; a perennial bulbous plant native to West Asia, North Africa and South-East Europe, but also growing elsewhere; often found in cultivated ground such as cornfields and vineyards.

[124]   *The Stoics in the third century B.C., with their assertion of the equality and brotherhood of man, made a valiant effort in this direction, but with their decline the emphasis to the present day seems to have been all in the opposite direction, towards defensive alliances, armaments and tariffs. If the Stoics had not been so soon submerged humanity might by now have learnt how to live peacefully together like rational beings.*

The Stoics were followers of the school of philosophy founded by Zeno of Citium c. 300 BC (who gave his discourses at the *Stoa Poikile* or Painted Porch in Athens, hence the name), and which flourished in Greece and Rome over nearly five centuries, before declining with the fall of the Roman Empire. The Stoics stressed self-sufficiency and equanimity in the face of adversity; they also held that reason is the governing principle of nature.

[124]   *We continued eastwards and came to the 'Devil's Wood'. It was a stinking, awful place of dead, shattered trees, with deep, narrow trenches everywhere. We scrambled along some of these, and all the time we passed wooden crosses with long lists of names, messages and pathetic poems of farewell pencilled upon them. We could not stand it and came back.*

WRP refers to Delville Wood near Longueval, the scene of prolonged fighting from mid-July to early September 1916, when the Germans were finally driven out: 'Its capture devoured six divisions' (Cruttwell, 270).

[125]   *Field Marshal Haig desired an attack in Flanders as early as January, 1916, and in May, 1917 he made his definite plan for it, and, after much trouble to get over the strong opposition of Lloyd George, started preparations for it for a date in July.*

David Lloyd George (1863–1945), Viscount, 1945; Liberal statesman; president of the Board of Trade, 1905–08; chancellor of the exchequer, 1908–15; minister of munitions, 1915–16; secretary for war, 1916; prime minister, 1916–22. In popular parlance, 'the man who won the war.' He is blamed in some quarters for not exercising more control over the generals, Haig in particular, and thus for not preventing the disaster of Passchendaele; the disastrous outcome of that battle was as he had feared, and he subsequently had particularly bad relations with Haig.

[126]   *Portugal had kindly come into the war recently. We wished they had not bothered.*

In fact Portugal had entered the war in early 1916 following the German declaration of war against it, 9 March.

[126]   *However on this day our efficient battery clerk, Bombardier Willis, came to me and said that I had the equivalent of £30 owing me, and wouldn't I like to draw it before somebody else did, or words to that effect.*

A large sum in arrears, the equivalent to £1,877.30 in 2016.

[127]   *In these days we think of armies 'breaking through' and continuing in victorious advance without pause for days and weeks, as happened in the second war. The extraordinary thing is that military leaders in 1914 apparently thought along the same lines; they apparently thought that men and horses could go on and on and on, as motor lorries go on and on. It was because living things are not machines that the Germans were held up at the Marne.*

The headlong retreat of the BEF and French left wing during August 1914 was arrested south of the Marne at the beginning of September, and at 22.00 hours on 4 September Joffre issued his famous 'Instruction no. 6': '[the] time has come to profit by adventurous position of German First Army and concentrate against that Army all efforts of Allied Armies of extreme left.' On 6 September began the counter-offensive that drove the German armies back towards the Aisne.

[128]   *The next day we passed along pretty by-lanes towards Cassel Hill, that extraordinary mountain visible for miles.*

WRP refers to Mont Cassel, a prominent hill in the Nord *département* of France; it overlooks French Flanders, standing 176 metres above sea level at its highest point.

[128]   *During a pause, as I lay on the grass, I looked up and saw a little, old brick or stone shrine by the roadway, a little thing with a small image in its cavity. On it were written in old lettering the following words:*

Indienst Gott.
In Sturm, Waeter, Donder und Fyr
Fur Drei Hunderd Jaeren
Bin Ich Noch Hier.

The lines rang in my head and still do even now. It had survived.

The correct spelling is: *Im Dienste Gottes, / In Sturm, Wasser, Donner und Feuer, / In dreihundert Jahren / Bin ich noch hier.* This translates as: 'Serving the Lord, / In storm, water, thunder and fire, / Even in three hundred years / I will be here.'

[130]   *Heavy work ammunition running. On most nights we had some 2,000 rounds in boxes to unload from a Decauville train a hundred yards away.*

Decauville railways, named after the manufacturing company founded by the French engineer Paul Decauville (1846–1922), utilised ready-made sections of light, narrow-gauge tracks which could be easily transported and assembled. Originally used in agriculture and for industrial purposes, the system was adapted by the French government for army use, and during the First World War the French and British relied on it heavily for front-line transportation.

[130]   *One quiet day I explored a short distance on this flank, and came to a minute pond, which actually had not been disturbed by any shell. It was a peaceful little place, full of water beetles, and water-boatmen, and water buttercups. I made a sketch of it. A few days later, after much shelling, I went there again. A shell had fallen right into it and it had just become a shell hole of mud and water: destruction* ueber alles.

WRP employs, with ironic intent, the key phrase in the *Deutschlandlied* (Germany Song), *Deutschland über Alles* or 'Germany beyond/above everything else', a phrase that can be read either as a call for sacrifice for the Fatherland, or (less charitably) a chauvinistic statement of national superiority.

[131]   *On 17 July we heard that Zero Hour would be on the 29th.*

In fact, zero hour was postponed due to bad weather: it became 03.50 hours on 31 July.

[131]   *Somewhere a shell caught them and Sergeant Gore and Gunners Havens, Bevan and a D.A.C. gunner all wounded. They got to a dressing station somehow and were sent back, but the Sergeant developed shell-shock and went to the rear.'*

Shell shock began to be understood during the war: it was mentioned as a case study in an article in the *British Medical Journal* as early as 30 January 1915 (192/2) (OED), and was reported in *The Times* as early as 15 February 1916 ('Officer's Suicide After Shell Shock', 5).

[133]   *Consequently, the country which Haig had chosen for his greatest of all offensives was an area where trenches of whatever depth would fill with water in wet weather and soil which, in spite of duds, would be churned up into mountains of loose, slimy, waterlogged earth by the terrific bombardments that was now going on, a bombardment which was to entail on our part the firing into this bog of an estimated 4¼ million shells.*

'In country as flat as the Somerset flats, it was impossible to sleep in dug-outs – a 6ft dug-out would have a foot or more of water in 24 hours' (*240th Brigade*, 28). The ten-day bombardment before Third Ypres 'destroyed all the surface drainage and created not merely the usual crater-field but an irremediable slough. British Headquarters had been warned of such a result by the Belgians, but obstinately disregarded the local knowledge born of long experience' (Cruttwell, 440).

[133]   *Another important piece of information which the Army's meteorological department supplied, was that on the first day of every August, with the regularity of a tropical monsoon, in this bog district of Ypres the weather always broke on this date, and had never been known to fail to do so.*

Brigadier-General John Charteris, Haig's chief intelligence officer, would speak after the war of the weather breaking in Flanders in August "with the regularity of the Indian monsoon", a notion that GHQ's official meteorologist later dismissed as "too ridiculous to need formal refutation" (Terraine, *Educated Soldier*, 348). Regardless of this detail, the weather that August proved 'exceptionally unkind', the rainfall being more than twice the average: 6.76 against 2.80 inches (Cruttwell, 440, n. 1). GHQ had clearly been worried about the weather in advance, and knew that the likely forecast would not be good. Charteris wrote of the preparations for Third Ypres: 'My one fear is the weather. We have had most carefully prepared statistics of previous years – there are records of eighty years to refer to – and I do not think that we can hope for more than a fortnight, or at best, three weeks of really fine weather' (Terraine, *Educated Soldier*, 343). Despite collecting eighty years' of weather statistics, and receiving from Tank Corps Headquarters (until it was ordered to desist) a daily 'swamp map', in which the colour blue was 'used to denote the bogs created by the destruction of the drainage dykes', GHQ remained ignorant of the condition of the battlefield. Of this remarkable fact, John Terraine, in his biography of Haig, observes: 'the hard fact remains that the full import of ground conditions did not sink in, either at Fifth Army Headquarters, or at GHQ' (342). How this was possible Terraine does not satisfactorily answer. 'The fact that the rainfall was pitiless and unrelenting certainly made a bad situation worse, but it was command errors, rather than the unexpectedly heavy rainfall, which made this the worst battlefield in history' (Philip Warner, *Passchendaele* (Barnsley, 2005)).

[135]   *At about this time came terrible news from the east, that is, the farther east. We knew there had been a revolution in Russia, but Kerensky seemed a good sort of person, and we were not interested anyway.*

The abdication of Tsar Nicholas II of Russia on 15 March 1917, and the establishment of a provisional government on 16 March, during the 'February Revolution' (i.e. by the old-style calendar), were reported in the British press; initially the changes were thought to signify a renewed Russian commitment to winning the war against Germany, when in fact they ushered in a process of disintegration and retreat that ended with the humiliating Treaty of Brest-Litovsk, 3 March 1918, by which the Bolshevik government extricated itself from the world war in order to concentrate on securing the Revolution. The moderate Russian socialist Aleksandr Fyodorovich Kerensky (1881–1970) joined the March 1917 provisional government, becoming prime minister from 21 July 1917; his authority was already damaged by the failure of the 'Kerensky Offensive', 1–19 July 1917, which proved to be the last major Russian action of the war, and after the October Revolution brought the Bolsheviks to power, he fled into foreign exile.

[135]   *But now we heard that Russian resistance was collapsing, in fact had collapsed, their armies just disintegrating and going home, as the French had been doing on a small scale. This, it was said, would enable the Germans to transfer forty divisions from that front to this. We had every sympathy with the Russian people, but we wished they had not decided to do this just at this particular time.*

After the signing of an armistice between the Central Powers and the Soviet authorities who now represented Russia on 15 December 1917, the Germans were able to move more than forty divisions from the Eastern to the Western Front over a period of months.

[139]   *7th. While preparing to put up barrage at 21.00 hours, Germans counter-attacked. Fired gunfire on S.O.S. Report said the Glosters, who were preparing to go over, met the Germans halfway, that the latter caught a cold, and that the Glosters took the remaining half of St Julien.*

St Julien had been captured on the first day of Third Ypres, 31 July, by troops of the 39th Division, but in the coming days it was subjected to German counter-attacks, and had to be temporarily abandoned; on 3 August it was reoccupied.

[139]   *The young Captain introduced himself to me as being the brother of a family friend. He was Captain L of our A.S.C.*

We have not been able to identify 'Captain L', who is given thus by WRP in his original typescript.

[144]   *The stunt was supposed to have gone well, but history records it as 'a disappointing action'.*

WRP refers to the Battle of Langemarck, 16–18 August 1917: on the opening day, Thursday 16th, eight British divisions, of Gough's Fifth Army, advanced along a front of around 12,000 yards, protected by a creeping barrage. The British artillery, however, had failed to silence the German batteries which, with machine guns mounted in pill boxes, directed devastating fire on the attackers: the 16th and 36th Divisions, on the slopes of the Zonnebeke spur, and the 56th Division on the Gheluvelt Plateau, all suffered very heavy casualties, and by the end of the day the remnants of most units were either in or near their starting lines.

[146]   *Actually the attack failed and from now on till the end of the month Inverness Copse was taken by us and lost again eighteen times! Wolff says: 'the senselessness of it all grew like a cancer into the minds of the Allied troops. One historian writes that "these strokes, aimed at the morale of the German army, were wearing down the morale of the British".'*

WRP quotes Leon Wolff's In Flanders Fields (London, 1958). He gives the reference as p. 159, but the quotation is not there, and the edition has no index. The 'one historian' is Dr C.E.W. Bean, otherwise known as the Australian Official Historian

(Major-General Sir John Davidson, Haig: Master of the Field (Barnsley: Pen and Sword, 2010), xvi and 36).

[146]   *On the 31st I went down for a rest. The wagon-lines now were by a château at Vlamertinghe. Walked down and it was a relief to be away. Had no work to do and could lie about. Things fairly quiet except for a high-velocity 'India-rubber' gun.*

Army slang for a German high-velocity gun.

[148]   *4th Borrowed bikes off Quarter and went off all day with Gunner Havens. Went through Poperinge and on to Watou. Here we had our hair cut by a Belgian soldier on leave at his home. He suggested that the war would last another two years. I suggested that the League of Nations might be the only way, to which he said 'Ah oui Monsieur, by fighting the war will last another two years.*

The idea of a League of Nations to guarantee world peace was famously articulated by the US President Woodrow Wilson in the 'Fourteen Points' that he outlined to Congress on 8 January 1918, but the idea had been in evolution for some time, and in a speech at Cincinnati on 26 October 1916, Wilson had advocated 'a league of nations after the present war to maintain peace' (*The Times*, 27 October 1916, 7).

[149]   '*Spent the evening at Talbot House, where we lay in hammocks in the garden and smoked Egyptian cigarettes, ending up with a cinema. I am not sure, and it sounds ridiculous, but I think that cinema was the first I ever went to.*'

Talbot House in Poperinge (known to British soldiers by the abbreviation 'Toc H'; see next note) was a popular social venue that opened its doors to all ranks in December 1915. It was an 'Every-Man's Club'; a notice by the front door warned visitors: 'All rank abandon, ye who enter here'. To accommodate the increasing number of visitors it was extended in 1916: the first floor of a neighbouring hop store was acquired, and used for church services, lectures, debates, concerts (it became known as the Concert Hall) and even films. WRP appears to have visited a cinema before: see above, p. 116.

[149]   *The result was that by the end of it Don Battery had been literally and completely blown away and had ceased to exist in any form other than scattered fragments.*

WRP refers to 'D' Battery, identified here by the phonetic alphabet, or 'signalese', used by the British Army in 1918: A=Ack, B=Beer, C=Cork, D=Don ... T=Toc, etc. For a comprehensive list of the various alphabets in use at different times see www.royalsignals.org.uk.

[150]   *13th. On this date began the preparatory bombardment of the Battle of the Menin Road which was launched on the 20th. On the position we noticed nothing unusual and only heard rumours that there was going to be an attack on St Julien.*

Overall responsibility for the Third Ypres battle front passed from Gough, commander of the Fifth Army, to Plumer, commander of the Second Army, with effect on 10 September, and the latter planned the Battle of the Menin Road Ridge, 20–25 September 1917, with characteristic thoroughness. Recognising the overwhelming importance of artillery in the infantry's advance, Plumer insisted on a long preliminary bombardment, which intensified in the forty-eight hours before zero hour, when counter-battery fire was the primary objective. At 05.40 hours on 20 September, 65,000 troops advanced across an 8-mile front, and by the end of the day they had secured their main objectives on the Gheluvelt Plateau.

[150]   *General Plumer, who had command of the operation, had his 2nd Army to the south of this line, and General Gough's 5th Army was to the north, the latter comprising our XVIII Corps of Maxse on the left and Fanshawe's V Corps on the right, their dividing line being the Wieltje-Gravenstafel road.*

Herbert Charles Onslow Plumer (1857–1932), created 1st Viscount (of Messines) 1929; commanded Fifth Army Corps, 8 January–8 May 1915; Second Army, BEF, 1915–17; GOC Italian Expeditionary Force, November 1917–March 1918; Second Army BEF, March–December 1918; Army of the Rhine, December 1918–April 1919. Ivor Maxse (1862–1958), KCB, 1917; commander, XVIII Army Corps, January 1917, and engaged with it throughout the fighting in Flanders, July–November 1917, and at St Quentin, January–June 1918; Inspector-General of Training to the British Armies in France, June 1918–March 1919. Hew Dalrymple Fanshawe (1860–1957), KCB, 1925; 1st Indian Cavalry Division (France), 1914–15; British Cavalry Corps, 1915; Fifth Army Corps, 1915–16; 58th London Division, 1916–17; 18th Indian Division (Mesopotamia), 1917–19. It has not been possible to verify these army depositions.

[150]   *Our 48th division in front of us had been replaced by the 58th, a second line London Territorial Division, which had done good work, but had not yet been in a major action.*
WRP describes here the order of Maxse's XVIII Corps at the Battle of Polygon Wood, 26 September–3 October 1917: 11th (Northern) Division, 48th (South Midland) Division, 58th (2/1st London) Division.

[152]   *Of course we all knew who was playing and, looking up, there we saw him, our popular Levy, playing his violin lying on his back on a lot of bags on the G.S. wagon, with his legs up in the air. He always played quietly and in tune, and when he sang it was the same; he never played jazz, but always quiet little ditties reminding us of home.*

'Jazz' was appearing on the bills of London variety theatres soon after the war, but one of its antecedents, ragtime, was already in vogue before 1914, and this is perhaps the genre WRP means here.

[152]   *'19th. All the previous night the most concentrated heavy firing I ever remember went on. Our heavies appeared to be firing at their maximum. We now learned that the*

210

big battle, (which was later to be called the Battle of the Menin Road) was to commence at 05.00 hours next morning.'

Also known as the Battle of the Menin Road Ridge, 20–25 September 1917, the third general British attack of Third Ypres. Its ultimate aim was to capture the Gheluvelt Plateau. Zero hour on 20 September was determined by the weather, 05.40 hours being decided upon at 01.45 hours.

[153]   *'21st. Barrage again early, but firing slower. A lovely bright, fresh autumn day. Rubber-nosed devil in trench by 'B' shack; enormous hole.*

Perhaps a German high-velocity shell (i.e. from 'India rubber gun').

[154]   *Some weeks later at Wimereux Base Hospital near Boulogne I received a letter from Sergeant Gore: 'we came out four days after you went. They have put us on road repair work. There is a rumour we are going to Italy. I do miss you so much, old fellow.'*

On 21 November 1917 the 240th Brigade entrained at Aubigny, Tanque and Savy, bound for the Italian front: it detrained at Bovlone and Cerea, in the province of Verona, on 27 November. The 48th Division was part of a substantial force sent from Britain to bolster the Italians following their disastrous reversal at Caporetto. French and American troops, and crucially American war materials, were also sent to the Italian front. The 48th Division saw fighting on the Asiago Plateau in June 1918, and was in the vanguard of the advance of the Sixth Italian Army following the disorderly retreat of the Austrians at the end of October. The division took the surrender of Trent, the capital of Trentino, from its Austrian commander, shortly before the armistice on the Italian front, which was signed at 15.00 hours on 4 November.

[154]   *'The outstanding feature of military leadership at this time, it has been said, was that the only defence known was indiscriminate slaughter. Earl Haig relied apparently entirely upon what he was told by Charteris, his information officer.*

'At one time the view was widely held that Haig arrived at his erroneous conclusions regarding the imminent collapse of German morale through the incompetence of his chief of intelligence, Brigadier-General John Charteris. The release of Haig's comprehensive diaries throws doubt on this judgement. It appears, rather, that Haig's sanguine temperament disposed him towards these conclusions, and that, if anything, Charteris was influenced by Haig rather than the other way round' (Robin Prior and Trevor Wilson, 'Haig, Douglas, first Earl Haig (1861–1928)', ODNB).

[155]   *On the first day of Third Ypres the latter was somewhere behind the lines watching our wounded coming back. He saw one man on a stretcher make the thumbs up sign. He probably meant it when, describing the incident to Haig, he intimated that the man's words,*

which he obviously didn't hear, were to the effect that it was a great victory, that the enemy was on the run; in fact it was a case of 'on les aura'.

'We will get them!' – a slogan of defiance that assumed a special significance in France during the war. It was widely attributed to Général Philippe Pétain, who rallied French resistance during the Battle of Verdun with an order of the day, 10 April 1916, that concluded with the words: '*Courage. On les aura!*'

[155]   *Poor man. What that man was saying was 'I've got a Blighty one. I'm out of this bloody lot.' It was a good thing that the troops did not know Haig's interpretations of Third Ypres thumbs up. It would on the other hand have been an immense relief to the troops if they could have known that Lloyd George, in the words of Lord Derby, 'was to spend the rest of the war attempting to prevent Haig from launching offensives' for the simple reason that no more reinforcements were available.*

WRP here quotes Randolph S. Churchill's *Lord Derby* (London, 1959), 287. Edward George Villiers Stanley (1865–1948), 17th Earl of Derby, was a Unionist politician; Director-General of Recruiting, 1915–16; Under Secretary for War, 1916; Secretary of State for War, 1916–18.

[155]   *The Allied casualties of Third Ypres (including Cambrai) for the period July to December 1917 have been estimated as nearly double those of the Germans, but it seems impossible to find reliable figures.*

WRP here brackets the Battle of Cambrai, 20 November–7 December 1917, with that of Third Ypres for the purposes of estimating casualties only. Cambrai is some 70 miles south of Ypres, and the operations there were distinct from those in the Salient. WRP's estimate of comparative casualties here seems distinctly implausible. Figures for Cambrai suggest that German and British casualties may both have been in the region of 40,000, while those for Third Ypres suggest that German losses may have exceeded Allied losses.

[158]   '*À bas la guerre*'.

'Down with war!'

[159]   *he was a Reservist, his H.Q. was Bruges; he was even now in touch with his Colonel; Indo-China was a trouble; he might have to report to Bruges at any time because he thought there might be war within three weeks.*

It is not clear to what trouble in Indochina this refers: there was a growing communist insurgency in South Vietnam in the late 1950s, backed by the North Vietnamese, but its escalation into a war that would involve the United States was still some way off.

[160]   *But the time came when I read wonderful Trevelyan's accounts of Marlborough's battles, and his vivid descriptions of the actual battlefields, their fields, hedges, roads and villages, which he had himself visited and walked over and identified; his description of how the 'field of Blenheim' had altered since those days, and how it looked to him standing on it and trying to visualize its outlines in the past; also his descriptions of the 'fields' of Ramillies and Oudenarde.*

In his acclaimed work *England under Queen Anne* (London, 1930–34, 3 vols), historian G.M. Trevelyan (1876–1962) considered the political consequences of British participation in the War of Spanish Succession (1701–14), and the notable career during it of the British commander John Churchill (1650–1722), 1st Duke of Marlborough. Trevelyan's battle scenes are thought to be brilliantly described, and *The Times* reviewer of the second volume, *Ramillies and the Union with Scotland*, observed: 'It should be a commonplace to say that Professor Trevelyan knows how to make the best of a battle-piece; one gathers, however, that he has visited nearly all the scenes of fighting which he describes' (*The Times*, 6 October 1932, 11). WRP alludes here to Marlborough's important victories at Blenheim (1704), Ramillies (1706) and Oudenarde (1708) during the War of Spanish Succession.

[161]   *I returned to the car and drove on a little and then stopped and consulted the map for the hundredth time. I was on Pilckem Ridge.*

Scene of the Battle of Pilckem Ridge, 31 July–2 August 1917, the opening engagement in Third Ypres.

[162]   *Of all the armies which fought in the First World War from its start in August 1914 until 1917 and 1918, omitting the remnant of the Belgian Army, which carried on bravely to the end, the French Army was reduced in potential perhaps by a half by loss of morale due to desertions following upon Nivelle's fiasco of April 1917; the Russian Army, demoralized by incompetence, starvation and politics, just walked home at the end of July 1917; and the Italian Army could practically be written off as from Caporetto in October 1917.* [See above]

[163]   *White roads leading faint and far / Into the land where the good dreams are.*

It has not been possible, despite some effort, to identify either the poem or the poet.

INDEX

If you enjoyed this book, you may also be interested in…

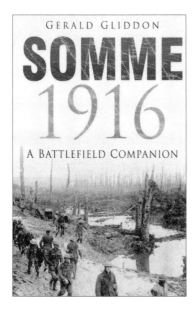

Somme 1916

GERALD GLIDDON

978 0 7509 6732 7

Gerald Gliddon's classic survey of the Somme battlefield in 1916, first published in 1987 to great acclaim, has been greatly expanded and updated to include the latest research and analysis. Supported by a wide selection of archive photographs and drawing on the testimony of those who took part, this new edition covers the famous battle sites, such as High Wood and Mametz Wood, as well as the lesser-known villages on the outlying flanks.

It includes a day-by-day account of the British build-up on the Somme and the ensuing struggle, British and German orders of battle and a full history of the cemeteries and memorials, both 'lost' and current, that sprang up in the years following the First World War. The author also provides thumbnail biographies of all the senior officers to fall, the winners of the Victoria Cross and those who were 'shot at dawn', as well as Somme 'personalities' such as George Butterworth.

This new edition honours the centenary of one of the bloodiest battles of the First World War.

Visit our website and discover thousands of other History Press books.

www.thehistorypress.co.uk

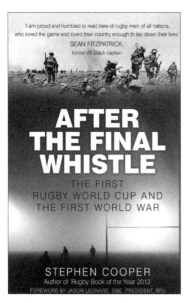

After The Final Whistle

STEPHEN COOPER

978 0 7509 6999 4

When Britain's empire went to war in August 1914, rugby players were the first to volunteer: they led from the front and paid a disproportionate price. When the Armistice came after four long years, their war game was over; even as the last echo of the guns of November faded, it was time to play rugby again.

As Allied troops of all nations waited to return home, sport occupied their minds and bodies. In 1919, a grateful Mother Country hosted a rugby tournament for the King's Cup, to be presented by King George V at Twickenham Stadium. It was a moment of triumph, a celebration of military victory, of Allied unity and of rugby values, moral and physical. Never before had teams from Australia, Canada, New Zealand, South Africa, Britain and France been assembled in one place. Rugby held the first ever 'World Cup' – football would not play its own version until 1930.

In 2015 the modern Rugby World Cup returns to England and Twickenham as the world remembers the Centenary of the Great War. With a foreword by Jason Leonard, this is the story of rugby's journey through the First World War to its first World Cup, and how those values endure today.

Visit our website and discover thousands of other History Press books.

www.thehistorypress.co.uk